D. J.

D. J. Dorothy Jean Ross
1891–1982

Barbara Falk

with Cecile Trioli

MELBOURNE UNIVERSITY PRESS

MELBOURNE UNIVERSITY PRESS

PO Box 278, Carlton South, Victoria 3053, Australia

info@mup.unimelb.edu.au

www.mup.com.au

First published 2000

Text © Barbara Falk with Cecile Trioli 2000

Design and typography © Melbourne University Press 2000

Designed by Melissa Graham

Index by Kerry Biram

Typeset by Syarikat Seng Teik Sdn. Bhd., Malaysia, in 12 point Garamond 3

Printed in Australia by RossCo Printing

National Library of Australia Cataloguing-in-Publication entry

Falk, Barbara, 1910– .

  D. J.: Dorothy Jean Ross, 1891–1982.

  Bibliography.

  Includes index.

  ISBN 0 522 84881 8.

  1. Ross, Dorothy J. (Dorothy Jean). 1891–1982. 2. Women educators—Victoria—Biography. 3. Educators—Victoria—Biography. I. Trioli, Cecile. II. Title.

370.92

To my daughter Anne Elisabeth Lloyd Thomas,
an Old Grammarian

Contents

Illustrations

Preface

'O rest in the Lord, and He will give thee thy heart's desire.' D. J. winced as if the pure contralto tone of Kathleen Ferrier's voice was a stiletto aimed at her heart. It was the day after she had resigned as headmistress of Melbourne Church of England Girls' Grammar School. She had sought refuge from telephones in my house in Studley Park. We had found pause together on other occasions in times of stress during the twenty-six years of a friendship that had survived years of separate lives and would continue until Mary Davis rang me to forestall the public notice of her death.

This book is a tribute of the kind D. J. would have wanted. It seeks to place her life in its historical context, to paint a picture in words that do not evade issues but seek to clarify what she did and who she was.

There are, for me, problems in defining public and private spheres which I have tried to solve with sensitivity and respect. Anecdotal evidence may reflect a passing mood, occasional weariness of spirit or a lapse from high seriousness. Reliance on such private moments can contribute to a distorted image. The reader is entitled to know that I am proud to inscribe myself her friend.

Barbara Falk

Acknowledgements

I would like to thank the following for permission to include quotations from published works: Professor W. F. Connell, 'Innovative headmistress—D. J. Ross', in C. Turney (ed.), *Pioneers of Australian Education, vol. III*, Sydney University Press, Sydney, 1983, pp. 209–10; Melbourne Girls' Grammar School, *Nisi Dominus Frustra*, Arbuckle Waddell, South Yarra, 1953, pp. 171–2; the extract from Isaiah Berlin, *The Sense of Reality: Studies in Ideas and their History*, Henry Hardy (ed.), Chatto & Windus, London, 1996, pp. 45–9 is reproduced by permission of Henry Hardy; Melbourne University Press for Janet McCalman, *Journeyings: The Biography of a Middle-Class Generation 1920–1990*, Carlton, 1993, pp. 147, 149 and 150.

I am grateful to the following people for their support: Christine Briggs, Professor W. F. Connell, Lesley Cunningham, Dr Katie Holmes, Professor Renata Howe, Pamela Lloyd and the library staff at Melbourne Girls' Grammar School, Rosslyn McCarthy, Nicole Muir, Professor Susan Rowley, Professor R. Selleck, Helen Spry and Don Wirth.

I am indebted to my supportive editor Teresa Pitt, academic colleagues and the administrative staff of the History Department at the University of Melbourne.

Dr Cecile Trioli is properly acknowledged on the title page for her contribution as co-worker in research and interviewing and for her academic skills in preparing the manuscript for publication and for many clarifying discussions. I am responsible for the words and their implications and express my indebtedness for her generous friendship.

Barbara Falk

Abbreviations

ACER   Australian Council for Educational Research

ATTI   Associated Teachers' Training Institute

IARTV   Independent Association of Registered Teachers, Victoria

IECD   Institute of Early Childhood Development

KTC   Kindergarten Training College

MBE   Member of the British Empire

MGGS   Melbourne Girls' Grammar School

MCEGGS   Melbourne Church of England Girls' Grammar School

NEF   New Education Fellowship

SCM   Student Christian Movement

WEF   World Education Fellowship

Introduction

Dorothy Jean Ross in her adult life chose to name herself D. J. to her friends. As a child Dorothy had responded to her given name. Her mother, when she was angry with her daughter, called Dorothy Jean to account. These names were signs the adult adopted of the conventions of her family home. The professional educator she became retained much of her early rearing. She signed Dorothy J. Ross on professional documents indicating her acceptance of herself as a public person, as teacher, headmistress and an educator of teachers in training. She was Miss Ross to colleagues and acquaintances. D. J. became the signature of her private self. This book retains her distinction in order to create the breadth, depth and dimensions of a remarkable human being. The facts of her life are signposts to understanding. Jane Welch Carlyle once wrote:

> And now the only sort of journal I would keep should have to do with what Mr Carlyle calls 'the fact of things'. It is very bleak and barren this fact of things as I see it very, and what good is to result from writing it in a paper book is more than I can tell.[1]

Miss Ross, D. J., kept no journal recording the bleak and barren facts of her daily life. They have had to be discovered in archival materials, in documents, in a few letters, in photographs and in the reminiscences of people who knew her. There is a dearth of documentary material about her early life. An advertisement in a daily paper and enquiries of all persons with whom I have discussed her life over seventy years produced few handwritten letters or records of private meetings. Reliance has had to be placed on deductions from what has been preserved.

When she was headmistress, Miss Ross always kept her study door open. This 'fact' tells us little about the reasons and emotions which caused her to decide to do so. I have chosen to look for incidents that are compatible with this practice, so that I may ask whether some relatively permanent trait of Miss Ross' personality is revealed in the decision to be accessible. Each such 'fact' will be woven into a pattern, one of many possible patterns chosen to mesh with the conventions of biographical scholarship, and is constrained by a particular linguistic discourse. The narrative is coloured by an interpretation of the historical time 1891 to 1982, which was Dorothy Ross' life span. Readers will be aware, and are occasionally reminded, that Dorothy Ross (D. J.) lived in 'the worst century that has ever been in wanton destruction of innocent human life and in murderous unreason masking itself as reason'.[2] This backdrop to the stage on which her life was performed cannot be ignored. The pace of technological change was so rapid that successive generations of her pupils inhabited worlds in which horizons of space were extended and communications revolutionized. Social and political upheavals changed the lives and perceptions of women in the industrialized nation states during her ninety years.

A chronological, reflective narrative has seemed the appropriate genre in which to record D. J.'s life. The convention that the narrative be broken into chapters has given the opportunity to distinguish a main theme for each time-span chosen as a period in her life. The final two chapters gather the threads emerging from the previous chapters—as D. J. herself tried to do in her old age.

The presence or absence of the author in reflective narrative requires a decision. In the chapters that follow, I will, as far as possible, within the friendship acknowledged in the Preface, be present by implication, rather than explicitly. There are many who will bring their own version of who Miss Ross was to their reading. For some, chapter 1, 'The Making of an Icon', may be an unwelcome examination of the legendary figure who is forever the ideal headmistress. There are for these readers no other dimensions to her life. The visual evidence that portrays her as a child and as a maturing and ageing body introduces the idea that Dorothy Jean was not born a headmistress. The theme of the first chapter is the creating of a legend. It begins with her early forays into the world of education in Victoria. There was a quality, consistently observed, which separated this apprentice teacher from others in her position. There are many comments quoted which show she made an impact on His Majesty's Inspectors of Education, on Professor Browne, whose Diploma of Education she abandoned in 1914, on members of her staff and on her student teachers. 'The crisis' which followed her resignation from Melbourne Church of England Girls' Grammar School enshrined the Miss Ross regime in public memory as paradise lost, and herself as the paradigm headmistress of her generation.

Chapter 2 begins the search for the living woman within the frame of the ideal headmistress. Her individual way of absorbing ideas and examples in the then current theory and practise of education tells us much about her. She was fortunate in her contact with leading personalities in education in Victoria, and through the New Education Fellowship in England and in Europe. In particular, her virtual apprenticeship to Miss Gilman Jones was formative and opened the way for her to become supervisor of the Associated Teachers' Training Institute. As a housemistress at MCEGGS, and as a supervisor, Miss Ross began to develop her skills as an administrator. No view of her would be complete which ignored her hard-headed grasp of the practicalities of organizing an institution.

After five years as supervisor of ATTI, D. J. took the step forward that is recorded in chapter 3. Her second voyage to England in 1935 celebrated personal and professional independence. She experienced a significant conflict, as the chapter tells, between current educational theories exemplified in the schools she visited, and in her personal life in assimilating and assessing the challenge of psychoanalysis to her evolving view of her own sexuality.

She brought her questions back with her to Australia in 1936 and surveyed the scene in Victoria as she continued her work at the ATTI. She was experiencing some of the problems inherent in trying to reform a system from within, and her study leave had given renewed impetus to her efforts.

She was soon to respond to the great challenge of following Miss Gilman Jones as headmistress of MCEGGS. Chapter 4 reports the fifteen years she devoted to developing 'her' school as her ideas of what was possible grew firmer and more coherent. Her achievements within the school assured her a position of authority in education in Victoria. Her influence extended to other States. These were her years of personal flowering: she is portrayed as a charismatic leader, secure in a long-lasting relationship, extending herself beyond her physical strength.

Chapter 5 explores her activities in the community and leads to a study of the relationships she formed as she acted in many organizations. Chapter 6 looks at these relationships in the context of what being a single professional woman involved in those years of the twentieth century in which she lived her maturity.

D. J.'s story is that of many professional women of her generation. When she was a young woman they had a choice of profession that was limited to nursing or teaching. Later in her life more options became available, for example, in law, medicine, biological research and journalism. Successful women of her age presented as public figures: energetic, dedicated, in control. Within that image there was the private female seeking a secure foundation in rapidly changing technological and psychological social constructs. The metaphor of the icon and the woman behind a facade dramatises their struggle. D. J. had to choose what private life was compatible with her profound conviction that education was the key to a better world. The vitality that fired her professional life is seen in her personal relationships and in her changing understanding of her own sexuality.

The final chapter, chapter 7, takes us to the nursing homes in which D. J. spent her last years. Her own words examine crucial decisions she made during her active professional and personal life. She retained the reticence of her generation but old age gave her some freedom to reveal her struggles. Her hold on life, her refusal to accept that her own life, like every other, was unfinished business makes poignant reading. She fought bravely to the end.

I

The Making of an Icon

The word 'icon' can mean a re-presentation, a portrait, a picture, a venerated image. It is as the venerated image of an educator that Dorothy Jean Ross is re-presented in one published memoir and in chapters of learned publications. Appropriate respect is paid to remarkable achievements, but as one historian of education has remarked: 'I have no idea who she really was'.[1]

In this chapter, I look at the construction of the icon, the venerated image, and begin a search to understand who the woman D. J. Ross became. An icon is *visual* so I look first at pictorial representations of D. J. Ross. There is a painting of Miss Ross by A. D. Colquhoun on the wall of Melbourne Girls' Grammar Assembly Hall. The headmistress in 1954 is among past and future colleagues. She is, as is the portrait, the property of the school, object not subject. The viewers for whom the portrait was intended were 'the family of the school', present and past students and their parents, members of staff, school councillors and the hierarchy of the Anglican Church. The artist has portrayed her seated, in three-quarter profile, the gaze is withdrawn behind her spectacles, the sensitive full lips are closed. Her hair is severely brushed back from a high forehead, the tapered quiet hands are folded. A high-necked white blouse, ornamented with a discreet chain, blends into a long-sleeved, dull blue gown which obliterates her body. The emblematic significance of the dress defines her status. She appears a sad, professional woman of sixty-three.

There are many different photographs which catch moments in D. J.'s long life. There is the body of the child, the adolescent, the woman in her flowering and in her old age.

> An instant photographed can only acquire meaning insofar as the viewer can read into it a duration extending beyond itself.
> . . . We are lending it a past and a future.
> . . . The truth it can tell is a limited one.
> . . . It seems likely that the denial of the innate ambiguity of the photograph is closely connected with the denial of the social function of subjectivity . . . In the positivist utopia when something is visible it is a fact and facts contain the only truth.[2]

'The enigma of appearances' will not tell us the 'truth' about D. J. . . . The photographs become true, lose their ambiguity in the context of a lived life.[3] Miss Ross is pictured in one photograph in 1941 with a narrow face, finely cut, wide, open grey eyes, her mouth controlled, but at this moment widened into a cheerful grin. Her body is somehow still innocuous, there but unnoticed, a space of indeterminate tweed, posed on low-heeled laced shoes. She bends to pat the current black cocker spaniel. The hand that caresses is long-fingered and narrow.[4] Looking again, the cropped hair that is fine, soft, vaguely brown, seems designed for ease of care. This woman is on her way, but is caught by the camera in a moment's pause. If a passing girl greets her she will look up in friendly recognition: 'Well Mary, has your sister recovered from the flu?'

This is how, half a century later, many of her MCEGGS Old Grammarians remember her. They revered her then and later. She knew them; she was a presence, available yet remote, human because of the dog and the informality she often allowed herself, but formidable if angered or on official occasions. She was, and is,

'Miss Ross' to them. This figure has no past, no present except as headmistress. 'She was very influential in my life. I owe her a lot.' I entertained five classmates in November 1996. They were unequivocal in speaking of their happiness in her 'democratic school'.

This is not how she began as headmistress in 1939. In her first year, pictured with her healthy looking, cheerful prefects, she appears uncertain of her position. She has yet to acquire the poise and easy authority of the icon. Her body in this photograph is rigid, her lips tightly closed as she looks grimly at the camera. The knuckles stand out in one closed fist, the other hand holds a cocker spaniel in his place. A studio portrait of her in this year is milder, but the intensity is there. She is consciously presenting herself in her new role.

These re-presentations merge with the figures described in words by those who remember Dorothy Jean and D. J. in the flesh. A body is always clothed in the fashions of the time. The early photographs of Dorothy Jean reflect her middle-class Melbourne and Geelong upbringing. The clothes she wore, the way her abundant hair was dressed, were the conventional styles of her mother's choice. When she bobbed her hair as a young teacher there was nothing outré in that choice. Her cheeks were rounded, the wide, open innocent eyes and the ample body seemed to have little resemblance to the attenuated form and the drawn face of the mature woman photographed with her colleagues in 1947 at the United Nations Educational, Scientific, and Cultural Organization post-war conference at Sevres in France.[5] In the years between, it seems that her body had accommodated itself to the picture she was gradually forming of herself. In her university days she retained much of her socialization into the upper reaches of the provincial middle-class. The understated suits and hats were worn by earnest young women of her social group. She melded into the family background and later into the pictures of members of the Princess Ida Club and the tennis team at Melbourne University. 'Facts' which bolster this interpretation are found in the photograph of three members of the tennis team she captained in 1912 and in the dresses of the friends with whom she holidayed at Lorne in 1916.[6] She would have been unremarkable in the photographs of the family group.

Her place in the society of her early years is described in her birth certificate of 3 November 1891: female, born in Toorak, Victoria, to Alfred George Ross, Gentleman, who was married on 23 April 1888 in Geelong to Lottie A. Walden now resident in Westbury Street, St Kilda. The birth was attended by two doctors. Alfred George Ross, of Scottish Anglican descent, was born in 1857 in Toorak. Dorothy Jean's mother Charlotte ('Lottie') Walden, a descendant of a cleric of the Church of England in Ireland, grew up with her widowed mother in Geelong in close friendship with the family of George Morrison, headmaster of Geelong College.[7] It was a financially secure upper middle-class background in which Dorothy Jean, an only child of parents in their thirties, spent her childhood. But there were underlying currents of unease. Lottie took Dorothy Jean to live for a year in Geelong with her maternal grandmother when she was three years old. Her musical, play-fellow father was an alcoholic and Lottie was concerned to protect her daughter from the knowledge of his failing. When he was well he played a vital role in his daughter's life. He encouraged her to learn to play the piano, and to be a tomboy (her mother had longed for a son). The precious only child was dispatched to boarding school in St Kilda when she was fourteen as her father's condition worsened.

June Epstein bases her account of these early years on what D. J. told her in her retirement. Describing (Alfred) George Ross as an alcoholic tells us little of the impression he made upon his infant daughter, nor what a 14-year-old thought of her exile to boarding school. Her later life reveals the extent to which he was her role model. She shared and identified with his musical talent. She played piano and flute. His humour and active physical life became part of her way of coping.[8] Lottie Ross did not forbid her daughter to climb trees or sit behind her father on his bicycle. Her mother is a shadowy figure; knitting warm woollen stockings, preserving her daughter from winter cold and the evidence of her father's losing fight with alcohol. Dorothy continued to live in the modest bungalow at 10 The Avenue in Windsor with her mother after her father died in 1910. In 1930 she was still controlling the asthma which could have been, in part, a physical manifestation of unconscious anxiety about the family secret. She was sleeping in a wired-in verandah in the family home—sleeping in the fresh air was advised for asthmatics.[9] D. J. had occasionally shared a flat in South Yarra in which her mother spent some years. Mrs Ross died in a small private nursing home in 1948.[10] It seems reasonable to infer that D. J. as an adult preserved a loving relationship with her widowed mother. There is no evidence of any deep intimacy; no grounds for surmising that Lottie understood the life her daughter was living. Grandmothers and maiden aunts, like her mother, appear as models of God-fearing, upright, intelligent ladies. D. J. could accept both her womanhood and the enrichment the male parent contributed. The pictured image is of a middle-class, coddled, only child of loving mature parents in an extended family that is intellectually and musically stimulating. Childhood and youth coped with the invisible control of a 'secret' which dictated the separation at intervals from parents and home. The world outside the family built an icon on this pedestal.

Formal academic records tell something of an enquiring mind within the pictured head. From kindergarten in Geelong to matriculation in Melbourne, 1895 to 1909, the image of a highly intelligent girl emerges, moulded by the private schools in the suburb of Windsor in south-east Melbourne. Dorothy passed from Miss Alice Corr's sub-primary school in Williams Road to Miss Adderley's Appin Ladies' College, Windsor, and at fourteen as a boarder to The Priory, in Alma Road, St Kilda. In these schools she enjoyed the education suitable for a local girl. Her mother was a friend of the headmistress of The Priory: no doubt Dorothy saw her mother when she played bridge at the school.

The prizes Dorothy gained in each year 1907 to 1909 were awarded for excellence in scholastic, artistic and sporting activities. There were 100 girls in the school and she was pre-eminent among the young ladies. Dorothy's father could compensate for his own deprivation of a university education by encouraging his clever daughter's matriculation. The records of her career at the University of Melbourne show that she passed her Junior Public Examinations and in 1908 the Senior Public. Her accumulated subjects of Latin, English, German, French, Algebra, Geography, Anatomy, Physiology and Biology entitled her to enter the Law Faculty. She matriculated on 11 February 1910[11] and enrolled in First Year Law. She had won a non-resident Exhibition to Trinity College and with her good results in the Senior Public Examinations her expectations must have been high. But there was a problem.

The Womens' Disabilities Removal Bill passed by the Victorian Parliament in 1903 ('The Flos Greig Enabling Act'), allowed the first Melbourne female Law graduate to be admitted to the Bar in 1905.[12] There was only one more woman graduate in Law by 1909. There is a photograph of Dorothy as a barrister in a play presented by the Princess Ida Club c. 1911. But for her, Law was an enforced choice. The schooling at The Priory had not provided a good preparation for Latin I and she had studied no Greek, which was a compulsory component of an Arts degree. Her first year Law was completed with the passing of Latin I in the supplementary examinations in 1911. She could then enter second year and completed that year with Honours in English II, French and German. She transferred to Arts and completed her third year of Arts passing English, French and German in December 1912. Greek I remained a stumbling block and until she passed, with the aid of a tutor in March 1914, she could not take out her Honours degree in Modern Languages and Literature. She did so in April 1914, after supplementary studies which qualified her for a Master of Arts without further examination. To fail Greek I three times before achieving a pass was a salutary experience from which she gained sympathy for pupils who worked hard but had limited ability and little interest in compulsory studies.

This is the story told by the formal records of the university undergraduate but they reveal little of the experience of the young woman pictured in the photographs. Dorothy's generation was the last in which female undergraduates were largely segregated from their male colleagues. She had to be chaperoned by an older woman at evening parties, and she was with her mother at the opera on the evening her father died in 1910. At the university, the Princess Ida Club had outlived its function as the social and cultural centre for women. 'By 1914 it was considered advisable that the Princess Ida Club should disband, rather than remain as a mere vestige of a former influential society.'[13] Women students, who now paid a compulsory union levy, were well provided for in the new Union building, with a separate common room and eating arrangements.

Before the turn of the century the History and Science student clubs were co-educational, as were the Student Christian Alliance gatherings, and during World War I the proportion of women increased 'from eighteen per cent to thirty-two per cent of the total student' body.[14] The increase in the proportion of women did little to broaden the social mix. Students, with the exception of the few on scholarships, paid fees, so the majority of Dorothy's fellow students were, like herself, from the non-government schools. Contemporary photographs confirm that dress and social behaviour were conventional. By 1928 it was pearls and twinsets. Photographs have shown that Dorothy conformed to prevailing sartorial fashion; it would have been difficult to query the need for a female student to present herself with womanly decorum. It was indeed difficult for either male or female students to voice heretical views of politics or religion. To the young women of the 1990s these female students of the late teens and early twenties appear strangely girlish. Their innocent frivolities—putting on their plays and their musical evenings, picnicking and gossiping together—tell of another era. It is difficult to give them full credit for the intellectual adventure they had chosen. A girl who had grown to adult-hood in a Melbourne suburb would have appeared naive if con-trasted with her English counterpart separated from her by six weeks of shipboard travel. The Australian young women were, however, exceptional women and they later achieved robust indi-vidualities in their professional careers.

The segregation of men and women in those years in Australia was a fact of social life. It was mitigated in families which included boys and girls. The rare cases in which brother and sister were first at day schools and, later, university together ensured the female partners for the chaperoned occasions when the sexes mingled, and at mixed tennis parties. In Geelong, Dorothy met the Morrison boys, but in her Melbourne life there are no recorded early friend-ships with boys and young men. Nothing is known of her feelings as an adolescent. Did this physically attractive girl attract male overtures and how did she feel if they were made? In her gener-ation, her studies in Biology presumably informed her of 'the facts of life'. It is highly probable that she would otherwise have re-mained uninformed.

After her degree was achieved, Dorothy spent some months as part-time teacher of a 4-year-old girl, Joan Wisdom: a daughter of a friend of her mother's.[15] She began to teach in a one-to-one relationship with a receptive pupil and this, no doubt, convinced her of the joys of teaching. She was later to see that this was the best way for an intending teacher to understand that each single child had to learn in a classroom. This principle was satisfied in various ways at the ATTI and later at Mercer House.

She was now committed to a profession and the appropriate next step for an Honours graduate was the Diploma of Education. D. J. began to emerge as Dorothy embarked on her professional studies. The Diploma of Education (DipEd) was a year's work not designed for this Honours graduate who had early in life chosen her voca-tion. Close links between the Teacher Training College and the Faculty of Education indicated that DipEd was appropriate for students intending to remain in or enter the teaching service of the State of Victoria.

The Diploma of Education in 1914 set out to respond to a hypothetical student who had asked: What is the relation of education to ethics and logic? Will I learn about my pupils from recording experiments and observations of sensation perceptions, ideation, memory and fatigue? What special problems will I meet in teaching specific subjects of the curriculum? How will I maintain discipline in the classroom? This same student would feel it necessary to know about the history and philosophy of education and be avid to compare Australian educational systems with those of other countries.

For 'the born teacher', practice once a week for three terms under the close supervision and criticism of experienced practitioners in schools approved by the Faculty, did not allow relationships with pupils to develop. As a student D. J. did not have an equal right to criticise compulsory demonstration lessons, nor could she question the appropriateness of spending three hours each week on blackboard writing, blackboard drawing and voice production. For graduate students, the DipEd year was 'busy' rather than rigourously challenging. The timetable for students was so full there was little time to ponder. Teaching procedures did not always exemplify the principles they advocated while the range of subjects was such that for an Honours graduate treatment must often have appeared to be superficial. These are some of the common criticisms made by graduates then and later of their DipEd year. Add to them the frustrating delay that the compulsory passing of Greek I had put on Dorothy's purpose. Milton's *Tractate on Education* and Bosanquet on *Education of the Young from Plato's Republic* (rather than Plato!) might have appeared as further hurdle requirements. At this stage in her life, she wanted to teach not read a list of books, some banal, on pedagogics. And the teaching practice that the course entailed was directed and formalised. Often the real teacher would remain in the room or a visiting subject supervisor would be present. The pupils knew this was a performance not a real lesson.

They either behaved well, conscious of their teacher sitting in the back row, or they enjoyed their freedom in her absence. In neither case could the student teacher establish even an ephemeral relationship with the group. For D. J. this must have been a travesty of what she had imagined teaching to be.

The declaration of war on 14 August 1914 was more than halfway in her DipEd year. No record has been found of her reaction to the event which marked the end of the nineteenth century. For this young woman in her twenty-third year the surge of British–Australian nationalism in Victoria must have been radically disturbing. She had been active in the Student Christian Alliance. Did she respond to 'the bugles of England' as a Christian pacifist or was she caught up in the fervour of a righteous cause? The university men of the Student Christian Alliance made choices that affected their lives. Some became conscientious objectors as pacifists, others volunteered for non-combat positions in the armed forces. They served as padres or paramedics. If D. J. had volunteered for a job open to a young woman supporting the war effort, how she dealt with the conflicting claims of Christian pacifism and nationalism could be inferred. There is no such evidence.

It can easily be understood that at this tense moment an already frustrated and irritated young woman would turn to action, to *do* something. There is ample evidence of fervid patriotism in the independent schools of Victoria, and though D. J. now had no father, no brothers and no first cousins to bind her personally to the conflict she must have heard among fellow students and intending teachers talk of what should, in conscience, be done. At the end of second term, she withdrew from the diploma course. D. J. had an educational sensitivity which she could not acquire from formal instruction or from theories of education. She was fretting to try her hand on what she was later to call 'the mud and dust' of the classroom. The syllabus of the DipEd at Melbourne University in 1914 offered her answers to questions that she was not at that moment asking.

We find her responding to her subjective feelings and judgement that this course was not right for her. Her estimate of the DipEd as an introduction to teaching was confirmed by Miss Gilman Jones, the headmistress of MCEGGS, when she supported Frank Shann, headmaster of Trinity Grammar School, in 1919 when he asked that the Independent Association of Registered Teachers, Victoria draw up a scheme to promote a more efficient system of teacher training.[16] Miss Gilman Jones played an important part in the development of Miss Ross' theory and practice of education. She was one of the older generation who was quick to recognise the quality of a young woman who joined her Association staff in 1923. She promoted the career, and provided a model for her protegé which became a significant aspect of Miss Ross' public image. Her judgement of Miss Ross as a teacher was confirmed by Dr Ethel McLennan, a senior lecturer in the Botany department of the University of Melbourne who, in a reference written in March 1928, portrayed an efficient and scholarly young woman, and stated: 'it is entirely due to her enthusiasm and constructive criticism that the syllabus for the school Intermediate and school Leaving Botany has been recast along modern and we hope rather model lines'.[17] During the 1920s and 1930s Miss Ross served on the Botany standing committee of the Schools Board of the University of Melbourne. She also won the approbation of Rev. A. M. Tonge at Trinity Grammar School and of Miss Addie Garton when she taught at Oberwyl. There was a quality consistently observed which separated this apprentice teacher from others in her position. This quality is visible on the face of the icon. It would grow and develop into various specific abilities but it was there from the moment she began to teach. The subjective contact between some human beings has an unusual flavour. Her capacity to communicate in this way failed her sometimes. She did not reach everyone with whom she had professional contact, but the overwhelming majority refer with delight, even if they cannot define the source, to what it was like to be her pupil or colleague. Isaiah

Berlin has sought to isolate and describe this quality in a brilliant passage which it is appropriate to quote here:

> . . . we do not readily suppose [he wrote of the capacity for political judgement] that this capacity can literally be taught . . . We speak of some people as possessing antennae, as it were, that communicate to them the specific contours and texture of a particular political or social situation an ear, a nose, or a political sense . . . we mean something perfectly ordinary or quasi-aesthetic in the way that it works . . . it is a species of direct acquaintance, as distinct from a capacity for description or calculation or inference; it is what is variously called natural wisdom, imaginative understanding, insight, perceptiveness, and, more misleadingly, intuition (which dangerously suggests some almost magical faculty), as opposed to the markedly different virtues—very great as these are—of theoretical knowledge or learning, erudition, powers of reasoning and generalisation, intellectual genius . . . What are we to call this kind of capacity? Practical wisdom, practical reason, perhaps, a sense of what will 'work', and what will not. It is a capacity, in the first place, for synthesis rather than analysis . . . Whatever can be illuminated, made articulate, incorporated in a proper science, should of course be so . . . There is no natural science of politics any more than a natural science of ethics. Natural science cannot answer all questions.[18]

Nor, I will argue, in this book, is there a science of education which can explain why, among the many talented headmistresses of her generation, remembrances of Miss Ross have made her into the symbol for that group. Her contemporaries have added to the impressions of her elders. They did not always like her, or agree with her, but they recognized her stature. The most acute of estimates by a contemporary comes from Professor William Connell. He and his wife Margaret cherished an enduring friendship with D. J. He wrote about her in many different contexts and he summarized the essential points in 1983:

> Miss Ross was not a radical innovator in her educational ideas and practices. Her genius was of a different kind . . . [it] lay in two directions. She had a remarkable ability to see relationships between a

number of ideas in which she was interested and to build them into a logically defensive and warmly held conviction which gave drive and consistency to all her educational activities . . . She had a genius also in human relations.[19]

Later still, in 1995, Arthur Sandell, a former teacher of mathematics and secretary to the Victorian branch of the New Education Fellowship wrote of Miss Ross: 'in her thinking, in her speaking about education, and above all in what she accomplished in her school, she was a living embodiment of NEF principles . . . Her profound influence was primarily through example'.[20] He quotes with admiration Miss Ross saying, in a retrospective analysis of a visit to Melbourne by Professor Ben Morris, 'Have we looked at our educational practice to see if we are, in fact, embodying them [Morris' prescriptions] in it or are we just letting him come and go?'[21]

Margaret Connell added to her husband's professional judgement, from a student's perspective at ATTI.:

> We always thought she was so much better than Mr Richardson, for instance, who was a bit of a muddler. He was on the staff there, he taught Maths method and Miss Ross was always interesting and always opened up new lines of thought and in actual practice teaching she was very helpful. I did my teacher training at Ruyton and she used to come there, of course, for the classes for two years, and the girls were a particularly nice group of girls. I keep in touch with quite a lot of them actually and very often they ask: 'Do you still see Miss Ross who used to come and see you teach?' and I think that's pretty good. She [D. J.] was tremendous, everybody looked forward to her lectures.[22]

'Tremendous' her older adult students found her. Among fellow headmistresses and headmasters perceptions differed. The monthly meetings of the Headmistresses' Association of Victoria tried her patience. On an occasion (in 1954) sitting beside her while I was waiting to present the report on Mercer House, she was listening quietly to an inane exchange between tired and irritated women. She leaned towards me and muttered fiercely in my ear: 'While there is death there is hope'. The more conservative of her colleagues found her views and practice disturbing. The 1939 minute of appreciation of the council of the IARTV records the public appraisal by her older colleagues at this stage in her career. In 1939 Miss Ross became the headmistress and World War II began to destroy the world in which she had lived her first forty-eight years. Those who had observed her development reveal nothing of her reaction to the 1930s Depression. Did her mother suffer financial hardship as a widow in those years? Were the knitted stockings, darned in various colours, worn by choice or of necessity? Did Miss Ross bicycle to save money? Did anxiety about finance contribute to the asthma which was particularly severe when Miss Ross lectured and supervised at ATTI? When she was too ill to travel to the office she telephoned her lecture so someone could read it for her.

A photograph taken in 1939 contributes a glimpse of the effort behind the recorded achievements. In a simple black frock, facing the camera across her desk, hair severely cut back from a thin tense face, eyes behind the spectacles hardly daring to twinkle and sensitive lips controlled, the new headmistress seems thin, anxious, burdened. What have people written and spoken of her sixteen years as 'an innovative headmistress?'[23] Professor G. S. Browne of the Faculty of Education contributed to her legend; his students were advised that MCEGGS in Miss Ross' day displayed the principles of the New Education in action as did no other school in Victoria.[24] A younger, noted educationalist, Dr Gwyneth Dow, had been a pupil at the school in the Gilman Jones era, and during 1950 taught at MCEGGS: 'The most progressive school open to me'.[25] Her comments on her time at MCEGGS are quite critical of Miss Ross as headmistress, yet she was foremost in attacking the reversion to a more conservative form of organization under her successor. Dr Dow's later career reveals a more radical perspective: 'Dorothy Ross', she wrote in 1991, 'seemed to me to be on the right wing, not the left wing of radicalism'.[26] The differences in their educational theories will become explicit in chapter 2.

What is relevant to the present theme is that any criticism of Miss Ross' position on specific points of either theory or practice have been obscured by Gwyn Dow's spirited defence of the Grammar Miss Ross had built on the liberal legacy left by Miss Gilman Jones.

Gwyn Dow was herself an exceptional woman. Strong-minded, intellectually able and, when she taught in Miss Ross' school, had her own deeply felt views on social and educational issues. She found a comfortable niche in MacRobertson Girls' High School from 1953 to 1956, under the headship of Rubina Gainford and Daphne Barrett, and in her experimental Course B in the Faculty of Education at the University of Melbourne.

Other staff members and educationalists have left more uncritical, admiring writings about Miss Ross than those of Gwyn Dow. Where criticisms are chronicled they have been, as were Gwyn Dow's, glossed over as Miss Ross' achievements acquired a patina over time. There were seventy women on the teaching staff in the last year of Miss Ross' position as headmistress. It is now not possible to salvage a representative sample of those who have contributed to the social memory of her rule. It is by chance that some are alive or have left written records. Among them are Wilga Rivers who taught French from 1953 to 1958 in a team led by Margaret Davies. She spent 'three years under Miss Ross whom she clearly worshipped'.[27] When Lyndsay Gardiner interviewed Wilga Rivers she was Professor Emeritus of Linguistics at Harvard University: 'She [Rivers] had undertaken the care of the SCM at Grammar and she liked the School Executive Council. The Head had sufficient veto in vital matters. It was a great learning experience and she liked also the consensus-type discussion style of the staff room and staff meetings'.[28] These are the reported words of another formidable, talented woman looking back at a far distant past episode when she had joined the group who had resigned from Grammar when Miss Ross was no longer their leader.

It has been said that Miss Ross' contemporary headmistresses staffed their schools with women of similar physique. The short, generously proportioned and high-bosomed senior staff at Firbank are referred to as evidence by me. Miss Ross' staff were formidable in intellect and character, rather than physically similar. Among them Gwendolen (Gwenda) Lloyd (1899–1965) to the left of Miss Ross, politically and educationally, is remarkable. She was the second daughter of well-known surgeon Wilfrid Kent Hughes and his wife Clemantina Jane (née Rankin), a pupil at MCEGGS and captain of the school for six months in 1915. She joined the staff of her old school as assistant housemistress to Miss Ross at St Cecilia's House in 1925, and with only an interval from 1934 to 1940, she was a close collaborator. She became joint chief of staff in 1951 and resigned in 1957, 'as the school has changed completely since the film [*Living and Learning Together*] was made in 1955'.[29]

In the context of the creation of the icon, Gwenda Lloyd provides the foil to the reputed, balanced wisdom of the headmistress. She criticized Miss Ross for being authoritarian. She pressed for Social Studies as a complement not a replacement for History at Higher Certificate level. She supported wide powers for the elected school council and was prominent in devising its constitution. She was married to a communist, and was known to be the adoptive mother of the Aboriginal singer Harold Blair. Miss Ross was held guilty by association by certain right-wing parents. She appeared moderate by comparison.

A different contribution to the image of Miss Ross is made by the memoir *A Golden String: The Story of Dorothy Ross*, written by June Epstein who was a member of the music staff from 1946 and in her own right was a solo pianist for the Australian Broadcasting Commission. There are two sources of the picture she paints. One is 'the cherished family friend'[30] whose childhood, professional and personal life she records from this perspective.[31] The other is in the correspondence which led to her appointment on the music staff as successor to Mrs Ruth Alexander. June Epstein initiated the exchange of letters with an enquiry from Frensham School in Mittagong in New South Wales asking 'if there would be a vacancy on your music staff for 1946'.[32] Her letter speaks of five years teaching in Australia and adjudicating music festivals, and gives an account of her progressive ideas of teaching music classes in both England and Australia, her home country. Miss Ross was quick to offer her a position: 'I should be glad, if you intend to accept this job if you would do so in writing as soon as you are able to'.[33] The decisive reply indicates that some unseen wires may have been carrying messages of an opening and of availability. June hedged:

> There is some possibility of work in connection with broadcasting and also other school work, but I am most strongly drawn to class music along the lines I have discussed with you, and the opportunity you are offering me for its development seems to be just what I am looking for.[34]

June Epstein accepted the position, no doubt reassured by the prospect that 'as music as a class subject throughout the school is in its infancy here the job would be what you care to make of it yourself'.[35] Here was a headmistress eager to recruit experts to her staff and ready to trust them to implement their expertise as she had already found their educational ideas broadly in conformity with her plans for the school. She welcomed variety in personal styles and appearances. Among her supporters were two teachers of mathematics who differed as widely in their educational ideas as they did in appearances.

The more conservative Elizabeth Pownall—tall, lean and tweedy —who had been appointed by Miss Gilman Jones was a strong supporter of her headmistress. She said: 'Miss Ross established from the outset a rapport with the teaching staff'.[36] During World War II, Miss Pownall often rode her bicycle from Camberwell to the Eastern Golf Club where senior school forms 4, 5 and 6 were accommodated during the evacuation. She became chief of staff after the school returned to South Yarra. Part of her duty was to act as liaison with the Archbishop, who was chairman of School Council during 'the crisis' in 1958.[37] She was among the first group of staff to offer her resignation to Miss Mountain, Miss Ross' successor, and subsequently joined the teaching staff of the Department of Mathematics at the University of Melbourne.

By contrast, Mrs Blanche Merz—small and unorthodox in dress and ideas, who taught Biology and Mathematics in the Middle School—considered the staff who resigned were mistaken in thinking that this resignation was the only course open to them.[38] She thought they should have considered that the future of the school demanded they sought reconciliation of ideas with Miss Ross' successor.[39] She considered Miss Ross was conservative in delaying the introduction of specific teaching of human sexuality to year 8 until a predator in the school brought the subject into the forefront of discussion. She reported 'over to you' was the form of permission given when she sought to include overt instruction in human sexuality in her middle-school biology classes. She was then five months pregnant, and resigned at the end of 1956 to care for her children.

The more educationally radical teachers on the staff fretted at their principal's conservatism, while those who espoused traditional educational practice were wary of some of the 'advanced ideas'. Miss Ross was confident of her ability to weld diverse individuals into a successful working team. Confirmation of her success comes from an ATTI student who held herself fortunate to train as a teacher of mathematics and junior housemistress at MCEGGS in 1952:

> I consider my time at Grammar and my association with Miss Ross as a great privilege. The best preparation I could have had for teaching. Some of the things she said at staff meetings and at mark readings I have never forgotten. For example, the girls couldn't help being born privileged and it was our job to give them good attitudes.[40]

This young woman, a communicant member of the Church of England, comments on Miss Ross' piety: 'She was a Christian, an Anglican, if not always an orthodox one . . . Her Scripture syllabus for the school was a masterpiece'.[41] From the recollections of this random selection of members of her staff, Miss Ross is seen as a woman of broad sympathies, able to choose persons to work with who could be sufficiently united to promote her plans for her school. The events which culminated in her resignation, and the interregnum under Mrs Sylvia Martin before and after her successor, Miss Edith Mountain arrived in Australia, have had a retrospective effect on the memories so far recorded. The duration of our memories and the clarity of recollection is in proportion to the force of the original impression, and to reinforcing by later related emotional experiences. Memory of an emotion felt in the past may be 'triggered' and enhanced by subsequent pain or pleasure.[42] The women so far recorded in this chapter regretted in varying degrees 'the crisis' at MCEGGS which came to a head in 1958, four terms after Miss Mountain had taken up her post at the school. How this series of events coloured the memories of her contemporary educationalists is the present concern. What the 'crisis' meant in D. J.'s life is another matter, to be considered in depth in chapters five and seven.

That crisis is still spoken of almost half a century later in tones tinged with deep emotion by those for whom Miss Ross was a loved headmistress. The high status of MCEGGS in the Victorian community led to the daily newspapers highlighting each development in a series of events which led to thirty-six members of staff leaving the school including the most highly qualified women, and the withdrawal of approximately sixty pupils months after Miss Ross' successor had taken up her post.[43] The publicity surrounding the controversy has enshrined Miss Ross' regime in public memory as paradise lost.

For Wilga Rivers, Gwenda Lloyd, June Epstein and Elizabeth Pownall, it meant a profound change in personal life and loyalty. For Gwyn Dow and Blanche Merz, it meant a revaluing of Miss Ross' regime in accordance with a heightened perception of what they would fight to preserve. For some it meant a conflict of loyalties between church and educational beliefs. Distress gave a rosy hue to the Ross years. Coverage in newspapers and radio dramatized events: noisy meetings, a teacher crying in front of her class, what the staff were reported as saying in an interview with the Archbishop.

A crisis was created, and deepened the impression on the memory of those who had been happy in professional association with Miss Ross. 'The crisis' must be seen in a broad perspective. Victoria was a polarized community in the 1950s. The Nazi and Japanese enemies had been vanquished, and in the wake of 'the good war' victorious allies had become enemies. Fear of the communist ally (USSR) and of socialists and communists within America, Australia and Great Britain influenced many who feared loss or diminution of privilege or deeply felt beliefs. MCEGGS had on its Council and among parents and Old Grammarians, men and women who shared these feelings. 'Progressive education' at MCEGGS, already on the wane in Great Britain, was viewed by them as a dangerous nurturing of the young. Miss Ross had acquired a stature and authority among them which restrained overt criticism. Excellent academic results, enthusiastic students and loyal staff had bolstered her position. The two years under a temporary head during which only two new staff members were appointed, had exposed a policy which required Miss Ross' reputation to make it palatable. That Miss Ross was 'the school' became obvious. Her reputation was thereby enhanced, though her policy was criticized and later changed in the direction she had anticipated.

The resignation of so many experienced, talented mistresses had a long-term effect on the Ross legend. Those who had resigned were welcomed to single-sex girls' schools in Victoria and to universities. They brought the principles which had inspired their work at MCEGGS to their new appointments and this reinvigorated memories of Miss Ross' school. Gwyn Dow and Wilga Rivers spoke of her and her school at the University of Melbourne. There were others who had resigned with them. Dorothy Fitzpatrick, a historian, taught in Miss Ross' way at Lauriston and susequently at Monash University. Elaine Brumley and Elizabeth Stephens brought their scholarship in classics and English to Lauriston. Miss Ross' influence on Mary Davis at St Catherine's was reinforced by Alison Winfield as school counsellor and by Dorothy Irving as head of senior chemistry.

These teachers testified to the high academic standards of Miss Ross' school. They maintained a sense of grievance and loss which kept alive their experiences as members of 'a democratic school'. Gwenda Lloyd taught at the Kindergarten Training College (KTC) from 1948 to 1959, and taught primary and secondary teachers at the ATTI and in its later form as Mercer House from 1948 to 1962. Her work on subject committees at Australian Council for Educational Research and addresses to educational bodies continued after she resigned from MCEGGS.

Miss Ross' longevity contributed to her reputation. She lived on, a respected figure in Australian education. Her presence as president of the Australian NEF and as a visitor to schools during her years at Mercer House continually refreshed memories of her contribution to education as headmistress. The MBE she received in 1959 kept her in the public gaze. She was still there, a living legend, and her rumoured 'pink' past was reinterpreted in the light of her wise old age. The Cold War came to an end, and towards the end of her life the educational pendulum swung further towards the logical development of her policies than she had envisaged.

An article in the *Age* paid tribute to the ninety years of her life. She was dubbed 'a woman of vision and principle who saw rebellion as a good thing and kept cocker spaniels'.[44] Her democratic school was described as embodying her vision and her principles. This is the icon she read about in Camberlea Nursing Home as she pursued her courageous endeavour to make sense for herself of her life and her work in education.

2

'Nosing My Way' Towards a Theory of Education

It is appropriate that in her later years the woman who kept cocker spaniels saw herself as 'nosing' her way towards a theory of education. The way in which her intuitive understandings were enriched by reading, by contact with other persons and by the experiences open to her explains her use of the metaphor. In following her mind's journey many of the educational ideas popular during her professional lifetime are revealed. When Dorothy taught her dolls as a child she was imagining herself as an adult in control, telling the young ones she owned what she thought they ought to know. As a child she conceived her role as didactic, authoritarian. She was playing at having power over others; for their own good.

How far her own upbringing and her schooling modified a childish idea of the function of a teacher is also a matter for speculation. When Mrs Ross took her only child, aged three, to the Geelong Kindergarten the head teacher (Miss E. Cathcart) had been trained in Germany by Friedrich Froebel, a pioneer exponent of children's gardens (kindergartens) in which children could grow as flowers. Dorothy's first experience of institutionalized education was of procedures based on Froebelian assumptions about the development of the whole child—body, mind and spirit in a functioning social group. Froebel had written in 1834: 'No community can progress in its development while the individual who is a member of it remains behind. The individual, who is a member of the whole body, cannot progress in his development while the community remains behind'.[1]

The emphasis on social relationships enlarged the life of an only child, while the unquestioned kindly authority of adults was in tune with life with mother and father, grandmother and aunts. It was a gentle introduction to schooling on which later conscious ideas could be based. The moulding of childhood home and early schooling is transmuted but seldom entirely lost in later life. In her most radical years D. J. retained something of her very early upbringing in the last decade of Queen Victoria's reign.

Miss Ross' published ideas on theory of education are expressed in speeches, short contributions to magazines, annual reports and reported contributions to debate. Attention to the audience to whom they are addressed must always be part of reading them as expressions of Miss Ross' thoughts. Anyone who heard one of her public addresses would add to the reported words the magic of her transparent honesty, the depth of conviction which added weight to what were sometimes normative assumptions or undefined slogans. To understand the way her mind functioned it is sometimes helpful to work backwards, as it were, from her practice to the ideas which justified them. Miss Ross seldom explicitly stated the conceptual frameworks within which she evolved her plans for schooling or for the training of teachers. To consider the development of her thinking we look first at a narrative of experience as a teacher, then conceptualise her thoughts as a theory of education. Until she abandoned the study for the Diploma of Education in 1914, her experience as a schoolgirl had been among genteel young ladies in small classes, taught by gentlewomen who could afford to be kind and allow some leeway for individual quirks. They were, on the whole, benevolent models.

There was time to fill in and in a move which showed her determination to pursue an independent life she approached the Deputy Director of Education, Frank Tate, and obtained a temporary position at Coburg Higher Elementary School as an assistant from 17 September to 31 December 1914.

This was a new world to Dorothy. The school was a pioneer extension of Coburg Primary School. It had been set up in 1911 to bridge the gap between primary and technical school for boys and girls who chose this alternative to the Secondary High School.[2] Coburg Primary lay under the forbidding wall of the State prison, Pentridge, in a rough working-class area. The control of a class of working-class children was something new. Also new was confronting a State system of education which could, through a headmaster, require her, a freshly registered teacher, to teach a subject, Science, which she had not previously studied. Her first independent move away from her mother's sheltered world was testing. D. J. much later confided to June Epstein: 'I didn't get on at all well at that school. I couldn't manage my classes, they were beyond me. I wanted them to listen to what I was saying and they didn't want to; they much preferred to talk themselves'.[3] The inspector reported favourably of the set lesson he observed: 'She is a good teacher. Has an easy familiar style of address and gets a good response in the shape of notice from her class'.[4]

Dorothy had thought of teaching as a process of 'opening windows' to knowledge of the world. As a lonely only child she had projected her own eager curiosity on to the dolls she had taught and on to the little girl to whom she had briefly been a governess.[5] At Coburg real working-class children and a State system began the education DipEd had failed to provide. Dorothy would become Miss Ross educationalist.

Her time at Coburg was very short. In the personal emergency created by her withdrawal from the course in 1914 her mother's Anglican network came to the rescue. Registration as a primary teacher could be recorded after a period of supervised teaching in a registered school if fitness to teach was attested by an inspector of the Department of Education. This 'back door' into teaching was open in the independent schools. The Rev. A. M. Tonge was happy to assist a friend of the family and Miss Ross became a junior member of staff at Trinity Grammar School in Kew. The school had been modelled on an English choir school for boys aged seven to eleven years, but was developing as a primary and secondary school. The inspection of a lesson and the recommendation of the headmaster satisfactorily achieved gave a passport to teach in the State system or in the independent schools. Through a friend, Ethel Ross (no relation), Dorothy was introduced to Miss Addie Garton who offered her a position at her small private school in St Kilda, Oberwyl, to become available in 1915.[6]

She retreated to Oberwyl as a resident mistress 'just as she was beginning to make some progress with her pupils'.[7] The retreat was into the female middle-class in which she had grown up, but her brief experience of young boys and a male headmaster had given her a professional ease with male colleagues.

Miss Ross embarked on her first full-time paid employment as a teacher before she had clearly formulated her educational ideas. She explained to June Epstein that her headmistress at Oberwyl, Miss Addie Garton, was conservative in her ideas and in her practice. Miss Ross was to teach modern languages but she accepted an invitation in an emergency to teach physiology. Stimulated by the private study necessary to conduct those classes she enrolled in Botany I as a single subject at the University of Melbourne in 1918 and achieved marks equivalent to first-class honours in the December examinations.

The four years she spent at Oberwyl enhanced her confidence in herself and clarified her interests. She could continue to develop her musical talent, playing the flute and the piano for the boarders. While conforming to Miss Garton's insistence on mannerly orderliness she could experience the pleasure of opening windows for well-behaved girls. The discipline she exerted came of the necessity to satisfy Miss Garton's concept of the Edwardian classroom. Miss

Ross was not authoritarian by choice in those early years. As she conformed she was deciding the first of the principles she would later embed in the knowledge she would gain from the books she would study, from following a model Miss Gilman Jones, from the conferences she would attend and from formal and informal contacts. She knew that a relationship with each pupil was a prerequisite for learning if the multiplication table or memorized poetry or the dates of the kings of England were to be absorbed into the minds of her pupils and become usable by them.

She accepted the responsibility such a relationship entailed when she exorted Jean Victoria Goodman, aged fourteen, to continue to study despite her father's insistence that she leave school and prepare for marriage and motherhood. Mrs Jean Cohen remembered the young teacher who inspired her until her death on 12 November 1997 aged ninety-one.[8] She had studied secretly at night while outwardly conforming to the plans of her patriarchal Jewish father. During World War II she was directed to work as a shop assistant at Longmore's pharmacy in Bourke Street, Melbourne and finally achieved her pharmaceutical qualification in a then male-dominated profession. Her own pharmacy in East Malvern marked a pioneer achievement for Australian women.

Miss Ross, young as she was, had recognized a quick mind and a resilient personality and was determined even then, that the potential of each of her pupils must be given scope. The demands of her practice were leading her to formulate a principle.

During these years 1915 to 1919, what she had absorbed from the DipEd study had to be reconsidered in the light of experience at Coburg and the demands of satisfying Miss Garton. At this time in her life, Miss Ross had no time to delve into the competing claims of idealism and realism, nor to speculate about psychology of mind. 'How to get Beryl to understand French grammar' was the pressing problem.

She brought with her into the practice of her profession the Anglican faith of her upbringing. Throughout her teaching life a defining Christian belief in the spiritual equality of all created beings formed a cornerstone of her ideas about education. Her studies in the biological sciences were important in her personal development. She gradually learned to understand the significance of body and of physical inheritance and growth when planning for a school. 'Mud and dust'[9] and body, the physical was real! A deference to the physical was later to be expressed in concern for the physical environment in which staff and students worked.

D. J. has left no record of her intellectual and emotional reactions to World War I. A small private school in Melbourne may have been insulated from the patriotic fervour that swept through much of the continent. Were newspaper items read to the boarders? Did any member of staff or a pupil suffer the loss of a 'heroic' relative at Gallipoli? Did Miss Ross find her ideas about education affected by the conflict 'over there'? 'War is horrible and brutal', wrote Frank Tate, Director of Education in Victoria, 'but it is not therefore to be ignored even in schools'.[10] He spoke of the primary schools of Victoria which were his responsibility. It seems probable that the sensibilities of young ladies in a small private establishment would be protected from the more realistic reports of the battlefields.[11]

Botany I had whetted her appetite for knowledge of the physical world. She resigned from Oberwyl in order to embark in 1919 on full-time study for a bachelor degree in Science. In that year she passed Chemistry and Zoology and gained first-class honours in Botany and the Brunning Prize for first place in the class list. She experienced a focused enthusiasm and a sense of mastery which was translated later into the second building block of her 'theory of education'. A passionate thirst for knowlege of a particular field was a prerequisite for the sustained effort necessary for mastery of a subject. The dullest pupil must, at least, be willing to learn, to find interest in a subject.

Dorothy was twenty-eight when she left Oberwyl; it was a decisive moment in her life. The age of extremes: 'the short twentieth century had begun in 1914', according to Eric Hobsbawm.[12] For

Dorothy, the gradual emergence of D. J. began in the first decade of that new century. Hobsbawm calls the years 1914 to the aftermath of World War II, 'the age of catastrophe'. This was followed, he writes, by twenty-five to thirty years of economic growth and social transformation. These are the years in which Miss Ross practised her profession and tried to formulate a coherent justification for what she achieved.

We have seen that she had become aware of two principles for educators: first that a relationship with each pupil was a prerequisite to satisfactory learning; and second, that interest in a specific field was essential. These simple generalizations appear in various developed ideas in her writing and speaking and in the practices she designed and implemented. It is important to remember the turmoil of 'the age of catastrophe' lest we do less than justice to those who then worked hopefully for a more humane world in dark days. While the economy tottered, the institutions of liberal democracy virtually disappeared between 1917 and 1942 from all but a fringe of Europe and parts of North America and Australasia, as fascism and its satellite authoritarian movements and regimes advanced.[13]

It is hard to realize now how slow and laborious connections to Europe and 'the Mother country' then were and to estimate the significance of this for a young woman trying her wings as she emerged from the chrysalis of an Edwardian upbringing. It was books, visitors and migrants who cast new light on the provincial society of Victoria before telephone, radio, television and air travel promoted speedy reaction to events overseas.

The end of the war and her re-entry into the University of Melbourne in 1919 brought D. J. sharply into the twentieth century. Among her colleagues in the Faculty of Science were returned servicemen.[14] 'One hundred and forty-six Victorian teachers in the State service had been killed. They taught the nation how to die' wrote Richard Lawson of the Melbourne Teachers' College.[15] Many returned servicemen took advantage of guaranteed entry to the

University of Melbourne. Like those who had survived military service, D. J. was older than the fellow students who had come straight from school. Absorbed in her studies as she was, this community differed sharply from that of her sheltered childhood and the life of Oberwyl. In her first year (1919) she was Exhibitioner in Botany I. In her second year she gained first-class honours in Botany II and was awarded a third-class honour in Physiology I. She then interrupted her course to do part-time temporary teaching at the KTC in Kew, presumably to earn money to finance her third year of study.

Miss Ross brought to her teaching at KTC some pleasant memories of her own first experience of institutional education at the Froebel kindergarten in Geelong. From 1917 to 1965 all training of kindergarten teachers was undertaken by the Free Kindergarten Union following Froebel's precepts.[16] No government money was made available, so the Union trained kindergarteners for the kindergartens established by the various Christian denominations, as well as for its own preschools. Training was a very restricted operation conducted part-time in small poky rooms in Clyde House, Collins Street, in the city. In 1920 there were only fifteen to twenty trainees who worked as unpaid assistants in designated training kindergartens. The fees they paid (£10 and 10s per annum) were higher than the Education Department demanded of its sub-primary students. Working in a kindergarten as a philanthropic endeavour was socially acceptable to middle-class parents in the southern and eastern suburbs of Melbourne. The entrance standard was not demanding, only the junior public certificate or a pass at Year Ten was required.

Teaching Nature Study at KTC at what was virtually sixth form level was not, for her, an intellectual challenge. But it was an opportunity to create a programme which would contain the content which the students would need to know and to implement. She also had to show them how to adapt that knowledge so it would interest very young boys and girls. The Free Kindergarten Union was a charitable venture; it had been listed in *The Charities Society Booklet* of 1912 as being designed for children of working-class parents. Miss Ross could take this into account as she remembered her fleeting experience at Coburg. This was a new challenge and she realized the opportunity for planning on a miniscule scale. Miss Ross taught Nature Study, and English with Mrs Warren, Physiology with Mrs a'Beckett.

The pittance she earned for this work was supplemented in 1921 by part-time teaching at St Catherine's Girls' School, Toorak. In 1921 St Catherine's co-principals, Misses Ruth Langley and Flora Templeton, were in the process of moving their day and boarding school from 247 Williams Road to a beautiful and spacious home in Heyington Place.[17] They had combined forces when Miss Langley found she could not sustain the school she owned in Castlemaine, although it was sponsored by her uncle 'The Lord Bishop of Bendigo'.[18] Miss Templeton, a well-connected older woman, brought to the merger her pupils from her small school of Blair House in St George's Road, Toorak. When Miss Ross joined the staff of fifteen at St Catherine's there were approximately thirty boarders and between fifty and one hundred day girls gathered in what Dame Elizabeth Murdoch was later to describe as 'really quite appalling' conditions.[19] The principals had been ordered to leave the premises by the Health Department.[20]

This school was familiar ground for Miss Ross. The pupils were the daughters of the professional fathers and wealthy industrialists of 'leafy' Toorak. Miss Templeton refused admittance to the daughter of a local pharmacist: trade as distinct from large-scale industry was barred. Miss Ross was recruited to teach Physiology, Botany, and Tennis. The hours were not onerous (10 a.m. to 12.30 p.m.) classes were small, and the girls of a familiar, if wealthier, social group.[21] Miss Langley was a serious educationalist. She experimented with the Dalton Plan and established a 'lectores' (readers) class for those girls whose parents disapproved of public examinations for their daughters. Miss Ross' time there was not wasted:

she could expand her previous experience at Oberwyl and gain assurance with teenage girls.

She returned to the university in 1922 to finish her degree. This she concluded triumphantly with first-class honours in Botany and second-class honours in Physiology. She was Exhibitioner in both subjects. Ethel McLennan, Botany Associate Professor, regarded her 'as the most talented student she ever taught'.[22] Despite these results, in 1923 the Faculty of Education refused her permission to embark on study for a Master's degree in Education (M Ed) unless she first completed the Diploma. By then, Miss Ross had been teaching for nine years. Finding herself as a scientist was a crucial step in her development as a teacher. She now had a subject, Botany, which she delighted to teach to girls of different levels of understanding. To be forced to adapt a beloved discipline to school lessons tests both mastery of the subject matter and a comprehensive knowledge of the intellectual, emotional and physical growth of children. D. J. demonstrated mastery in her science course and in her language studies. How did she develop her intuitive understanding of young people into a theoretical knowledge of child development and methods of teaching and administration of a school?

She learned much in what was virtually an apprenticeship to the headmistress of MCEGGS, Miss Gilman Jones, an Englishwoman, born in 1880, who had studied the Maths Tripos at Cambridge. After wide teaching experience in England and South Africa she became a partner in a girls' school, Ascham, in New South Wales. Financial stress led her to accept the post at MCEGGS. She provided a link for D. J. between her early experiences and her evolving self-image, for Miss Gilman Jones was a formidable personality, mellowed by a sense of humour. She was assured in her position of authority within the school and in the hierachy of the Anglican Church. Her educational and feminist activities included membership of the Council of Public Education and vice-presidency in 1922–23. She was a member of the Schools' Board and member and president in 1923–24 of the Headmistresses' Association of Victoria. She was involved in the establishment of the ATTI (later Mercer House) and the maintenance of the Homecraft Hostel (later Invergowrie). Miss Gilman Jones found time to become president of the Australian Women's Voters' Association in 1922 and to serve as vice-president of the National Council of Women of Victoria in 1925 and as vice-president of the Victorian Women's Citizens Movement in 1930–34. She could not have pursued these outside activities without devolving responsibilities within the school. A building programme in 1919 resulted in a hall, laboratory and new classrooms. Her care for her staff reflected her feminist stance. The salary scales at MCEGGS were used in 1940 by women teachers in their struggle for a wages board and, unlike many independent schools and all government schools, she employed married teachers.[23]

Miss Gilman Jones was regarded by her pupils with awe and affection. Her nickname of 'Jonah' was appreciated by her and she named her holiday cottage at Barwon Heads 'The Whale'.[24] She was an innovative head of her school. She brought with her to Australia her association with the NEF and in her relatively small school was able to implement the flexibility of grouping advocated by the NEF. She was, for example, acquainted with the Howard Plan, an experiment carried out at Clapton Secondary School for Girls by Dr M. O'Brien Harris, the headmistress. The Howard Plan for Middle School was an adaptation of Dr Maria Montessori's extension of her principles to secondary schooling. Choice of activities within a strictly controlled range had been a feature of Montessori preschool and preparatory grades. In the secondary school a three-year basic programme to be covered by all students before they could proceed to the intermediate public examinations was based on the same principle. Miss Gilman Jones and her staff interpreted this to mean that some subjects—English, Scripture, Current Topics, Civics, Singing, Gymnastics and Games—would be studied each week as a class. There was some choice for individual pupils in the balance of the curriculum, and some choice also in the order in which all subjects were studied and in the location in which pupils worked during free study periods. This flexibility was promoted by a vertical division of pupils into 'houses' in preference to the conventional horizontal division by chronological age into classes or forms.

This division into houses under a housemistress illustrated the New Education emphasis on the importance of stable peer and tutorial relationships in groups, in which loyal and amicable feelings could be fostered among diverse individuals. Wartime stress and postwar hope had given these ideas currency in Great Britain. Miss Gilman Jones brought them to the staff and parents of her school. Among those who chose to become a housemistress was Miss Ross. Miss Gilman Jones had been quick to recognize the quality of her new recruit and had directed her to teaching senior and middle school Science. The new organization offered Miss Ross an opportunity to test her conviction that personal relationships were essential for optimal learning.

Miss Ross made some comments on the benefits and difficulties of the Howard Plan as she administered it under the direction of Miss Gilman Jones. The Howard Plan as it was implemented at MCEGGS served to divide a heterogeneous population into workable groups. The school was comprehensive in an intellectual sense, restricted by fee-paying in a social sense, and restricted by gender (except for small boys in the prepatory grades). Several principles were involved in a vertical rather than a horizontal method of division. Basically the Plan assumed an hereditary-based intelligence measured by chronological age and facility in certain sections of the culture (mathematics-based 'subjects', linguistic subjects, manual dexterities). It was expected that each girl could master, given time and incentive, an appropriate syllabus. A basic core of necessary knowledge and skills could be extended by individual choice of alternative subjects (Mathematics, Science, Languages). The key word was mastery. During the three years of the Plan, five stages of each subject must be mastered one by one. 'Mastery', not time spent on the subject, was the criterion for progressing.

Incentive was to be found in the satisfaction of mastering the corpus of knowledge and in the socially cohesive house grouping. A house consisted of sixty girls studying during those three years, with the key figure, the housemistress, in a supportive administrative role. Emphasis on individual study habits entailed free study periods allocated in each individual timetable. The Howard Plan placed an administrative burden on the housemistress. Parental pressure on 'free choice' complicated timetabling. Individual teaching had to be resorted to when timetable clashes could not be resolved. Cross-age teaching was a possibility and the opportunities for leadership were increased. Inter-house competition was accepted as a proper stimulus to sporting, charitable and intellectual endeavour.

As an organizational principle, delegation of authority by the headmistress to house and subject mistresses was adopted. Miss Ross could experience and observe this procedure, the interest it generated counterbalanced the low salaries and the increased effort entailed by the Plan. It was consistent that at fifth form level Miss Gilman Jones continued the policy previously introduced by Miss Edith Morris[25] of an alternative programme for those older girls who for various reasons did not intend to sit for the public examinations. It was still customary for affluent Australian parents to send schoolgirl daughters to be 'finished' in Paris or London. A local alternative for the girls whose parents disliked 'bookish' girls gained some support from the Parents' Association which was formed in 1928. MCEGGS was still a small school in today's terms: in 1931 there were 350 girls in the 'Big School' and 150 in the Junior School at a time when an Infantile Paralysis epidemic disrupted schooling throughout Victoria. This record portrays a formidable headmistress. Miss Gilman Jones was a fine example of a life dedicated to education and to her Anglican faith. Miss Ross acknowledged her formative influence for Miss Gilman Jones had consolidated a school in which Miss Ross, the successor she had moulded, would fit comfortably. At the time of Miss Ross' appointment as headmistress she was able to congratulate the school in 'having as headmistress a woman of such brilliant gifts as Miss Ross who moreover knows the school well'.[26] Miss Ross, however, was no Gilman Jones clone. She was nineteen years younger, born in Australia into a comparable social group but exposed to different intellectual and social currents. It was to become important that in the broad spectrum of Anglicanism Miss Ross was no church woman in the sense in which Miss Gilman Jones contributed to her church. Miss Gilman Jones had seen the school in its setting as a church school, so did Miss Ross but she did not consider that her position as headmistress required her to take public positions in the hierarchy of the Anglican Church.

Miss Ross sat with Miss Gilman Jones when she heard Professor John Adams give a series of lectures in Melbourne in 1924. He would have spoken directly to her concerns as she implemented the Howard Plan as housemistress of St Cecilia's House. His treatment of theory in ordinary language showed him to be a down-to-earth practical man. The term 'paidocentrism' was deflated as he explained that 'verbs of teaching govern two accusatives, one of the person, another of the thing—*Magister Johannen Docuit*—as the master taught John Latin'.[27]

This is now a truism but in 1924 it stated for Miss Ross what she had already discovered: that personal relationships between teacher and pupil were essential if John were to learn Latin. It would not have appeared to her odd or reprehensible that Adams spoke only of John and his master; Jane hardly ever appeared. Miss Ross herself followed this convention in much of her own writing. She also wrote and spoke in ordinary language but it would be facile to interpret her public communications as an index of her depth of thought at this time. John Adams had written a comprehensive study, *The Evolution of Educational Theory*, in 1912 and when he spoke in Melbourne in 1924 he was adapting his discourse to what he knew of primary teachers and what he had no doubt been told about his colonial audience.

He was bringing the New Education to the unenlightened.[28] Neither Miss Gilman Jones nor Miss Ross were his target audience but he could confirm and extend what Miss Ross had already formulated for herself. Unlike her experience of the syllabus for the DipEd, the Adams lectures attracted her attention. In September 1924 Miss Ross appeared as editor of the *Australian Educational Quarterly* published by the IARTV. Miss Gilman Jones' guiding hand can be assumed. As joint editor with F. E. Grieve (MA, DipEd, a master at Wesley College) Miss Ross shaped the *Quarterly* and contributed to the April 1929 issue. In her editorial notes of 15 September 1929 Miss Ross shows her firm balance looking at the 'bewildering mass of tendencies and new methods continually arising, and books defending or criticising these new methods [that] are continually appearing'.[29] She draws attention to some problems in testing this 'bewildering mass' in practice. Frequently, when dealing with new methods, schemes and plans in education, the personal factor is completely forgotten. It takes a Dr Rouse to maintain a Perse School, a Caldwell Cook to make a success of 'Littleman'.[30]

In 1928 Miss Gilman Jones fostered the next step in Miss Ross' education as a teacher. It was on her recommendation that Miss Ross was appointed late in that year as supervisor of ATTI, contingent on her obtaining an appropriate formal qualification as a secondary school teacher. She was to take up her appointment at the begining of 1930 and in the interval was enrolled in the 'Course for Teachers of Experience' at the London Day Training College (later the Institute of Education of the University of London). Miss Ross journeyed to England in the company of Miss Ethel Colebrook, a fellow member of staff of MCEGGS. There is a vivid picture of their life at Crosby Hall, a residence for academic women in Chelsea, in a letter written by a fellow resident, Miss Constance Tisdall, to her family on 31 May 1929. She had met Miss Ross at the Australian table at the Hall on 6 May, with Miss Colebrook, 'who is a dear', and they shared expeditions to theatre, concerts and the Rachel Macmillan Nursery School.

> we have breakfast at eight in the big hall. That's a thrill in itself, when you think of the people whose memories are bound up with it. We sit on benches (backless) and the principals sit on the dais. There is a huge fireplace, where there is a fire most days even now. The roof of course is wonderful . . . I pay £3 a week, but that doesn't include lunch or tea: for which I pay 1s. and 6d. respectively. There are rules to be kept. I paid 2/6 deposit for my latch key so am quite independent there! At breakfast, lunch and tea we help ourselves from a warmer arrangement. There is Indian or China tea (I mix them) and coffee and all the usual things to eat. Most of the vegetable dishes are of pewter—and the bread and fruit are on wooden dishes. Dinner is at seven, and then we are waited upon. The waitresses and maids are all ladies—some of them, I think, graduates. Perhaps they all are . . .[31]

Life at Crosby Hall was regulated in a way reminiscent of a girls' boarding school. It was plain living for hard-working women who were experiencing London life in the company of women familiar to them in their Australian professional lives. If the visit was to be a broadening social experience, it depended on contacts outside Crosby Hall. Miss Ross found an enriching experience through her membership of the NEF. She was already acquainted with the ideas of the 'New Education' and of the work of the NEF. She had the opportunity to consolidate and develop her understanding of NEF principles when she attended the Fifth World Conference at Elsinore, Denmark, in August 1929. The report and comments on the papers and discussions at the conference give a clear picture of the confused idealism which confronted Miss Ross.[32] In the pages of this report we find statements of the response of educators in countries relatively untouched by the legacy of World War I: Denmark, Sweden, Norway, Latvia, Finland, and of those in countries seeking national rehabilitation: Germany, Austria, Poland, Russia, Turkey and England. In hindsight, after World War II and the death of the hopes enunciated in the early 1920s it requires an effort of the imagination to understand the atmosphere in which Miss Ross imbibed the ideas which led to her later educational practice. There were juxtaposed reports of the evolution of 'folk high schools' in Denmark, with the development of the German educational system under the Weimar Republic, with the theory and practice of Soviet education in Russia and accounts of American and British experiments. There were sessions devoted to discussion of the methods of learning and teaching, of the content of curricula and of testing and examining, and of the appropriate training of teachers. The philosophical and psychological bases on which the new education was devised were discussed. Miss Ross recorded some of her impressions of the conference in letters to friends at the IARTV.[33] They give a picture of the social life of the conference and the reactions of a lively young woman enjoying her contact with the persons who had been 'famous names' to her in Australia. She wrote:

> The whole affair is excellently organised . . . I imagine every house is being used . . . We sit down to table all together—four Australians, one Irish, three Finns, two Swedes and waited on by a Danish lady and her two daughters . . . Language is a problem for social encounters and most notably for some lectures . . . The big bug of the conference is, of course, Madame Montessori. She really is a most remarkable woman. I believe she speaks English perfectly, but her boss in Italy, Mr Mussolini (to whom I will always refer in future as Mr Smith—we all call him Mr Smith here!) will not allow her to speak publicly in any language but Italian. Also, every public lecture here may be given in the speaker's own language, but a printed translated summary may be obtained in at least three languages. Not so Montessori. When she spoke, she spoke in Italian, and, standing beside her—pin for pin alike in height and age and appearance, was an interpreter who translated her speech sentence by sentence into Danish—in compliment to the hostess country. But no English, French or German printed summaries for love or money. It was an extraordinary method of making a speech. But the marvellous thing was that she held without a sound an audience of over 1,000, of

whom only about 50 could understand her, and only about 60 per cent could understand Danish. Fortunately an English woman who understood Italian was able to get down almost everything, and she redelivered the lecture afterwards to the English members of the audience in another room—with Madame Montessori sitting amusedly at the back of the hall. Fortunately I was able to get down almost every word of the very fine lecture it was, to send to the AEQ [*Australian Educational Quarterly*].

. . . It is by no means a holiday, as we are cramming what might be a term's work into a fortnight. We have courses and groupwork and lectures . . . What I like about it is meeting and hearing and talking to men whose books I have known for years, or whose work I have known about.[34]

Contact at the conference with Dr Dengler, substituting for Franz Cizek who was ill, took Miss Ross with her compatriots to Vienna to visit the Cizek School of Art.[35] Back in London she followed up her meetings with Dr Montessori and attended a term's course of lectures given in London (this time in English). Professor William Connell, who was one of the sixteen Australians at the conference, has commented on those participants with whom Miss Ross was particularly impressed:

The general topic under discussion was 'The New Psychology and the Curriculum'. In the exploration of this topic speakers expounded the behavioural, gestalt, psychoanalytic theories of the time, looked at the reconstructive possibilities of education for current society, and discussed various pioneering schools, methods of teaching, and ways of reorganizing curricula. Short courses were offered by various lecturers such as Maria Montessori and Harold Rugg. Dorothy Ross attended both. She was greatly excited by the whole conference and particularly enthusiastic about Montessori whose lectures and demonstrations deepened her own growing conviction of the importance for teachers of the study of child development and the significance of early childhood education. The American educators, whose views she had 'rather liked' when she had read their books, she also found congenial. From them, particularly Rugg, she heard views on ways of reconstructing the curriculum both to make it more socially responsive and to provide opportunity for more individual self-expression. She joined a group for eight lectures and discussions on teacher training by the heads of teachers' colleges throughout Europe and America. She listened to Elizabeth Rotten and Paul Geheeb, the most talented and sensitive of German progressives, to Helen Parkhurst and Carleton Washburne, the originators respectively of the Dalton and Winnetka Plans, to William Boyd and Beatrice Ensor, mainstays of the NEF in the United Kingdom, and to Decroly Roger Cousinet, the most esteemed and influential progressive in the French speaking world. It was a rich and seminal experience.[36]

She had also been attracted to Dr Susan Isaacs and to her use of Freudian concepts and made contact with her when she returned to London. As she fulfilled the requirements of the teacher training course in one year instead of two and travelled in Scotland and in Europe it can be assumed that there was little time for consecutive critical analysis of the whole indigestible experience. It can safely be assumed that the impact of the international character of the NEF convinced her that serious attention must be devoted to sorting out the principles, if any, that were common to the numerous presentations at the conference. Her return to Melbourne in 1930 as supervisor and designate mistress of Method at the ATTI marks the end of her initial period as a classroom teacher. She now had to develop a theoretical position from which to educate intending teachers.

Her early training as a linguist and subsequent studies in biological sciences formed a basis for her thoughts. At this moment she was fundamentally an empiricist, her feet firmly on the earth. All concepts were for her derived from experience. 'I must have lived ideas in the world if I am to believe them to have meaning' she could have said. Pragmatism went hand in hand with a firm Christian faith. The world of the spirit had another vocabulary. In her first year at the ATTI the presence of her predecessor, Miss Catherine Remington, would not have been a heavy constraint. Miss Ross was again in tutelage, albeit that of a congenial erudite woman whose quality is attested by the inspectors of the Council of Public Education in the final report on her work in September 1930: 'The inspectors desire to place on record their appreciation of the work of Miss Remington. By her sound scholarship, her compelling personality, her breadth of vision, her stimulating influence over her students, she has contributed largely to the standard of primary teaching in registered schools'.[37]

Miss Ross had her experience as a teacher at Oberwyl, St Catherine's and Coburg Higher Elementary School and MCEGGS to draw upon, and the limited experience of training teachers at KTC. This was good preparation for the variety of schools and the broad range of school supervisors with whom she would have to deal. There was much to do and much to learn. She had, no doubt, absorbed John Adams' advice not to attempt 'premature synthesis'.[38] The New Education was 'making use of a great variety of principles'.[39] Certain key ideas could be adopted tentatively. while she cultivated the necessary practical skills. She continued to publish substantial articles in the *Australian Educational Quarterly*. In May 1930 her notes of Maria Montessori's lecture at Elsinore as translated into English appeared:

> The environment must be revealing not formative; one that reveals the child's inner spirit, and does not impose an adult attitude on the unsuspecting and plastic mind . . . By creating an atmosphere natural to childhood one may stand by and see the child revealing himself as he really is . . . the child's inner satisfaction is the act of polishing not the finished work. Adults have ulterior motives for their work; children work for the work itself. So the child does not really need competition and external prizes and stimuli . . . The development of the child represents a series of conquests of the environment. At different stages he shows 'sensitive points' which must be used to help him realize himself. Instinctively these sensitive points direct the child towards the material things which help him to unfold at the right moment the powers within him. These points are psychologically very important. If they are not used at the critical stage they can never be recaptured . . . his spirit in work will ever remain that of the creative artist or poet-the spirit of joy in doing.[40]

In the following year (1931) she contributed an article on the Danish folk high schools, and in April of the same year 'Random but expurgated thoughts of an examiner', with a characteristic opening sentence: 'Some examiners do have thoughts, many of which however are unprintable'. Some of her printable thoughts as examiner of Intermediate Botany in December 1930 are displayed as she writes:

> They illustrate points of wider and more general interest. I feel that in teaching Botany ideas should be taught before terms and the terms should be introduced, insidiously as it were, only when the class is thoroughly familiar with the idea (from object to idea to classifying term). The term will be easier for those students to remember if they can relate it to its Greek or Latin root . . . and why [call it] Briza when Shell grass is so much nicer.

The article concludes with a plea for treating Botany as a subject worthy of intelligent study equal to the physical sciences and mathematics:

> I do not wish to deprecate the aesthetic side of the subject which, at bottom, is the side that matters most, but I do want to maintain that the very fact of its scientific character adds aesthetic weight to the subject, because an appreciation of the beauty of the world of Nature is immeasurably enhanced by an understanding of the wonders of its workings.[41]

What she had learned in her travels had to be tried in practice; but there were constraints. The council of the IARTV through its Executive Committee was responsible for policy to the independent schools. Inspectors annually assessed the work of the IARTV on behalf of the Council of Public Education. Recruitment of full-time students was restricted by the prerequisite that they find employment as a pupil teacher in a registered school. The premises in McEwan House at 343 Little Collins Street were too small to accommodate the students for their lectures and classes on two afternoons a week. There was also pressure on the space from the inservice lectures which the ATTI had provided since 1921. Miss

Ross had not appointed her staff. She enjoyed working with Irene Webb and Alice Crowther, lecturers in Drama and Speech, but neither she nor the students found Mr Richardson inspiring. He taught and was also secretary to the IARTV.

The supervision of the student teachers in their schools was labour intensive and placements in Melbourne suburbs and as far afield as Geelong, Mount Macedon and Berwick made the work of the supervisor and her staff physically demanding. Miss Ross drove everywhere, often with her cocker spaniel beside her. It was for Miss Ross an opportunity to develop the skills in managing people that St Cecilia's House had required and to try her hand at working with an overseeing committee and liaising with H. M. inspectors of schools. She did not make advances towards a theory of education between 1930 and 1935. She found time to edit R. H. Yapp's *Botany: A Junior Book for Schools,* to harvest the work she had done in collecting specimens when she had taught at MCEGGS. She did not have leisure to study and resolve the theoretical differences in the works of Froebel, Montessori and Susan Isaacs.[42] She did find time to lead one of the two reading circles set up by the Assistant Mistresses Association, an unofficial form of inservice teacher education. The *Australian Educational Quarterly* reported:

> Miss Ross has taken the following subjects: (1) Thinking, (2) Freedom, (3) Body, Mind and Spirit, (4) Education and the Adolescent, (5) Play and the Aesthetic, (6) Growth of the Mind, and in connection with these has set various books including *Every Man's Psychology*, Adams; *Instinct, Intelligence, Character*, Stanley Hall; *The New Children*, Radica. Circle discussion has ranged over such problems as hero worship, the religious ideas of the child, and the child's appreciation of art . . . The circles had much difficulty in securing a sufficient number of text-books . . . The circle led by Mrs Thorne is using *The Aims of Education and Other Essays* by A. N. Whitehead in which he voices his protest against inert ideas.[43]

She was learning her trade as a teacher of pupil teachers. A snapshot of the educational world in which she worked is needed to put her achievements in perspective. It was a small world in many senses of that word. Some constraints on the development of her ideas when she began to work at ATTI have already been discussed. It was a unique institution. In Victoria the number and prestige of the independent schools was higher than in the other Australian States. Like their counterparts in the UK, school councils and heads did not place great value on trained teachers. The boys' schools preferred to choose their man for scholarship and character or sporting prowess, and imbue him with the ethos of their school. Techniques of teaching would be acquired by accepting advice of more experienced members of staff. As a classical education was deemed to be an adequate training for serving the state as ambassador or civil servant, so, too, no gentleman needed formal training to become an adequate teacher of young gentlemen.

This 'back door' into teaching appeared to be a suitable means of acquiring staff for single-sex independent schools. Trainee student teachers were poorly paid. They could be influenced by a supervisor in the school while the business of registration and teacher training could be left to the ATTI. The schools formed and financed the IARTV. When a weak supervisor led its training branch the ATTI supervisors in the schools criticized anything in the training which did not suit the policy of their school or college. Miss Ross inherited from Miss Remington, a dignified and respected scholar, the reputation her predecessor had created at the ATTI. Miss Ross had made her mark in NEF circles but she was not yet well known in the schools. It would be some time before she could hope to find supervisors in schools who would welcome students with progressive ideas. The heads of the non-government girls' schools 'found response to the challenge of the New Education somewhat easier'[44] than did the boys' schools and the State schools or those in the Catholic education system. The pressure on schools to prepare a girl for a professional future was not so intense. The influence of A. S. Neil, Bedales and Dartington Hall could be seen in Preshil school. This school was an exception.

The heads of schools were members of the governing body of the IARTV. Miss Ross' students had to be considered employable by them. She had grown up happily in this milieu and held fast to the religious and scholarly values it embodied. During the first four years the changes that she inaugurated were not confronting. Her annual report to the IARTV in March 1932 gives a picture of one of her immediate concerns, the academic preparation of her students: 'The year 1931 closed with a roll of forty-two of whom twenty-five were first year and seventeen were second year students'.[45] The academic standard is revealed by her comment that primary registration was attained by only a few second year students as some lacked compulsory Intermediate (fourth form) Arithmetic:

> The entrance qualification for ATTI is matriculation which is ultimately required by The Council of Public Education for Primary Registration ... A bare Leaving Certificate [fifth form] is a very slender qualification for primary teaching. A year in an Honours Class helps to give a wider background and greater poise, both much needed qualifications for a teacher. To attempt to broaden this academic base during teacher training, evokes the comment 'Academic work and professional training both suffer if attempted together'.[46]

Miss Ross believed students came to their training with an inadequate general education. By 1933 she was sufficiently confident in her position to press for a new document defining the responsibilities of the ATTI committee and ensuring that the supervisor had the power of appointing staff subject to committee endorsement if additional expenditure was incurred. She had taken the first cautious steps towards enlarging the role of the Training Institute and gaining the powers that would enable her to bring the challenge of fresh ideas.

Miss Ross had become a member of the Executive Committee of the ATTI on her appointment in 1930, and in the ensuing three years she began to put her own imprint on the ATTI. She was thirty-eight years old and had quickly perceived the necessity of recognition of her sphere of independent action by the governing body of the heads of independent schools. She knew that if she permitted, the formidable heads of schools would dictate policy, yet their co-operation was essential for the functioning of the programme of teacher training since the intake of students was determined by the paid posts offered to student teachers in the schools. The conditions of their employment had to be negotiated. Miss Remington had already commented 'while a student's life should not necessarily be easy, it should not be so hard as to dim the brightness of the gifts of youth—vitality, initiative and eagerness to work and play'.[47] In 1932 Miss Ross' hand can be seen in new regulations proposed by the Executive Committee of the ATTI to the Council meeting of the IARTV on 5 October:

1. Student Teachers. The school should arrange for one ordinary observation lesson a week.
2. That the student should have at least 9 free periods (40 minutes) per week. Miss Ross estimated that the study time required by the students apart from the actual attendance at lecures averaged nearly 10^1/$_2$ hours per week for the three terms of the year. This calculation included no provision for reading.
3. That no student teacher should be required to spend more than 20 periods in actual teaching, of which at least 10 must be in the primary department.
4. The sub-committee recommended that the ATTI refuse to accept students for training unless they were definitely employed on school staff and paid a salary.[48]

This is unmistakable Miss Ross, a clear vision of the actual working week for a student and the translation of a benign purpose into definite plans. In 1933 salaries for student teachers were set at £40 per annum for fifteen periods of teaching per week with an additional £2 per annum for every additional weekly period. The same sharp perception of the reality of institutional organization is seen in the other proposals Miss Ross put forward in 1932. Through the ATTI Executive Committee the IARTV retained the right to appoint the staff of the ATTI. In August 1933 the AIRTV Council resolved as Miss Ross had requested: 'All staff of the ATTI shall be under the control of the supervisor who shall have power to make and cancel appointments, reporting to the next meeting of the ATTI Committee'.[49]

In 1932 Miss Ross brought to the 5 October meeting of the ATTI Executive proposals for a new course in sub-primary teaching. The endorsement of the Department of Education was required and collaboration with the KTC was desirable. A visiting supervisor of sub-primary students would be required. A trial of the course was to be held on thirty-two Saturday mornings in the following year. The Department inspector criticized the course because it provided no opportunity for observation or criticism lessons. Miss Ross was satisfied that the theoretical content of the trialled course could form the second year of a sub-primary course and proposed a restructuring of ATTI courses. Primary and sub-primary students would share a common first year and specialize in the second year. A third year was to be required for double registration.[50] The new courses were approved by the Education Department and the schools.

These changes could be welcomed in the schools as could the development of a more adequate ATTI library. In 1933 the library committee (of the Executive Committee) of the IARTV changed the system of depending on gifts of books and charged a one shilling donation from each student per term. In future £1 per term was allocated to the library from each student's fees. As early as 1934 Miss Ross was telling the Conference of Heads of Schools and the ATTI Executive Committee:

> At present classes were very large, it was a mistaken kindness on the part of schools to accept as teachers more students than really necessary for then such students could not attain sufficient practical experience. If too many students were trained then no positions would be later obtainable for them. On the other hand, certain schools gave more work than was proper to student teachers. *Young teachers should not be given too much teaching or too great responsibility.*

Sufficient spare periods should be allowed for preparation of notes of lessons and for observation work. With graduands the case was different; they could be given more periods of work than younger students *and more salary*.[51]

In the debate that followed Mrs Limcock (Penleigh) doubted the wisdom of paying students £40 in their first year. She thought they should be paid less and given less work, but that conditions of work set out should be adhered to rigidly. Against this Miss Ross thought that there could not be sufficient training unless fifteen to twenty periods were occupied in teaching.[52] To watch Miss Ross overseeing the practice she considered essential for the professional development of her students is to begin to understand how she demonstrated her ideas. Folding her body into a desk intended for primary school height in a junior school classroom, Miss Ross noticed a 6-year-old-girl sitting in the third row. What had attracted her attention? The restless hands turning and turning a pencil, the dark blotches under unfocused eyes, the slight movement changing body weight from side to side? Something, she thought, might be wrong here. The lesson ended, and in the staff room the student teacher turned expectantly to her supervisor, and mistress of Method. The first question was unexpected: 'What is the matter with that dark-haired child, second from the right in the third row?' The startled student consulted her seating plan: 'That is Lucy Norton, Miss Ross. I haven't had to speak to her'. Miss Ross, like her mentor Susan Isaacs, had a penetrating eye for the bodily signs of inner distress. She did not rely on theory to emphasize to a raw, inadequately prepared young woman that she must *look*, must ask herself: 'Is each of my pupils healthy, well fed, free enough from crippling anxiety to be able to attend to a carefully prepared lesson?' This one-to-one teaching of her students was more important, Miss Ross said, than the lectures she gave in Little Collins Street.[53] She was 'nosing her way' towards the administration of a small enterprise and demonstrating to her students and to the schools in which they taught that individual pupils learned, as students themselves did. Each individual learned in a relationship with a teacher who shared enthusiasm for what they taught, whether it was Intermediate Botany or techniques of class-room management.[54]

By 1935 D. J. was ready to deepen her understanding of what she was doing. She had unfinished business from the Elsinore Conference. She could learn more from Susan Isaacs and from the schools in England which embodied the New Education. It was time. She was on her way. She applied for three months' leave and when it was granted set out in the mid-year break in 1935. She was no longer an apprentice. She was a proven professional woman. She would now choose from whom she would learn. This expedition would mark a new phase in her professional development and widen her perception of the world outside Australia. It is interesting that there is no mention of the Depression in the records of the IARTV meetings nor in Miss Ross' reports to that body. The major independent schools seem to have been largely insulated from communal hardship during the years 1929 to 1933.[55] D. J.'s vision of her world was about to change.

3

A Step Forward

D. J.'s second voyage to England in 1935 celebrated personal and professional independence. She did not go to England as a student but as the accredited head of an institution with the assurance of a successful first five years. The IARTV had granted her £100 towards her expenses. She had learned to deal with her governing body, with the State Education Department and a variety of independent schools. She had impressed and charmed her students and led her small staff. When she visited schools and teacher training institutions she was received as a visitor of consequence. She knew by now that in England one prefaced a visit with a letter introducing oneself and tentatively suggesting available dates. She could make the most of her time.

It was not all 'education' in that short visit. There was music with Anne and Stewart Macky and their cottage in the country[1] where D. J. and Anne gave respite one weekend to a young Australian woman struggling to establish a relationship with a German refugee intellectual in the face of family reluctance. In that setting D. J. was relaxed, warm and cheerful. She quickly established an easy informality with a cautious young man with precise German good manners: and packed the pair off to a shared bedroom with no-nonsense good humour.

As always with D. J., the serious purpose of the visit took precedence over relaxation. She had come to learn more from Susan Isaacs and to visit schools and teacher training colleges. Susan Isaacs was an older contemporary, born in 1885 with many of her publications still to appear. D. J. had responded to her restful warmth and depth of understanding at Elsinore in 1929 and later in London. Susan Isaacs shared D. J.'s practical orientation. She had been principal of Malting House School, Cambridge, from 1924 to 1927 and by 1935 was head of the Department of Child Development at the University of London Institute of Education. She would become a member of the training committee of the Institute of Psychoanalysis from 1944 to 1946. Susan Isaacs had accepted Freud's account of the psychological development of human beings and interpreted them for parents and teachers in easily understood and untroubling language. She had written in 1928: 'to know in general that it is a matter of how much and at what age, or of the appropriateness of fixity of emotions is one thing; to be able to read the situation precisely in any given case is another'.[2]

During the ten weeks in which D. J. heard Susan Isaacs lecture she probably was not confronted with the complexities of Freud's metapsychology. Like D. J., Susan Isaacs was concerned with educating: helping mothers and nannies and institutional carers to understand children's development and to learn why their own reactions to children's behaviour was not always appropriate. The language and concepts of Freud's writings were not explicit when she taught these audiences.[3] D. J. may also have attended a series of lectures developed in the Spring at the Institute of Child Psychology by Dr Ian Suttie. Certainly she was able to purchase and read them in published form in *The Origins of Love and Hate*.[4] This volume was a basic source of some of D. J.'s ideas about the education of student teachers and of female pupils. Suttie wrote in his introduction:

> Formally the tentative theory I have formed belongs to the group of psychologies that originates from the work of Freud. It differs fundamentally from psychoanalysis in introducing the conception of an

innate-need-for-companionship which is the infant's way of self-preservation. This need gives rise to parental and fellowship 'love'. I put it in the place of Freudian Libido, and regard it as genetically independent of genital appetite.[5]

In 1935 the sociological consideration of ideas was becoming of growing concern among historians and political philosophers at the London School of Economics. Similarly, psychologists were considering Freudian theory in the light of their knowledge of domestic habits and conventions in Germany in the years in which Freud first wrote. The applicability of Freudian concepts (as then understood) to English middle-class homes was beginning to be queried.[6] It is not difficult to discern what Suttie offered to D. J. Suttie distinguishes between Freud's psychoanalytical clinical practice and his metapsychological theoretical formulations. Of the former he tentatively postulated: 'Freudian practice is a cure by love'.[7] Suttie's criticisms of Freud's theoretical position have been developed since 1935 and added to by many critics. On this second visit to Europe D. J. was ready to receive some of Suttie's key ideas. Her own childhood as an only and female child in an extended family of strong women would leave a residue of understanding of the significance of Suttie's emphasis on the centrality of relationships, with the mother as an alternative to Freud's patriarchal organization. D. J. had been schooled, as we have seen, in a Froebel's kindergarten and she had later taught his ideas in the Kindergarten Training College in Melbourne. Suttie's dependence on relationships in a social community as a key to emotional development would thus strike a familiar note. She may have also responded with relief to the 'English' denial of the primacy of a libido grounded in genital desire.

In 1935 in London Norman Haire and Dora Russell were shocking their contemporaries in the World League for Sexual Reform.[8] D. J. had already read and experienced some difficulty in assimilating Radclyffe Hall's *The Well of Loneliness*, published in 1928[9] and in Suttie's thought sexual elements would have no place in three of the four distinguishable but overlapping types of relationships between persons, which C. S. Lewis later described as affection, friendship, eros and charity.[10] Lewis' definitions provide a useful framework for considering the nuances of interpersonal relationships which are central to analysing the behaviour and beliefs of adult human beings.

Affection: 'the truly wide taste in humanity will similarly find something to appreciate in the cross-section of humanity whom one has to meet every day'. 'Because we are a social species familiar association provides a *milieu* in which, if all goes well, affection will arise and grow strong without demanding any very shining qualities in its objects'. Friendship demands more. It is 'in a sense not at all derogatory to it—the least natural of loves; the least instinctive, organic, biological, gregarious and necessary . . . It is essentially between individuals . . . a luminous, tranquil rational world of relationships freely chosen'. Charity 'is wholly disinterested and desires simply what is best for the beloved'. In Lewis' terms 'divine gift-love in the man enables him to love what is not naturally lovable'.[11] This is the apex of the pyramid of human loving and the place of eros, erotic love, lies between friendship and charity. The debate between Freud and Suttie is about the centrality of libido in the development of these relationships.

In her public image Miss Ross displayed affection, friendship and charity and these appear to be the aspects of relationships between staff and between staff and pupils and between the girls which the organization of the ATTI and later the 'democratic' school fostered. They can be seen to reflect the emphasis Suttie placed on them in his critical interpretation of Freud's theories in 1935. They accorded well with what Miss Ross had heard and had studied in John Adams' writing. Adams had written in 1922:

> Child study in moderation is an excellent thing, and has always been
> carried on to some extent. But the natural history stage of ped-
> analysis as exemplified in child study is something quite different
> from the application to children of a form of analysis that properly
> belongs to the resources of pathology, and should have no place

among ordinary wholesome children ... The teacher must be as
nearly normal as Stekel and Freud will allow him, and must above
everything carry on his work in school by dealing with his pupils on
a wholesome human footing.[12]

Wholesome teachers of wholesome children will realize that
although a 'plant must have roots below as well as sunlight above
and roots must be grubby. Much of the grubbiness is clean dirt if
only you will leave it in the garden and not keep sprinkling it over
the library table'.[13] Teachers should not concern themselves with
the genital impulses of their 'wholesome' pupils. An optimist in
England in 1935 might have brushed aside the evidence of anti-
social behaviour in children as pathological. Freud's pessimistic
belief 'that the mind of a man is so attuned that it is swamped by
arguments and rational considerations once it listens to them. But
just as arguments and rational considerations have such power over
him, he will, when comfort demands it, do all he can not to listen
to them' suggests a different emphasis.[14]

D. J. had inherited strong passions and sensitive nerves. Her
upbringing had led to controlled behaviour in conformity with the
social mores of her family group. The disturbing theses of Freud's
followers and critics challenged the orthodoxy in which she had
been reared. Her inner conflict between reason and the passions
reflected the debate between Freud, Susan Isaacs and Suttie. She
experienced a formative conflict during her second excursion into
a changing European culture. In that year she retained some of
the optimism of the inter-war years. She had taught her student
teachers to trust in devising modes of schooling which would educate pupils for an affectionate society.

Different expressions of 'this good working faith' were found in
the schools in England that Miss Ross talked about and visited.
A member of her staff, Alice Crowther, was an anthroposophist, a
follower of Rudolf Steiner. Alice Crowther had planned to spend
some time at the Goetheanum, near Basel, the centre of the life of
the sect.[15] She spoke with Miss Ross of the importance of Steiner's

belief in the educational significance of the concept of the trans-migration of souls. If human development was not constrained by a single lifetime educators could afford to take a relaxed view of slow developers. The rate of development was not necessarily an index of intellectual potentiality. Intelligence testing relied on checking achievement against chronological developmental norms for estimating IQ. This view was denied in Steiner schools where slow learners benefited from the relaxed and respectful atmosphere. This view conflicted to some extent with a reliance, then prevalent in Australia, on IQ testing (how Miss Ross coped with this is explored in chapter 4). From an entirely different theoretical basis Miss Ross was exposed to A. S. Neill's practice at Summerhill where, with the help of his son-in-law, a psychiatrist, working on Stekelian principles, he was 'bringing happiness to some few children'.[16] What Miss Ross found acceptable in Neill's statement of his stance was: 'At Summerhill it is his love that cures it is approval and the freedom to be true to oneself'.[17] She rejected his statement: 'Freud says sex is the greatest force in human behaviour. Every honest observer must agree'. And she also found unacceptable: 'Make the unconscious conscious and religion will have no function ... Hate and rebellion are only thwarted love and thwarted power'.[18]

Her faith as a Christian denied such scepticism. As noted in chapter 2, D. J. in her university days was a member of the Student Christian Alliance (later the Student Christian Movement). She had retained the belief of her Anglican upbringing and at the ATTI she had based her psychology lectures on the then published works of the Rev. Leslie Weatherhead, an erudite Methodist minister. Dr Weatherhead wrote with balance and logic of current psychological theories within the parameters of his professed religion. The convincing 'proof' of Christianity, he was to write in 1951: 'is to be found not in the intellectual reasoning by which this or that dogma is defended, impressive though this often is, but by the lives of people who have been changed by it'.[19]

The racist theories of *Mein Kampf*, for example, are not validated by the number of persons whose lives they changed. Fallacious as this argument is, it would have appealed to D. J. who tested a person's sincerity by the extent to which they implemented belief in action. Rev. Leslie Weatherhead made a succinct analysis of the variations of psychoanalytical doctrines in the works of Freud, Adler and Jung. He also considered the then popular purposive or hormic psychology of William McDougall and the Behaviourists. He undertook a Freudian analysis.[20] Through him and through other secondary sources, among them Susan Isaacs, D. J. was confronted with a more complex version of the nature of individual human beings. New dimensions were added to her thinking. As Professor Connell has observed, she selected from each of them ideas to which she responded. In the turmoil of ideas and practices she struggled to maintain her balance and to formulate a personal position on which she could ground her professional practice and an understanding of herself with which she could live. It was a testing time for her. A. S. Neill and Summerhill did not wholly convince her that Stekel had found the answer to emotional maladjustment in children.

Neill, like many who accepted Freud's emphasis, misunderstood him when they attributed to Freud the belief that education should give 'the power to subordinate thinking to feeling'.[21] In so doing, they contributed to the devaluation of a function of schooling which was to initiate children into the inherited culture. Curriculum and lessons were conventional at Summerhill. Attendance at classes was voluntary. In her own life and in her professional programmes D. J. never made this mistake. The educated heart for which she worked was intelligently disciplined feeling. To make the unconscious conscious, she realized, was to enlarge the ego and diminish the domination of the id.

When A. S. Neill visited Dartington Hall, he asked the children why they did not scribble on the walls. He was reacting to a progressive school which had its origin in a different tradition and drew its pupils from a different social sector of society. His own pupils were children of the left intelligentsia and some were in trouble with the law. Dartington Hall emerged in 1926 on the Dartington Estate as one of the enterprises designed by Leonard and Dorothy Elmhirst to revitalize country life and halt the exodus from the land. Initially it was established to provide an education compatible with Dorothy Elmhirst's ideals for her three children. Farming, furniture-making, housing, social welfare and the cultivation of the arts and education were to enrich rural living. The progressive school became a separate enterprise under the headmastership of William Burnlee Curry.[22] Located in the midst of a thriving community, at various times and in many ways the pupils could participate in the commercial and cultural activities. Compared to Summerhill it was a luxurious school. The pupil–teacher ratio was unusually generous, each pupil had a single bedroom study and until the war servants catered for domestic living. Fees were high. Curry had been influenced by Bertrand Russell's writings on principles of education:

> What is needed is reverence . . . The child is weak and superficially foolish, the teacher is strong and in everyday sense stronger than the child . . . The man who has reverence will not think it his duty to 'mould' the young . . . The man who feels this can wield the authority of an educator without infringing the principle of liberty.[23]

Through Curry, Dartington spoke to D. J. in a language she understood and could embrace. Dartington Hall showed her a school without prefects, where all pupils shared a democratic voice in government, where individual and group projects were a method of study and where co-educational boarding school life was based on the principle of trust and discreet oversight.

Bedales was the first of the New Education Schools.[24] It had been opened by John Haden Badley in 1893. He had served his apprenticeship with Dr Reddie at Abbotsholme, an earlier experimental boys school which showed him 'what to do, and how not to do it'. For Miss Ross Bedales was a school that still bore traces of its emergence from Arnold of Rugby's school for the sons of gentlemen. Bedales, like the Steiner schools and Dartington Hall, was co-educational: 'Badley thought in terms of the well-to-do late Victorian family in which brothers and sisters would learn to live amicably'.[25] Boys and girls were treated differently; the former called by their surnames and beaten by prefects until the early 1920s while the girls were subjected to highly charged 'little talks'. Students who formed emotionally fraught heterosexual relationships were characterized as 'silly'. Perhaps more important to Miss Ross than the mixture of public school emphasis on cold baths, physical exercise and physical punishment with 'exact scholarship', was a collective corporate life promoting self-reliance and individuality.[26] This was found in the Montessori-inspired junior school, Dunhirst. Madame Montessori made several visits to Bedales in the 1920s when Arnold Dolmetsch was influential in inducting young pupils into orchestral playing.[27]

These three independent schools displayed different strands in the changing educational scene. They exemplified the ferment of the New Education which had been discussed at Elsinore. The immediate challenge for Miss Ross was to search for a training which would better foster appropriate changes in Australian practice. Her task at the ATTI differed widely from that of the delegacy for Teacher Training at Oxford or the similar post-graduate course at Cambridge, where two of the terms required for the Diploma were spent in practice, one in primary and one in a secondary school. The theoretical courses were not highly regarded by young men and women who had recently concluded rigorous undergraduate studies. The various training colleges forming part of the University of London approximated more nearly to the ATTI. Relationships between training colleges and the schools in which the students spent apprenticeships and later found employment were, and are, often complex. The conservative schools may have found the advice given to students about either content of curricula or pupil–teacher relationships contravened their conventions and practice. Bedales, Summerhill and Dartington Hall would have been pressed to find courses for teachers in training which met their different emphases. The imprimatur of professional training for teaching was not in England a legal pre-requisite for practising as it was in Australia.

Miss Ross had planned a short visit to the United States on her way home but the needed grant from the Council of Educational Research was not forthcoming so she had to rely on published accounts of American developments. She needed to absorb more of the furore which had arisen over John Dewey's views on democracy and education. He had been followed by Harold Rugg and Ann Shumaker, George Counts and Theodor Brameld.[28] The idea that a new social order might be created by a child-centred education which replaced authoritarian indoctrination by free play ideas had threatened the political forces of the right. There was a warning here. In 1967 Miss Ross was to put in her own words the key idea she took from this debate: 'school practices often imply a belief that pupils can be educated for democracy only through authoritarian ways'.[29]

When Miss Ross returned to the ATTI in 1936 she still faced the problems inherent in seeking to reform the system from within. The relationship of the ATTI to the independent schools in Victoria had no parallel in England. The principals of the schools in which the ATTI students were employed were often on the governing body of the IARTV. Would Miss Ross find sufficient schools in Victoria where student teachers, educated as she wished them to be, would be employed?

Her problem must be considered in its social and political context. D. J. had been in England and in Europe in 1935. Violence had already been displayed in the 1931 Japanese invasion of Manchuria; the Italian invasion of Ethiopia took place in 1935. The failure of the League of Nations to act in either case was ominous. The German and Italian intervention in the Spanish Civil War followed in 1936. D. J.'s life, her acts and her feelings must always be displayed against the background of events in the world, even though distance from Europe minimalized the impact. Like her Australian contemporaries D. J. had a eurocentric view of the world in which she lived.

In 1936 educationalists in Australia were still talking of 'the democracy that may save civilization', and Miss Ross looked at Victoria's schools in the hope that increasing knowledge of child development, and of the social conditions that would foster benevolent adults, could produce a generation of citizens of a truly democratic polity. How closely did the reflection on schooling she had enjoyed during the period abroad mesh with the practice in the schools in which her students were employed? She found a variety of stated values and practices in IARTV schools. In some boys and girls schools, participation of students in school government was beginning to replace the conventional hierarchical structure through principal, vice-principal, senior staff, junior and visiting staff, prefects, probationers and form captains.

It was not until 1944 that the then headmistress of St Catherine's, Miss Sophie Borland, set up the School Students' Advisory Council, but a decade earlier her predecessor Miss Edna Holmes, had said in her annual report: 'There is too much stress on competition and co-operation is much more valuable'.[30] She had done away with ranking and girls were only judged against general criteria. She instituted tests of ability to help advise her pupils whether their ambitions for post-school careers were feasible. She was the only headmistress among the teachers who established a Victorian branch of the NEF and before her retirement in 1942 Social Studies was taught at St Catherine's.[31]

There had been some more radical small private schools in Victoria. John Lawton set up a preparatory school, St Andrews, in 1921 where Margaret Lyttle was head of the junior school. A pupil remembers: 'We had school meetings—it was run on very democratic principles, for all the school came to the meetings to do with running the school. It seems quite extraordinary but that is how it was'.[32] St Andrews closed in 1932 and Margaret Lyttle went on to register Preshil as a junior school in the following year. She followed A. S. Neill in some of his practices at Summerhill School. Meetings in 1934 at Methodist Ladies' College (MLC) to vote for conduct prizes had quite a different flavour:

> It is difficult, however, to convey something of the charm and sanctity with which the ceremony of voting is carried out. Take, for example, the Seniors. When the time for voting arrives, the Senior School and staff assemble in Fitchett Hall. Then with quiet dignity, the Principal and Vice-Principal enter between rows of standing girls, and take their place upon the dias. With due impressiveness the Principal then outlines the purpose of the Assembly and the procedure.
>
> The girls are reminded that not popularity, nor personal friendship must weigh with them, but worth. The girls chosen are to be the representatives of the School product in the outer world. On a quiet review of the year's conduct, what girl from among them do they think best carries the school standard and traditions? The silence is impressive, beyond that of many a church service. The address ended, the girls have the names presented to them, and must sit silently for a few moments ere they record their votes on the papers prepared for the occasion. Voting finished, the papers are gathered by the prefects and duly handed in. The results are not disclosed until prize night. Neither the girl selected nor the school assemblage could ever forget the importance of the occasion, nor the dignity and responsibility that the prize carries. It must, therefore, have great value in the moulding of their characters. The whole atmosphere is sacramental. The best traditions of a church school are made real.[33]

This school, a former pupil of MLC believed:

> emphasised the maintenance of the *status quo* by its emphasis on loyalty, respect for authority, politeness of speech and manners and special deference to special people. In the process it tended to inhibit criticism, either secret or overt, of the underlying assumptions of the *status quo*. The superiority of Western, industrialised, 'Christian' civilisation; the assumption that money should be able to procure privilege, the prestige of status associated with certain careers . . .[34]

There was another side to the emphasis on maintenance of the *status quo*. There was the excitement of hearing from women who loved the literature they were sharing with their pupils. There were the teachers who conveyed the satisfaction of a mathematical proof or the logic of Latin grammar. Within the formal structure of conventional schooling there was sometimes an intellectual adventure.

Miss Ross had student teachers in training at MLC. Her consultations with the principal about their progress are not available. Miss Ross, in her contact with the single sex boys' schools, found a similar range of theories and practices which often did not embrace NEF principles. In Victoria during the 1930s the girls' schools proved more acceptance of change than did the public schools providing education for boys.[35] Boys' schools with the longer traditions had influential 'Old Boys' who individually and through their organizations exerted a conservative influence. The schooling of boys was of serious concern to the media and it was not only in sport that pupils were considered rivals. The 'old school tie' was a factor in future appointments. It would have been harder for a progressive headmaster, if one had been appointed by mistake, to restructure his school. J. R. Darling, an English Anglican layman appointed to Geelong Grammar School in 1930 had the qualities and the confidence to introduce changes to curriculum and organization without fatally offending traditionalists among the schools supporters:

> He had two outstanding fields of vision. He saw the need for incentives, interest and perspective in school work if it was to be more than superficial, and he saw the vital need for individual and group participation in activities designed to develop that incentive, interest and perspective.[36]

He had to reduce a 50 per cent failure rate at the Leaving examination among a comprehensive school population. To do this, he sacked five staff in his first year and later introduced a modified Dalton Plan which enabled him to broaden the curriculum. A

Public Affairs sixth form catered for non-academic boys and in 1939 a nominal school representative council stressed that the school should produce leaders for a democratic community. Timbertop, a country estate for fourth form, taught the values of self-reliance and physical endurance. By the 1950s careful recruitment of staff enabled Darling to withdraw from personal commitment to the daily detail of the school. To balance the staff he had added some notable Australians, strong either academically and educationally or politically left wing, among them J. C. Nield, Russell Ward and Manning Clark. Art and music were encouraged by appointment of Herschfeld-Mack, formerly of the Bauhaus, an old *Dunera* boy.[37] Under Darling's leadership Geelong Grammar was similar to MCEGGS when Miss Gilman Jones was headmistress, in the balance of traditional and progressive practices. Melbourne Grammar, Caulfield Grammar, Scotch College and Carey Grammar adhered to their traditional ways.

Miss Ross faced a challenge in developing the small establishment which produced teachers for this wide range of non-government schools. The Catholic system, with its parish primary schools and the secondary schools of the various religious orders, also claimed her attention. Her reputation extended beyond those independent schools where she supervised her student teachers in training. The growth of State government secondary schools enlarged her field of interest. She made regular contact with the University of Melbourne where she represented the independent schools on the Faculty of Education. She was known as a member of the Curriculum Revision Committee and the Schools Board. The Education Committee of the Free Kindergarten Union and the Victorian Society for Crippled Children and the Australian Broadcasting Committee (ABC) relied on her advice, as did the Girls' Schools Committee of the SCM and the League of Nations Union. Her life for the next three years was busy and fruitful. The tasks at ATTI were well within her capacity and if the physical strain of travelling brought on an attack of asthma or migraine, she could read her lecture over the phone to a colleague from her home in Windsor.

In 1937 she took pleasure in meeting colleagues who attended the NEF conference which held sessions in the capital cities of Australia between 1 August and 20 September.[38] Among the twenty speakers were old friends and acquaintances. The conference title, 'Education for Complete Living: The Challenge of Today' emphasized the optimistic outlook that universal schooling would combine with increased leisure to provide opportunity for raising the general level of human life to heights never yet attained.

This rhetoric and the methods advocated for the achieving of the ideal were familiar ground for Miss Ross. The session on the training of teachers conducted by William Boyd, the head of Education of Glasgow University, criticized contemporary courses and spoke in familiar words of the desirability of sound scholarship as a base for a training which synthesized theory and practice. But it was the president of the NEF, Laurin Zilliacus, a headmaster in Helsingfors, Finland, who challenged Miss Ross with his opening address entitled 'The race between education and catastrophe'.[39] He considered that it was likely that there would be a rise of Fascism with support of the right wing in some democracies. He concluded:

> Man must set about establishing the Democratic State which is the Educational State, or blunder from one holocaust into another, until he perishes from the earth . . . The schools must as a matter of great urgency give knowledge required by the citizen and provide practical training in citizenship . . . The school should not only give practical ability and knowledge, it should foster the development of the will to citizenship: it should not only change the mind, it should touch the mind and heart of the growing generations . . . It is in the last resort to the social conscience of the teacher that democracy must look . . . At bottom, it is the problem of the haves and have nots.[40]

At another moment he feared the violence of a communist revolution. The dilemma of political liberalism was displayed for D. J.

to consider in a post-Depression Victoria.[41] Her second experience outside Australia had confronted D. J. with a testing variety of ideas and practices. The strength of her will and her intelligence enabled her to weave her own way through a bewildering time of change. Her professional focus on the schooling of middle-class children possibly insulated her from some of the most disturbing effects of the inequities in European and English class systems. It is not of these that Miss Ross wrote when she returned to Australia.

Characteristically, she responded to the threat of impending global catastrophe by looking to the immediate practical steps that she could take to improve ATTI training courses. She appraised the Council of the importance of a distinctive course for first year students, allowing them more time for study and reflection, and limiting teaching periods to a maximum of twenty per week, with fifteen as a minimum: 'Students in training do not have the leisure, that is so valuable a part of university education'.[42] A salary of £40 for fifteen periods should be set and £2 paid for each additional period taught. The allocation of time required four mornings and three afternoons at school. The remaining working time, one morning and two afternoons was for supervised theoretical work.

She had to convince school councils and principals that their long-term interest would be best served by forgoing the immediate profit of cheap hours of teaching. The time gained for her students was to be spent partly in extending their general education and partly in acquainting them with what she had learned on her recent trip about developments in educational theory and practice. She included, for example, the work of Charlotte Bühler on their reading list as an introduction to the increased emphasis (then stressed in Vienna and in the United States by Arnold Gesell and Frances Ilg) on controlled observation and recording of development of children from birth to maturity. Statistical averages provided norms against which individual children could be checked. She noted also, the increasing reliance on measurement reflected in the use of IQ tests in schools.

There are records of the part Miss Ross played in supporting the Headmistresses' Association in promoting equality of treatment for her female students in relation to their male counterparts in both boys' and girls' schools. In August 1939 she spoke convincingly of this at the ATTI Executive Committee.

Former students have spoken with affection and enthusiasm of the magnetism of her sense of the importance of what she was teaching. Those who failed to respond to her demand for dedication to the task would experience her impatient distaste for a time-serving approach to a great profession. Many of her students took her love of the work with them into the schools. Her influence and example was felt beyond the small institution with its three members of staff. Miss Gilman Jones had once, according to June Epstein, agreed with her that she would never make a headmistress.[43] But, now she was a respected figure in Victoria and known by reputation in other States. Wide experience on a variety of committees had taught her to choose the moment to interject a fresh idea or end a fruitless interchange. She knew the independent schools and the State and Catholic systems. The stage was set for Miss Gilman Jones to suggest that Miss Ross apply to succeed her as headmistress of MCEGGS.

4

Challenge and Response

The position at MCEGGS for which Miss Ross was applying was prestigious and difficult. She would follow a formidable head-mistress who had had a long and distinguished career in the school and in the Anglican community. She was, in a sense, an applicant from within. Some women on the staff who had minimal formal professional qualifications had been senior to her when she had taught there. Her later career had earned respect among education-alists but she was not yet well known to the parents of junior school pupils at MCEGGS.

D. J. was realist enough to assess her situation. She had not thought of herself as a potential headmistress when she had applied to be supervisor of the ATTI. She had to consider whether she wished to narrow her activities to one institution, and one in which she would have to appear as a 'proper figurehead'. Her Council would have a majority of clergy and laity to whom she would be responsible, not only for the academic school but for the support staff in office, boarding house and grounds.[1] There were the Parent and Old Grammarian Associations.

Against this she had to set an opportunity to demonstrate her educational convictions in a living model school. She braced herself to accept the challenge remembering that she already had friends among the staff. There was her intimate friend Mary Davis who was teaching in the middle school; Alison Winfield was a friend on the staff of the preparatory school; and she knew well and respected Miss Elizabeth Lothian who taught Classics in the senior school. Her friend Gwenda Lloyd was available and would give support to fresh ideas if she appointed her.[2] Miss Gilman Jones had given strong leadership to a team of scholarly, efficient women. Parents were satisfied with the school's reputation for academic and sporting achievement. The girls who had come up through the school would be her prefects and sixth form. They were conformable to the ethos of a sound, liberal school in the best of English traditions. She wrote her application, and sent it, citing Miss Gilman Jones as one referee.

In making her final report as headmistress in 1938 Miss Gilman Jones said: 'the school is to be congratulated on having as headmistress a woman of such brilliant gifts as Miss Ross who moreover knows the school so well'.[3] The council of the IARTV, of which Miss Gilman Jones was president, confirmed her appreciation in an eulogistic comment on Miss Ross' services as supervisor of teacher training:

> She had brought to her work boundless enthusiasm and energy and has been happily successful in enabling her students to catch her own enthusiasm, and to approach their work with a similar energy . . . through Miss Ross's work at the Training Institution the work of the Primary departments in the Registered Schools has been wonderfully developed.[4]

It was a brave decision. Even at ATTI D. J. had experienced physical consequences of the nervous tension the work engendered. She was in her late forties, for many women a stage in life when fluctuations in health and mood are common. It can be a problem for professional women when promotion to a heavy responsible workload comes at this moment. D. J. was in her middle years a vigorous, physical presence, powered by an excitable nervous system which she dominated by strength of will. She was subject to attacks of asthma and migraine, exacerbated by the cigarettes she liked to smoke. She acknowledged the physical strain when she replied to an invitation on 6 April 1940 to join the newly constituted council of the KTC: 'I hope this will not mean a multiplicity of meetings. I haven't really much energy left by 8 p.m. most evenings'.[5] The selection committee of Council gave an adulatory synopsis of her career which showed how successfully she had coped with her troublesome body:

Miss Dorothy Ross. M.A. B.Sc.

Distinguished university career both in Arts and Science including exhibition in Botany and Physiology.
Diploma of Pedagogy of University of London with special credit.
Studied Education in Europe in 1929 and 1935.
After 14 years experience in teaching at Oberwyl, St Catherine's and MCEGGS was in 1928 appointed Supervisor at the ATTI.
Miss Ross' work there has been outstandingly successful and she has been a notable figure in the educational world holding the following positions:

  Member of Faculty of Education of the University
  Member of Curriculum revision committee of the Education Department
  Member of Council's Incorporated Association of Registered Teachers
  Member of Botany and Biology Standing Committee of the Schools Board.

Member of the Education Committee of:

  Free Kindergarten Union
  Victorian Society for Crippled Children
  League of Nations Union
  Broadcasting Commission.

She has been deeply interested in the religious side of education, is a member of the Girls' Schools Committee of the Australian Student

Christian Movement. Miss Ross was chosen from a large number of candidates from Australia, England, South Africa, New Zealand, India, and the Straits Settlements.[6]

It was an impressive record for her to rely on as she girded herself for the task. For the next fifteen years Miss Ross lived in the public view as the headmistress of the premier girls' Anglican school in Victoria. Under Miss Gilman Jones the school had been 'possibly more distinctly Anglican in those years than in any time before or since'.[7] The wording of the Constitution by the Provisional Council in June 1900 had stated:

> the system of education shall provide for pupils a sound general education, including instruction in modern languages, classics, mathematics and science, *and also* such regular instruction in the Holy Scriptures in conformity with the principles of the Church of England as may be approved by the Provisional Council.[8]

The School Constitution 1914, clause i, provided for the use of an order of daily worship in the School, approved by the Archbishop. Miss Gilman Jones had stressed many times the need for a school chapel to centre the religious education of the girls in their own buildings rather than in Christ Church, South Yarra, the parish church. The ceremonial rituals of Anglicanism were essential for Miss Gilman Jones. She infused an atmosphere of respect for their importance into the school community which included girls and staff of other Christian denominations, Jewish and atheist families. As Miss Gilman Jones had warned her successor: 'she would find the school a full-time job requiring all her strength and energy'.[9]

D. J. had found her religious way in Low Church Anglicanism. It was in keeping with her emphasis on principles demonstrated in practical actions of living that she would emphasize daily feelings and behaviour rather than the precision of ritual observance. This emphasis would enable her to hold together teaching staff and students selected on secular criteria. The school assemblies and her religious education classes had an element of challenge to girls.

'Clarify what you believe', she told them, 'then live as you believe'. She brought her own deeply felt faith into her first school assembly. June Epstein has given us D. J.'s moving account of her needing a draught from the school nurse to enable her to face this public appearance.[10] She was fundamentally reticent about her deepest feelings: she gave leadership at some cost to herself. D. J. wrote to a friend about an address to officers of the Australian Women's Auxiliary Services: 'If they asked me to speak of the price of leadership I might speak from the heart. As it is it will be another case of preaching what I find almost impossible to practise'.[11]

Much that has been written about the Grammar she created refers to the period when the school returned in 1944 to Anderson Street, South Yarra, after wartime evacuation. In the three years between taking up office at the beginning of 1939, and the evacuation (5 and 6 March 1942 to 15 August 1944), there were changes which forecast the school after 1944. Miss Ross had responded to the modifications in the theory of child development that the work of Susan Isaacs, Maria Montessori, Charlotte Bühler, and Arnold Gesell and Frances Ilg were producing. Some members of staff of the preparatory school had been appointed by Miss Gilman Jones before these developments had been reflected in Australian training colleges and schools. It would have been invidious to single out these long-serving and devoted women. Staff meetings and discussions had convinced her they were set in their ways. In her first year Miss Ross chose to spill all positions in the preparatory school and advise staff members to reply to the advertisements. In this way, five members of staff were replaced and the way cleared for a revision of nursery and primary curricula.

The appointment of her close friend, Mary Davis, as headmistress of the renamed junior school caused some comment. In 1946 the possibility of Miss Mary Davis being appointed supervisor of ATTI was abandoned as 'it was possible the Council of Public Education would not accept her'. She had been appointed a member of the executive committee of ATTI in July 1943. The question of her appointment as supervisor was raised with the registration committee of the Council of Public Education, 'as she lacked the academic requirements'. The official reply was 'no'.[12] Miss Davis had been promoted to teach in the middle school by Miss Gilman Jones. Miss Mary Davis was a handsome, tall women, gracious in demeanour, with an unusually deep and melodious speaking voice, secure in her upbringing in the Western District of rural Victoria. Loss of family money in a rural depression had led to her entry into education, first as a governess, then as a pupil teacher at Ruyton, where she had finished her schooling. She was a trainee at the Melbourne Teachers' College when Miss Gilman Jones appointed her to MCEGGS as housemistress and junior teacher. Miss Gilman Jones directed her to transfer her training to ATTI under Miss Ross. It was known to Miss Davis' colleagues in April 1936 that she had finally achieved her Leaving Certificate, and only then had she become a fully qualified primary teacher. Her appointment ensured that under Miss Ross' continued tutelage the junior school would prepare pupils for promotion into the secondary section. Miss Davis was formally underqualified for the position and suggestions of favouritism were made.[13]

It is relevant to remember that many girls' schools in Victoria, including MCEGGS, had grown out of private schools often owned and conducted by mother and daughter and a niece, or by sisters and other relatives (see chapter 6).[14] Special relationships as a justification for appointment or promotion to a position of responsibility were not frowned on as they would be today. The Council minute book of 19 July 1939 records that the headmistress' remarks about the preparatory school 'were fully endorsed by the Council who gave her their full support . . . Miss Ross was authorised to carry on. The future of the Prep. School being entirely in her hands'. Miss Davis, as head of the preparatory school, received a salary of £300 per annum; Miss Colebrook, who was to take charge of the highest form, was also paid £300 per annum.[15] There is an implied recognition of Miss Davis' lack of academic standing and the need for a member of staff in a supportive role. Miss Gilman Jones had fostered Miss Davis' career on her judgement of her utility to the school, as she had Miss Ross', though the latter's scholastic record added weight to that decision.

Having inaugurated changes in the junior school, Miss Ross was happy that in 1941 the first outdoor nursery school attached to a Victorian independent school was opened in the garden of Phelia Grimwade House. She had admired 'the Utopian' kindergarten at Bedales.[16] She selected Miss Alison Winfield, who had been reappointed to the staff, to be in charge of this development. Miss Winfield 'had a wonderful time' using her skills in carpentry to make equipment. [17] Miss Winfield was later transferred to the junior school, which gave her a further opportunity for creating teaching aids.[18]

The junior school was then to include an extra year for many girls. The age of entry to the secondary school was raised from ten and a half to eleven and a half years. Miss Ross was sensitive to the evidence she had heard in England about the maturing of young girls. Later, in 1939, she turned her attention to the structure of authority in the senior school. The staff were ready to accept some changes as they had come to realize that the dismissals of preparatory school staff did not portend similar action in the senior school.

In April 1939 Miss Ross carried the staff and the senior school pupils with her in her first cautious moves to increase the number of people who would share her responsibility for the organization of the school. An advisory council of seven girls and four members of staff was chosen to advise the prefects and the staff meetings of matters to be discussed. The number of prefects was increased from twelve to twenty and a prefects' executive committee was to be elected by senior school pupils, the headmistress and staff. By 1941 the advisory council had a written constitution and in that year was, for the first time, chaired by a pupil. In the following year (1942) the headmistress resigned her mandate to appoint the school captain in favour of voting by prefects. She informed the governing body of impending developments which reflected the changing notions of the education of late teenage pupils. The schools were extending their responsibility for the life of school children, as middle-class mothers lived more of their time outside their homes. This increased responsibility was extended to the schooling of girls who were diagnosed as 'non-academic', but whose parents preferred them to spend the same period at school as their contemporaries who were preparing for the learned professions. Miss Ross said:

> by adding an extra period to the Senior School day we can give an opportunity to girls to do part of their homework, at least, under supervision. For two other reasons it is felt desirable to continue afternoon school to four o'clock. It will give more opportunity for physical education . . . and it will allow girls to be at school longer instead of having to go home to empty houses or necessitating the curtailing of mother's afternoon away . . . From next year onward sixth form examination work will cover a two year course . . . No girl will be admitted to an Honour Sixth Form unless she is fully matriculated . . . Next year will see in the school, a Fifth Form and a Sixth Form for girls whose parents prefer they should be educated not through the medium of external examinations.[19]

Miss Ross had begun a search for means to ensure equality of respect for each individual pupil regardless of intellectual achievement. She was not moving towards the anti-intellectualism of some progressive contemporaries but was seeking for an organization appropriate for an intellectually comprehensive intake. She became aware that schoolgirls in the alternative Leaving (fifth form) classes were as sure of their inferior status as were their contemporaries in the academic stream, and friendships between the two groupings did not flourish as she wished. She had begun to experiment as she realized that for girls in the non-academic stream there were expanding job opportunities in nursing (a respectable occupation since World War I), in kindergartens, in domestic science, in secretarial positions, in libraries, and in mothercraft nursing.

More contentious was the decision of the sports committee to reorganize the whole sports programme of the school. In 1940 the Sports Day became a Field Day:

in which every girl took some part. It was a whole day programme and lunch parties in the gardens became a regular feature of the day. The Athletics Club was formed and throughout the year members practised a variety of athletics including javelin throwing and discus throwing, and so the Athletics Club events on Field Day reached a high standard.[20]

In that year 'the Sports Committee decided to withdraw from inter-school competition in swimming and concentrate on their own sports, inviting teams to compete there as in running sports'.[21] Since 1902 MCEGGS had cultivated team games. At times tennis, lacrosse and cricket were replaced by basketball, hockey and baseball. The value of participation in team games and competition within the school and with other schools was an unquestioned part of the inherited public school tradition. D. J. had eagerly participated in team sports at school and at university. Her conviction by 1940 that there were dangers for children and teenagers in competitive sport must be explained. In her Speech Day Report in 1948 she said:

> In physical education also, there is a basic curriculum for all, and only at the later stages is their specialization in certain forms of athletics when girls have developed their particular interest and have undertaken training for it. So in the Junior School Field Day the basic physical education work in the school is demonstrated, and in the Senior School Field Day there is a balance between the work of all, and the work of the few who are particularly good in certain lines. *This has nothing whatever to do with the desire to eliminate competition, as some people think, but is based on the same general principle* that the work of every girl in the school is important, and not just that of the academic or athletic. Competition in games is not only natural but necessary.[22]

She elaborated this in a newsletter to parents in May 1954:

> Competition in games is natural. We cannot play a game without a team to play in, and another team to play with. The 'playing with' another team is an attitude of mind. It could be a playing against

attitude, that is, we play hockey in order to beat another team, and it could be a 'playing with attitude', that is, we need another team to play hockey.[23]

She had become convinced that co-operation, not competition, must be the organizing principle of social living. As she was to seek equality of respect for academically gifted and less able pupils, so the physically gifted must not be encouraged to feel superior to the clumsy. Sport was an aspect of physical education. The health of girls was to be safeguarded by the school medical officer, a tuck-shop which sold nutritious food, appropriate furniture, ventilation and temperature control. Exercise was essential and must be under-taken by all, two hours per week were allocated for physical edu-cation.[24] Competitive games fostered aggression which must be restrained and they promoted élite cliques.

The executive School Council endorsed her view in a debate introduced by the girls on the abolition of school colours: 'we do not need any recognition for work or play other than our valedic-tory books and the team shield and letters', reflected Miss Ross' influence.[25] There were two strands to Miss Ross' thinking about sport. There was the rather puritanical view that it was only part of the health programme. Perhaps she had forgotten the sensual pleasure in a perfectly executed swing of a tennis racquet, or the delight of a graceful movement on the hockey field. The second strand was her aversion to a competitive spirit which relegated skill and collaboration in team work to a minor place. Competition as a primary motive for work or play was repugnant to her.

In her first two years as headmistress Miss Ross had, with con-summate skill, carried pupils and the majority of staff with her in changes which would have far-reaching effects. Perhaps she was fotunate that the war was creating problems which preoccupied Council and parents.

The even tenor of change was disrupted by the request to evacuate the school premises following an offer from the school, as Australia became fully involved in World War II. Melbourne

Grammar School, Wesley College, Melbourne High School and MacRobertson Girls' High School received requisition notices. Miss Ross reported to the School Council on 10 April 1942: 'At intervals from April 1940, I had been in touch with the Director of Evacuation concerning government controlled evacuation of school children'. She showed remarkable courage and self-control in going quietly ahead with her long-term plans for the school knowing that there was little prospect of the systematic progress that she desired. During this time, she dispatched Miss Davis with the school's medical officer, Dr Vera Scantlebury Brown, and other staff to search for suitable accommodation in the countryside within reasonable distance of Melbourne.[26] All was prepared; locations found, the finance committee consulted, parents informed that the arrangements they had agreed to were imminent and finally the press was informed. Miss Ross summarized the detailed plans for the School Council and informed the parents that there were additional boarding fees for those parents who had decided to let their daughters go with the school.

> The school was housed in seven locations, 338 girls at Marysville in groups as follows: in four boarding houses.
> 1) Marylands. 126 girls of the Middle School.
> 2) Roseleigh. 28 girls of the School Certificate Group [that is, girls who were not studying for matriculation]—to carry on their practical training and helping with the little ones, and 28 junior school girls.
> 3) Koorunga. 84 of the upper forms of the Junior School.
> 4) 72 children (boys and girls) of the youngest age groups of the Junior School.[27]

These moves were accomplished between 5 and 20 March 1942. On 13 March, Southern Command had ordered that evacuation be completed by 16 March. Miss Ross in conjunction with Captain Groves succeeded in finding premises for the boarders and the remaining day pupils; for them school work began at Eastern Golf Club, Main Road, Doncaster, on 23 March. The examinations forms missed six days of school work. At Doncaster there were 220 girls in seven classes of which one class, the rural class, was composed of seventeen girls from several classes who could not for various good reasons go to Marysville. The boarders were established in three private homes in Balwyn.

A wartime operation had been carried out by a civilian institution with efficiency and care for the young people involved. The teaching staff displayed flexibility and endurance in adapting boarding houses to schools and devising forms of education that were possible without equipment and full libraries and in inadequate premises. What was achieved was altogether admirable but compared with the evacuation of primary school pupils in the blackout of London, it was still a luxury story. The children lived with their teachers and their schoolmates. They were not billeted compulsorily with unwilling families. They did not have to share a host school for a half-day's schooling. There was food enough, and constant affectionate care. Yet the evacuation to Marysville was a traumatic experience for some of the children. For one little English girl aged eleven whose father was in the Royal Navy and whose mother was evacuated to Warrnambool for the birth of her son, the loneliness and the felt rejection by her Australian classmates is recollected with horror.[28] The teachers, preoccupied with providing the basic necessities for living—single beds, with the necessary rubber sheets, food cooked in clean kitchens, adequate heating and bath water—had, according to this pupil, little time left to comfort or distract the girls. The experience of children parted in wartime from parents varied, as had their previous experience of living in the family. The difficulty of exile from familiar surroundings was adventure and a challenge for some; for others, 'sending me away' was rejection and a sign of lack of love. At certain ages the ego is more robust and the child will cope when even months earlier independence is not easily achieved.

The wartime school was a different institution. Wildfell, the junior boarding house in Domain Road, could be retained as the central administrative unit but close central control of daily detail was weakened by the geographic spread of the various units, though the focal importance of the headmistress was enhanced. She was the link: she alone knew the whole picture. With the small car or the truck Miss Ross kept in touch with the dispersed units. 'I arrange as follows' she reported:

> Tuesday, Thursday and Friday at Doncaster, Wednesday at Wildfell for seeing parents and for executive work. Saturday, Sunday and Monday at Marysville. I choose the week-end at Marysville, because I do no teaching in that part of the school and because there is not room in the church for the whole school and I read a service with the girls who do not go to church. On Mondays I take assembly there, and visit the girls in their class. On Saturday I do administrative work. I visit the Balwyn boarding houses when I can after afternoon school, and when we are more settled I hope to have dinner in each house once a week at least.[29]

Such a punishing schedule took its toll. We get glimpses of what the cost was for D. J. from letters she wrote to a member of staff between September 1942 and the end of first term 1943.[30] She tells a story of continual physical exhaustion and mental fatigue. The record of her weekly timetable tells only of the distances to be covered and a broad indication of the work to be done in each place. In December and January of 1943 she had worked fifteen hours a day for nine days at Wildfell preparing the school time-table. Then she had driven non-academic girls to Marysville in the truck (the car needed unobtainable new parts), so that she and they could prepare to give a holiday to some seven-year-old girls from the Footscray Settlement. 'I can't see myself getting much of a holiday' she commented. 'I wish I were driving a yellow cab' or 'were a nice tidy tram running on rails'. Even when 'nearly all in' her chosen metaphors were of regulated, active employment.

A characteristic reflection heralds the beginning of term: 'But it has been a complete miracle that how much at the end of my tether I have been, when there was a job to be done requiring both spiritual and physical strength it has come quietly but surely'.[31]

As well as the unending demands of the dispersed school, D. J. bore the burden of responsibility for her mother. She had established Mrs Ross in Wembly Court, Toorak Road, South Yarra and joined her there when it was possible. In May 1943 she returned home to find her mother 'all of a jitter and the housekeeper on a bust'. It is no wonder that the overburdened headmistress longed to be 'on a bust' herself. It does not take too great a stretch of the imagination to realize that on each arrival at Marysville or Doncaster or Wildfell there were people waiting to present pressing problems they had saved for her to solve. She recorded that she felt that on each visit to a unit she must convey a feeling that the school still existed as a whole with its ideals and long-term plans. When the school could return to South Yarra the benefits of these strange thirty-two months must be realized. While D. J. was 'having fun with the gas producer', the staff and girls at Marysville and Doncaster were establishing new relationships as they shared domestic responsibilities and learned and taught in the way the temporary premises allowed.

Some of the benefits of this period were similar to those later sought by independent schools when they established country properties for pupils to find independence and understanding in shared living and love of rural pursuits. The downside was the 'stupid hot-house atmosphere at Marysville' where adolescents and their teachers lived in very close proximity during months when many had personal wartime anxieties. Everyone's quirks, previously lived outside the school, became known and a source of either increased affection or irritation. D. J. observed this and sometimes experienced the backlash during her routine visits. In her letters she refers to 'two devastating attacks' on her by a member of staff. The headmistress, like staff and girls, had revealed more of herself in the informal conditions and had become more vulnerable. The stress she surmounted increased her need for loving support. Comments on favoured treatment of individuals or units could be hurtful, even if she much later came to modify her claim that 'I have always kept my private and professional self apart and can be quite objective when thinking of people I love in their professional capacity'.[32] Logically, she could not have made such a claim on the basis of her understanding of the interpenetration of heart and mind.

Wartime conditions had loosened the formal structured relationships between levels of authority within the school, between members of staff, academic and administrative, as well as between girls and staff. As roles became interchangeable, modes of address and the content of conversation became more informal. These changes influenced the school as a social unit when the return to South Yarra was completed.

The reuniting of the school community in South Yarra was demanding for the headmistress, for the staff, the pupils, and for their parents. In 1943 Miss Ross had made clear to her Council in a letter accepting the renewal of her contract as headmistress that she did not wish to accept an increase in salary during wartime:

> My Dear Archbishop,
> At the last Council meeting you asked me to continue as Headmistress of this school for another period of years and offered to make my salary £100 a year more. The Council meeting was not the time or place for me to do more than say I should be glad to serve for another five years, but before the next meeting I want to say that I do not think that in war time I should accept a rise in salary. I think that even had it not been war time I should still have preferred to refuse the extra salary though this is a personal matter and I should not like it to prejudice the matter of salary conditions of my successor or successors. Mr Wettenhall knows of my decision in this matter as he rang me up about the new agreement. I hope you will accept my decision in this matter.
> I am looking forward to the next five years when we shall all have to be doing some hard work on reconstruction.
> Yours sincerely
> Headmistress.[33]

The 'personal matter' to which she refers in her letter reveals something of the spirit in which she set about the reorganization of the school. For her, teaching was a vocation. Her salary should enable her to live as the position of headmistress required. Her reward would be the opportunity that position provided. In October 1942 Miss Ross had considered that gains from the evacuation could be harvested by another year in exile. At the beginning of the 1943 school year, MacRobertson Girls' High School, part of Melbourne Grammar and St Catherine's were already back in their own buildings. Miss Ross was convinced it was time to unite the nine scattered units of MCEGGS into a visible single school. The Air Force was erecting buildings in Albert Park to house the 200 military personnel then in Anderson Street, but construction was slow. The school could not move as a whole. There had been reorganization of the wartime units since 1942 and the constant changes had added extra strain to staff and pupils. Miss Ross began a long process of recovering building by building, and moving section by section back to town. The process was debilitating for her. Living in domestic uncertainty diminished for both staff and pupils the relief of a war turning to victory. Miss Ross gave her account of the return to South Yarra in a paper she prepared for the School Council.[34]

The return to South Yarra was accomplished in wartime. D. J. never quite lost a frankness of speech and an occasional angularity of movement when the discipline she imposed on herself could not conceal a naturally explosive temper. When the fire penetrated her habitual defences the force was considerable. The inconvenience and frustration of what Miss Ross saw as military incompetence led to such an occasion when the 200 military personnel had not been removed from Anderson Street as promised. That such losses of her self-control were rare is attested by the importance placed on this event in the records of Desma McDonald, June Epstein and William Connell.[35]

> There was a confrontation between the RAAF officers and Miss Ross in which to use her own words, 'she vented all the rage and fury and frustration of two and a half years of coping with the inefficiencies of the local RAAF administration'.[36]

When the school was finally reassembled in South Yarra both staff and pupils from Marysville were accustomed to the informal sharing of domestic duties and *ad hoc* arrangements for lessons. At Doncaster, the golf club house and boarding houses had demanded a high degree of patriotic consent if normal study was to be achieved. Everything had been temporary. Groups of girls had changed houses as some girls left and others arrived. For some, the returns meant life at home with parents and siblings, public transport in school uniform, disciplined behaviour on the stairs 'at all times' and formal entry to the daily assembly. The freer life, being continually on the move, had suited D. J. Despite fatigue, a certain temperamental irritability had been satisfied. 'Any calmness I may ever show', she wrote at this time, 'is through prayer and fasting'. Some staff found this hard-won control too threatening. The return to South Yarra made demands on her to emphasize a strictly professional authority.

The informality of the evacuation months was an advantage for Miss Ross as she set about creating her 'democratic' school. The first cautious moves which she had already made could be built on, as the senior girls had gained assurance and a measure of responsibility for their own actions, and as they had cared for the juniors during the evacuation. It had been a torrid time for members of staff. They were wearied, as was Miss Ross. The war had not yet ended. The bombing of Dresden, VE Day, Hiroshima, and VJ Day were still to come.[37] The mood was sanguine, but as victory came closer the horrors of the years of conflict were becoming more public. It was in this flux that Miss Ross drew on the ideas she had accumulated and began to develop them in the running of her school.

Professor Connell, with his profound knowledge of education and as a professional colleague and friend of D. J.'s, notes that she did not begin her work as headmistress with a blueprint for her ideal school. She moved always within the guidelines of the possible, not tilting at windmills, but with a clear patient insight into her governing body, the people whom she selected to staff her school and the social mix of parents who paid the fees. MCEGGS was a chapter in D. J.'s life: the present study is not a history of the school but a study of the fifteen years in which being the headmistress dictated her public persona and thereby influenced her being.

Secondary socialization into a world of work,[38] being the headmistress, meant there was a language and role appropriate to that position: 'we become what we do'. Miss Ross had her model headmistress, Miss Gilman Jones. She insensibly modified her concept of herself to maintain her role. Her request to a boutique at the top end of Collins Street to dress her as a headmistress,[39] reveals her consciousness of the demands of her position, but this role never absorbed her whole self. She could not have carried her Council, her staff, the parents and the girls with her if she had adapted herself completely. The passionate seeker, the rebel, the witty iconoclast, dog lover, musician were reined in, but not extinguished. We become what we do—we must look at Miss Ross' speeches and writings and reports of those who knew her to form a picture of the headmistress in her school. In those postwar years she found many friends in the wider educational world. During the evacuation Miss Ross had been the spider in the web of institutions that had housed the school. When the school was reunited, delegation of authority had to become more structured, though the principles underlying the new forms remained and were crucial. The school became an A class school for the Intermediate (fourth form) examination in 1944 which simplified changes in curricula and organization.[40] The regular monthly staff meetings enabled any teacher to place an item on the agenda and it was very rare that the headmistress used her authority to force a decision.[41] Each teacher was expected to have individual opinions and a social sense of the welfare of the school community as a whole.

These meetings took place after the timetabled working hours, as did the many smaller subject committees to whom the details of implementing policy decisions were delegated. A member of Miss Ross' teaching staff experienced the cost in time and energy of sharing in the control of her working hours. Some members of staff gladly exchanged long working days for shared responsibility. Some found the demands exorbitant and sought simpler situations. There are testimonies, oral and written, of the open supportive relationships Miss Ross established. 'Her study door was always ajar' and however busy the moment, a welcoming interest could be assumed. As the size of the school increased, more and more administrative groups had to be formed. By 1953 the total school population, girls, office, domestic, teaching staff, and Council numbered '2,000 souls in all'.[42] 'My job was logistics', Miss Ross said of her function.

The units of management reflected the growth of a pupil from kindergarten to sixth form. The junior school, Morris Hall and Ross Hall had its headmistress, the middle school, its head, and the senior school, the second mistress or assistant headmistress. Miss Ross had to work more and more through others. Her own career had left her with a somewhat sceptical reliance on paper qualifications. The headmistress of the junior school (Miss Davis) had few formal qualifications; nor did Alison Winfield, the school counsellor (a rare post at the time). When Miss Ross felt that a young person had potential she would appoint her and foster her development. Alison Winfield had come to MCEGGS from the country in her fifteenth year and had spent an extra year in the sixth form, as she was too young to enter university. She enrolled at the KTC.

She had returned to teach in the junior school and when Miss Ross reinvigorated that section Miss Winfield had her chance to set up the kindergarten. That successfully achieved, Miss Ross ensured that she study Professor Schonell's course in Queensland in methods of testing,[43] and later sent her to a one-year course based on Susan Isaacs' principles at the London Institute of Education. Her expenses for these courses were paid for by the school. She was certified in England to teach pupils up to the age of eleven.

As school counsellor, Miss Winfield shared with Miss Ross the cards which recorded the results of the tests she administered on entry to all girls and the confidential records of each one's progress through the school. She gave vocational guidance and set up a library of information about careers. In 1947 she was vice-principal of the junior school and delegated for Miss Davis when she was on leave. Her work ensured close contact with Miss Ross, her mentor, with whom she maintained an appropriately formal relationship and became secretary to the NEF when Miss Ross was federal president in 1959.

Alison Winfield was formed by what might be called a long apprenticeship and her warm and outgoing personality matured in the process. Her judgement that Miss Mountain was inadequate as a person for the duties of headmistress caused her to resign in 1959 and to join another of Miss Ross' protegées, Miss Davis, at St Catherine's, first, for a few hours a week and in 1962, as full-time school counsellor.[44]

Since Miss Ross did not delegate her authority to appoint staff, she gathered around her like-minded women and through them her influence could be felt throughout the school. She maintained a presence through the morning assemblies she conducted in middle and junior schools and in regularly teaching religious education in the senior school. 'Mark readings' were another attempt to have some personal relationship with each girl. The intention is clear. Miss Ross visited each class, at least twice a year in middle school and senior school and in the presence of the class teachers spoke to each girl from notes of her academic progress and social contribution. The recollections of Old Grammarians of their reaction to this procedure are diverse. For some, it is remembered as an accepted routine, others spoke of a feeling of painful exposure in front of classmates. One Old Grammarian told of her intense dislike of being present when her friends were criticized.[45]

How did Miss Ross reconcile her respect for individuals with a public display of faults and virtues? She did not always succeed in overcoming her personal likes and dislikes of certain girls. 'She always talked to X for a long time. She was sports captain and very good at lessons too.'[46] She could be harsh if she had been told a girl was wilfully underperforming, or was anti-social. One Old Grammarian told of 'Cainey, a pupil, answering Miss Ross back when she had accused Nona of being lazy. Cainey said, "not so."'[47] Some spoke of kindly reassurance to hard-working failures.

This attempt to overcome the necessity for delegation of personal contact with each girl to others could not succeed. Her position as headmistress and the formal setting of the classroom gave a particular flavour to either praise or blame. Informal casual contact as she moved about the school revealed more clearly that she knew each pupil as a named individual.

Her concept of a democratic school in which each girl was known and could make an individual contribution was expressed in the development of the Advisory Council which had been created before the evacuation, into the Executive Council of the school.

> The Executive Council of the School—a body representing the following interests in the school:
> Staff.
> Clubs such as the Dramatic, Music, Art and Craft, Athletics Clubs, etc.
> Committees such as the Library, Magazine, Social Services, Minor Clubs, etc.
> Organisations such as the Seamen's Mission, Birthday League, etc.
> Sports Captains.
> The Seven Senior Forms of the School with one representative each.
> The Boarding House which is represented by the Boarding House Captain.
> General Members. These are elected over and above those with special jobs, as there are more jobs to be done than the special ones, for this body, besides being deliberative is also a working body and there are certain things which need to be attended to by appointment rather than by election.

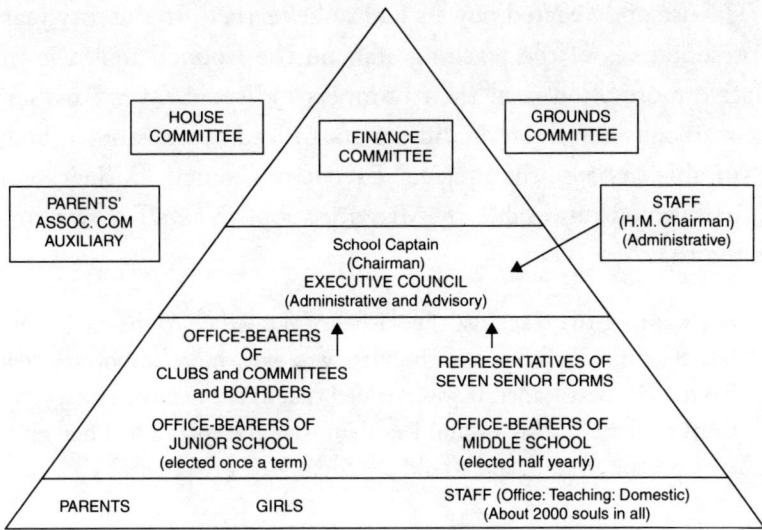

The elected body in turn elects its Chairman who becomes Captain of the School for the year. She allots all the extra offices such as the Secretary in charge of Grounds, Secretary of Buildings, the School Treasurer, the Secretary of the E. C. [Executive Council—the name was chosen to distinguish the representative body from the School Council which was presided over by the Archbishop of Melbourne], Secretaries in charge of Pound, Cloakrooms, and the Tuckshop, etc.

. . . At each alternate meeting, each Councillor gives a report of her particular job, and makes recommendations or asks for help in improving it. These reports are in writing and are handed in and filed in the special book for the purpose. They are thus available for the help and guidance of future secretaries.[48]

'The school as a democratic community' is the title often given to Miss Ross' school;[49] this is shorthand for *schooling as an education for democracy*.[50] *Nisi Dominus Frustra,* the Jubilee story of the school, expresses the situation succinctly: 'More people may send in suggestions, more people may take part in the discussion, the propositions will get a thorough airing, but the responsibility, the final judgement still lies, as it will in school life, with those who have the necessary wider experience'.[51]

The use of delegated powers had to be learned. In the first years representatives of the teaching staff on the Council took the initiative more often than their numbers indicated. Miss Ross and the staff considered the candidates nominated by the student body as suitable to be on the Prefects' Executive Council. In the case of a girl deemed unsuitable by Miss Ross and the staff it was suggested that:

> not wanting to go against the wishes of the P.E.C. in the choice. We felt that the confidence of the girls was even more important than having the best leader. It was decided that at the next meeting of the Committee Miss Ross should explain that the voting had not given a clear enough lead, and would ask them for a Preferential Vote . . .[52]

As the years passed, the girls grew into the Council and its place in school life was taken for granted. There were some pupils who saw Miss Ross' purpose as clearly as she did herself: 'If I needed more than one vote', she once said of her own contribution, 'I ought not to be Headmistress'.[53] Formal powers may be extensive or limited, the electorate may be wide or narrow, the power of veto may be seldom used. Progressive schools in England and in Australia had set up a variety of representative assemblies. MCEGGS Council was not unique; what set it apart was the degree of emphasis, the genuine concern that the Council should be seen by all pupils to have practical effect. Decisions should be seen to modify or introduce changes in the daily life of the school. Pupils saw the Council make a majority decision which did not work and had to be rescinded. Council meetings were more than role playing. This was so because the headmistress, through her staff, realized that the reality of responsibility would not be experienced in role play. Council minutes make interesting reading. Each meeting began with the council prayer: 'Almighty God, our Heavenly Father, give us courage to change what ought to be changed, serenity to accept what cannot be changed, and wisdom to know one from the other'.[54] Perhaps the choice of this prayer more than any other statement she made about her purpose in schooling encapsulates D. J.'s basic Christian striving that each girl in her school might attain courage, serenity and wisdom, under God, as an adult in society.[55] The means to this end are succinctly summarized in diagrams from *Nisi Dominus Frustra*.[56]

If some parents and some members of staff were concerned that too much time was taken by pupils participating in school government, they were reassured by the results of public examinations and the outstanding performance of former pupils in university courses. Miss Ross believed in the worth of the traditional curriculum for those girls who showed the ability to profit from academic studies.[57] Excellent results in public performance were ensured by careful attention to studies appropriate for each individual girl.[58] 'We are trying', Miss Ross said in the John Smythe Memorial Lecture[59] in 1954:

> to help girls live in the world that they already belong to, to give them interests for their leisure time, to raise their standards of taste, to prepare them for useful careers—but above all to make citizens who will be well-adjusted and not misfits with feelings of frustration because they have been unhappy while trying to follow a rigidly academic course unsuited to their needs . . . The fact that most of the girls are happy in work of this kind is shown by the much larger numbers who stay on for a post-leaving year after they have acquired the much coveted Leaving Certificate . . . This enjoyment of work is, I believe, a criterion of whether the work is suitable for the girl. A highly academic girl enjoys her work, takes examinations in her stride, and in fact even though she will not own up to it, rather enjoys them, gets a great deal of pleasure out of getting her teeth into something which absorbs her energies, and which she knows is leading her on to still more interesting work. The practical or artistic girl also enjoys her work and puts her energies into it, and will go to endless pains to produce a good piece of work, but because of the age-old tradition that if you enjoy your work it must be easy, she is sometimes afraid of being thought lazy by the more academic, who sometimes lay stress on their hard work rather than on their enjoyment of it. The

girl who finds her work a burden, who fears examinations, and who can never really get any pleasure out of it is most likely a misfit in the course she has chosen, and as a result feels frustrated and unsatisfied.[60]

It can be argued that the final sentence gives a simplistic view of the psychological origins of frustration and dissatisfaction with one's efforts.

These arrangements are often described as validating the concept of the 'comprehensive school'. MCEGGS under Miss Ross was selective in the sense that the majority of scholars were white, Anglo-Saxon middle-class; all pupils above the kindergarten were female. There was no formal physical or intellectual standard required for entry to the school at any level. Where the line was drawn between the intellectually and physically disabled is not specified. Within these limits, careful arrangements were made for differences in tastes, skills, abilities and wishes of girls and their parents.

A comprehensive school within the London County Council Authority had a much larger and more diverse population in background with which to cope. At MCEGGS some scholarship girls and some Jewish pupils were conscious of the social difficulty of sharing in the domestic life of the majority group. A former scholarship girl of the Ross era commented in an interview that she could not invite classmates to her home and was not often invited to parties or excursions with girls with whom she shared interests at school. The intention of equal respect and treatment for each individual, irrespective of ability or social status, operated in varying degrees in different age groups from year to year. Miss Ross was fully aware of the diverse group of old girls and parents who took an active interest in the school. She took steps to involve them in her design to create a socially cohesive yet free-thinking community. Her open personal approach played no small part in what she achieved. It was reflected in her relationships with Old Grammarians.

Dorothy J. Ross
as a young
woman, *c.* 1909

Dorothy J. Ross
as a young
teacher at
Oberwyl, 1916

Three generations of the Ross family: (left) Dorothy's grandmother, Ellen Walden, and mother, Lottie Ross, in 1911; (above) Dorothy in the garden at The Avenue, Windsor, *c.* 1913

Miss Dorothy J. Ross, the new headmistress of Melbourne Church of England Girls' Grammar School, 1939

Miss Dorothy J. Ross, headmistress, 1954

Miss Ross, in her first year as head-mistress, with her dog and prefects

Miss Ross in her study at the Melbourne Church of England Girls' Grammar School, with her dog Geordie, 1952

Melbourne University Women's Tennis Club Team, 1912: (left to right)
Hilda Kershaw, Dorothy Townsend, Madge Gaunt, Dorothy Ross (captain)

Colleagues at the Australian National Seminar, held at Melbourne
Teachers' College, 1949: (left to right) F. H. Beard, A. W. Stephens
(programme co-ordinator), Dorothy Ross, S. Wallace, Dr W. G. K. Duncan
(Seminar Director) and J. A. McCallum

The Lady who kept
cocker spaniels:
Miss Ross, Miss
Davis and Miss
Rosan Richardson
at the MGGS Field
Day, 1942

Mrs Martin, Miss
Ross and Miss
Davis, *c.* 1942

The truck Miss
Dorothy Ross drove
to the Doncaster
and Marysville
schools during the
war years

Miss Mary Davis,
new head of the
Junior School, 1940

Miss Alison Winfield,
Mrs Gwenda Lloyd and
Miss Dorothy Ross,
1940s

Sisters: Miss
Dorothy Ross,
unidentified
Soroptimist and
Miss Mary Davis,
1960s

Beau, 1972

Dorothy Ross on the
beach at Inverloch, n.d.

'I was a disadvantaged
child': Dorothy Ross,
aged twelve, 1903

Every life is unfinished business: Dorothy Ross at Camberlea Nursing
Home, Camberwell, 1970s

There had been a past students' society since 1904 'to help the school as well as keep Old Girls in touch with one another'.[61] Representation by three ex-officio members of the committee of the Old Grammarians on the School Council had given past students a voice in forming policy. The place the Old Grammarians Society (OGS)[62] played in the life of the past students of the school reflects the opportunities that became increasingly available for women, for work and rewarding social participation, after 1904. Since schools for girls offered a new freedom for females, they clung to the school in adult life as the place where they could retain purposeful relationships outside the family circle. In the OGS they could revive youthful enthusiasms and feel emancipated once more. From 1911 to 1913 the Old Grammarians Hockey Team won the State premiership, and at various times, 'Literary, Musical, Choral Societies and for a few years, 1926–34, a Tennis team' existed.[63] The Old Grammarians Committee had rooms in Collins Street. By 1938 associations of past students of the independent schools in Victoria were usually fund-raising organizations meeting a few times each year for social reunions. The need to provide stimulating occasions had been overtaken by the many organized opportunities to meet like-minded women, and there was an increase in heterosexual voluntary organisations.

Fewer women had time to play an active part as Old Girls. Those who did, reflected the views they had formed of their school as young adults. Some resented change to the site of 'the happiest days of their lives', while others applauded changes that accorded with their adult stances. The conservative Old Grammarians were to become important in the later years of Miss Ross' headmistressship. Miss Ross realized that she could not bring changes in the school which went beyond the understanding of the parents who paid the fees. There had been a Parents' Association since 1928, and since 1930 the organization sent two representatives to sit on the School Council.[64] The conventional three times a year meetings of the Association were not sufficient for Miss Ross to convince parents of the rightness of innovations. In 1952 a parent–teacher conference was organized to foster closer co-operation, with the pleasing outcome that a newsletter to parents began to be published twice a term and a handbook for parents was compiled.[65] Miss Ross succeeded in involving parents and Old Girls in her ideas for the school, as well as encouraging them to provide the money that would make carrying them out practical.[66] It is clear that Miss Ross herself played no small part in the affectionate links that bound Old Girls and parents to the school.

During her years at MCEGGS there was a deepening of understanding in the educational community of the way in which belief in one's own strengths and weaknesses was conditioned by the opinions of companions and teachers. In the early years, the part played in IQ test results by emotional factors was not fully realized.[67] When the school returned to South Yarra Miss Ross supported Miss Winfield in applying the testing procedures. On the basis of this battery of tests, and an interview with the school counsellor, a card was prepared for each pupil containing information from tests, performance in subjects, results of physical examination by the school doctor, comments by teachers and information provided by parents or guardians. The card index was confidential to counsellor and headmistress and was used in advising teachers if special consideration for a girl was appropriate. Some teachers resented the function of the counsellor[68] as intervening in the relationship of each teacher with her pupil.

The setting up of this system was consistent with Miss Ross' concern for the welfare of each individual pupil. It was not easy to administer, since some parents were unwilling to accept the school's diagnosis of a daughter's potential. Some of the Old Grammarians interviewed for this work expressed regret in retrospect that the system had acted as a disincentive to strive for academic success. Granted the possibility of error, it was still a courageous move forward at a time when a rigid academic curriculum and promotion by age, or repeating a year, was the norm in Victoria.[69]

One Old Grammarian recalled she had been asked by the counsellor: 'What will you do, because you are not going to pass Matric?' The dumfounded girl did not reply and had been advised: 'Perhaps you could be a nurse'. Her academic mother and father were outraged, and after passing the Matriculation examination the pupil went on to become a successful social worker.[70] The reliance on IQ tests as certain data for predicting academic performance was belated. As early as 1939 the Oxford Child Guidance Clinic in England was using a diagnosis, 'IQ coming up nicely', on certain patients.

Miss Ross' great strength lay in the administrative skill with which she created structures to carry out her convictions. The organization of the middle school had allowed each girl to follow an individually designed programme. After first year in the secondary school, 'girls were allowed to choose what other girls they wanted to be with in the following year, and class lists of three parallel forms were made following their choices'.[71] Some manipulation went on in the staff room to ensure that no girl was labelled unwanted. It was not until fifth form that girls were divided into academic and practical streams on the basis of career intentions rather than intellectual achievement. In her own career, Miss Ross had experienced the force of her intellectual ability in carrying out practical tasks. Since she felt little temptation to theorize what she did, she saw no reason to denigrate the girls who could act 'cleverly' or 'sensibly' in solving practical problems. In 1948 the extension of the A class category to the Leaving certificate allowed more flexible curricula in that year.

The programme for the academic stream was set by the Matriculation examinations of the University of Melbourne. To achieve a balanced experience for these girls, options, free choice of extra curricula activities, were provided, and sport was encouraged: 'Any group of girls wishing to form a club may apply to the Minor Clubs Committee (of the Council) for permission to do so'.[72] If a club had more than twenty members it became a major club and its president became ex officio, a member of the Council. Three final year pupils who were dissatisfied with the school magazine sought permission from Miss Ross to found an independent publication. Miss Ross gave them £20 for the first issue, but finding a printer and sponsors who would pay for advertising space was the responsibility of the editors. *Brick* survived the school life of the founders and was still being published in the 1960s, taking a more serious tone.[73]

It is significant that at a time when Miss Ross' regime was drawing to a close and her girls were finding her 'remote', that they sought her help and found her supportive of an initiative directed against the conventions of the school magazines of that period. Clubs came and went as enthusiasms waned, but the opportunity for girls to be with like-minded friends gave a flexibility to groupings otherwise dictated by formal studies.

The mixture of conservative and progressive in Miss Ross' academic vision can be seen in the academic programmes to sixth year. Modes of communication were progressive, secondary school pupils were encouraged to research projects in the public library, to work in teams, to play music in groups, to go on excursions. Tests were to be held without warning, to minimize tension and underplay significance. Examinations were kept to a minimum. The content of subjects was traditional. The exception was Social Studies, the brainchild of Mrs Gwenda Lloyd, an Old Girl and captain of MCEGGS in 1915, who had been a member of staff from 1925 to 1934. Mrs Lloyd was to the left of Miss Ross academically and politically. They sometimes clashed. On occasion Mrs Lloyd taunted Miss Ross with being 'autocratic', but mutual trust, support and affection were unquestionable. Perhaps it is in her dealings with Mrs Lloyd that Miss Ross' style of management is best exemplified. She recognized an enthusiasm equal to her own. Gwenda's husband, John Lloyd, used to say that she had three children: Jenny, Phillip and Social Studies.[74] Formal Social Studies were considered necessary to develop a comprehensive training in citizenship and an appreciation of the interdependence of all people. It was not to be a substitute for studying History but to be complementary. Both Mrs Lloyd and Miss Ross would be horrified to realize that by the 1990s Social Studies had played a part in the decline of the teaching of History in secondary schools in Victoria.

Oral testimony from past students refer to Mrs Lloyd's creation of respect for scholarship, her use of original sources and the sensitivity of her relationships. Mrs Lloyd had a fourth baby: the post-Leaving Certificate Form VI. Mrs Lloyd and Miss Ross fought hard for equality of recognition of the post-Leaving Certificate. It was finally 'recognized by the Nursing Board, the School of Occupational Therapy and the Kindergarten Union, but not the University's Schools Board'.[75] In the first years of the 1930s when both Mrs Lloyd and Miss Ross were seeking equality of recognition for practical and academic courses, Victorian academic and educational circles had not then begun to question the value of learning and of intellect which would bring that about. A transition sixth form made it possible for girls to transfer from non-academic to academic stream. Parents and their daughters tended to regard the post-Leaving Certificate Form VI as inferior, though the proportion of pupils leaving MCEGGS during the years 1945–53 and 1954–56 shows that those going on to university formed a numerically élite group: 'By 1950 they were only about a quarter of the total number of school leavers'.[76]

Having invited Mrs Lloyd to join her staff, Miss Ross backed her innovations and defended her against attack by conservative parents and clergy. They shared in the years of hope between the wars, the belief that education was the key to peaceful co-existence of nations and individuals. As that hope died, Mrs Lloyd moved further towards the militant political left than did Miss Ross.

'A good school curriculum' say Cunningham & Ross: 'enables a pupil to try himself out, but it will avoid like the plague any emphasis on failure or inferiority'.[77] Methods of assessment, for example, broad categories designated by letters rather than numbers, avoid detailed competitive comparisons. A core curriculum with sets (small groupings) for different levels of achievement allowed social contact between coevals to continue. In this way, it is possible to delay placing girls in different courses until they are mature enough to understand their own strengths and weaknesses.

The organization of curricula from junior school to the sixth form required choice of optional courses and subjects. Core subjects shared by parallel forms were to integrate girls of all levels of scholastic achievement. These were discussed by Miss Ross in the John Smythe Memorial Lecture and summarized in her last letter to parents under the heading 'The Comprehensive School' in December 1955:

> Miss Ross chose as her topic a subject that is very much the subject of controversy both here and in England, viz., 'The Trend Towards the Comprehensive School'. A copy of this lecture was sent to all parents at the beginning of the year because in it she sets out in some detail the way in which this School is organised as a comprehensive school, with courses to suit many varied interests.[78]

The endeavour to create equality of respect for differing degrees of academic achievement was extended by Miss Ross to other divisions in the community of the school. Very early in her years as headmistress she had become aware of the arrangements which excluded the boarders from the shared life of the day girls. In Miss Gilman Jones' day progressive educational ideas had not extended to the boarding houses.[79] Before the evacuation the boarding houses were staffed by women who had not studied contemporary developments in educational thought and practice. They were either women who needed to earn a living but lacked professional training, or widows with depleted resources. Few of the teaching staff wished to supplement their incomes by becoming residents. The boarders were subjected to an old-fashioned regime of study, church attendance and mild supervised recreation. The discrepancies in the lives of boarders and day girls disturbed Miss Ross. A quick practical response was to organize packed lunches for boarders which enabled them to share in the busy lunch time of options and sports. She joined the boarders' evening meal whenever possible and saw that outings and 'street leave' were less restricted. She was still not satisfied. In 1952 she wrote to a friend: 'I am worried about the boarding house but can put my finger on nothing exactly'.[80] In 1953 she:

> began a progressive reduction in the number of boarders. The reasons were threefold.
> 1) Decrease in the number of Junior Boarders (under the age of 11).
> 2) Financial loss mainly due to the necessity for there being at least six non-teaching members of house staff for three houses.
> 3) The great overcrowding in the day school at Morris Hall and the necessity for more school space . . . as the number of boarders had necessarily to be reduced, it was felt that this could best be done by taking only those country girls who would otherwise be debarred from a good secondary education.[81]

Miss Ross in this year altered boarding school life for the older girls:

> Batches of twenty-six of them take turns in living for a term at Wildfell, and there they take an active part in managing the house and providing the meals . . . The girls, in small groups, take their turn in doing housework, cooking meals, cutting lunches, and doing other chores. All available hands turn to the gardens on Saturdays . . . From all accounts girls at Wildfell enjoy their new way of life.[82]

Not all girls enjoyed doing the chores and gardening on Saturdays. Some girls of farm rather than a grazier background would have found the bright lights of Melbourne a more attractive change from home. The boarders were represented by the captain and vice-captain on the Executive Council, so their separate identity was recognized at the same time as Miss Ross sought to bring them into the life of the day school.

It was not only the girls who had to readjust to life in the reunited school. For many of the members of staff the disruption to ordinary living had been serious. Mrs Lloyd and her young son returned to town to resume home life with husband and daughter. Some single members of staff had to remake their personal living arrangements after the close community of the residential units. Miss Ross had to abandon her frantic peripatetic lifestyle for a regular round of duties and social obligations. It was a difficult time for her. It was not easy to reconstitute the school and plan for the future while Australia was still involved in hostilities. The threat which had resulted in the evacuation no longer existed, but bulletins of battles, war refugees and the horrors of the Holocaust were ever-present. On Sunday, 15 August 1944, the last unit from Doncaster came home almost exactly a year before VJ Day.

During that year the exhausted headmistress coped with refitting the buildings and grounds as a school. Tradesmen in Victoria were in war mode; both materials and services were hard to find. There was a flood of applications for entry to all sections of the school.[83] Beneath all the turmoil and distraction Miss Ross was implacably driven to maintain her thrust towards her vision of the school. She had an innate modesty which prevented her realizing the full significance of her own contribution to each move she made towards her end. She had not been elected head of her democratic school nor were the staff elected by vote of the community so that she tended to see herself as the constitutional monarch with reserve powers. If she negated a suggestion by staff or Executive Council, it was a rare use of her legal responsibility to the Council of the school. The following extract, written by Mrs Lloyd, conveys the working dynamic between Miss Ross and her staff:

> Sometimes her ideal of democratic rule broke down and when no arguments could win support for some action she particularly wanted she would suddenly announce that it would be put into practice anyway—staff would be speechless with astonishment at such a departure from her ideals. This happened rarely and usually ended with general acceptance and approval after a trial but sometimes with murmurs of discontent and passive non-cooperation which initially meant failure—for her ideas and methods relied on cooperation from the staff and if this was not forthcoming the ideas failed to work.
>
> More usual was a masterly handling of a staff meeting so that after throwing ideas out for discussion she would remain silent

while the more vocal opposition wore itself out—The meeting would close amicably with the opposition thinking it had its way—after a decent interval the subject would be re-opened at another meeting—meanwhile discussion would have been continuing in the staff room in groups large and small at recess and lunch time or in free periods—the new ideas would have become more familiar—its advantages clearer, its drawbacks recede—so that when it again came up for discussion more reasoned and thoughtful and calmer discussion could take place and in most cases the wisdom of the suggestion would have become apparent—because Miss Ross never made a suggestion without preparation and thought—If the idea was still unacceptable it would be dropped—and perhaps renewed a year or two later. It was seldom that she forced the pace beyond the capacity of the staff to understand what she was driving at—She taught the staff that the girls must be helped to grow—that they must not be pushed beyond their capacity to understand at that particular stage—and without ever stating this—she treated the staff in like manner.

At other times she would skilfully direct discussion so that the decision made was acceptable to all—and the ideas often appeared to originate from the staff. Of course there were occasions—many of them—when ideas did arise from the staff and were given the same serious consideration by Miss Ross as she expected her ideas to have from them—Always her criterion was—Will this help the girls? On the rare occasions on which she over-rode the staff it was always because she felt that they were blocking something which would really help the girls.

She would not be human if she did not sometimes lose patience —sometimes fail to live up to other ideals—and perhaps her main characteristic as a headmistress was just this—she was very human—never 'god-like' never infallible.[84]

After settling back in South Yarra Miss Ross needed a respite from the burdens she was carrying. Miss Davis, the head of the junior school, had applied for leave without pay in October 1946 and Miss Ross 'on the advice of her doctor subsequently applied for extra leave' from April to October in 1947. The finance committee of Council in approving her request noted, 'Miss Ross hopes to see something of developments of education in England since the passing of the Education Act'.[85] Miss Winfield would act in Miss Davis' absence and Miss Kathleen Hall would substitute for Miss Ross in the six months she would be away. Miss Davis departed at the beginning of 1947 and D. J. followed. She shared a cabin on the ship with an ATTI graduate, Margaret, the wife of her colleague and friend, Professor W. F. Connell. D. J. relaxed during the sea voyage and enjoyed reverting to an earlier role in teaching and entertaining Margaret Connell's children. She badly needed this six months when she could be a seeker, renewing acquaintance with her younger self. Nevertheless, she visited an impressive list of schools: Eton, Bryanton, French lycees, and small village communal schools in the remote highlands of Scotland.

Miss Ross had received a request from the High Commissioner to be a representative of Australia at the UNESCO workshop-seminars at Sèvres on the outskirts of Paris. Together with W. F. Connell and S. Wallace, she participated in the timely discussions of 'Education for international understanding'. It occupied six weeks of her vacation. A snapshot, taken at the end of the seminar, shows she was thin and weary.[86] When D. J. and Mary visited the Falk family in Oxford during 1947 she seemed to be avid as ever for new experiences and new ideas. For the first time, she met the Falk children. Their parents retained warm memories of her whole-hearted pleasure in their existence. Mary provided the steady background to D. J.'s adventuring.

D. J. returned by flying boat to be in time for the final 1947 term. She had under-estimated the effect of the absence of two headmistresses and she had to restore her firm control. During the six months she and Mary had been away her role as conduit of ideas between each section of the school had been missed, as had Mary Davis. For example, a letter Miss Winfield wrote to a parent: 'I am unable to help you with details of the syllabus but I shall hand your letter to Miss Davis on her return', suggests the difficulty the temporary head of the junior school experienced.[87] The maintenance of a cohesive school pursuing a single ideal became more difficult as numbers of pupils and staff increased. There was a turnover of staff and recruits had to be integrated into the team. The problems of organizing a fulfilling life for pupils were exacerbated by the smallness of the South Yarra site and the need to persuade Council to buy neighbourhood properties.

The post-war world differed in troubling ways from the years which had preceeded the conflict. As head of MCEGGS Miss Ross could not escape the question that was being raised about the relations of the Christian churches to the Holocaust. Her deep belief nurtured in kindlier years was tested by the erosion of belief among the parents who committed their daughters to her care. The population of South Yarra had changed during and after the war. 'New money' replaced some of the older established families and girls came to MCEGGS from the suburbs of an expanding city.

It was a time when 'our Russian ally' was metamorphosing into the communist menace of the Cold War. The fear of communism merged with the dread of the 'yellow hordes' who would descend from China upon a hapless Australia. In 1947 Arthur Calwell had estimated that there were 'twenty-five years before yellow races are down on us'.[88] Robert Menzies saw that the 'suspension of liberties and free speech . . . followed on logically from this new form of Cold War'.[89] He said what 'extremely good electoral sense the issue of anti-communism was'. Victoria, his home State, was still a relatively isolated conservative community. The fear of communism the media fostered, found ready acceptance among both rich and poor. The world of D. J.'s upbringing was disappearing with an influx of migrants.[90] The 1949 strike, the Petrov Affair, the Korean War, a financial crisis in 1951, kept Victoria in anxious flux until the Communist Party Dissolution Bill was declared unconstitutional by the High Court on 9 March 1951.[91]

It became increasingly difficult for Miss Ross to concentrate her activities on the school. A penalty of her success was invitations to chair, or be a member of outside, organizations. As the reputation of the school spread beyond Victoria, visitors were many and requests for help increased (see next chapter).[92] On 10 July 1949 Miss Ross wrote a reference for Miss Mary Davis who 'has been known to me for the past sixteen years' and now is headmistress of Morris Hall, the junior school. Mary Davis was the successful applicant for the post of headmistress of St Catherine's Girls' School. D. J., as always during the past sixteen years, supported Mary in her professional development (see chapter 6).[93] D. J. considered Mary's induction into her new role required that she attend St Catherine's regularly, each week. This was an added distraction from her work at her own school and also made more difficult the task of establishing close links with Miss Gamble, the newly appointed headmistress of the junior school.

It is understandable that Miss Ross relied increasingly on trusted and long-serving members of staff. They were an impressive group of women. Mrs Sylvia Martin had been seventeen years in the school, as chief of staff in 1941 and assistant headmistress since 1944. Elizabeth Pownall (1933–55) was senior mathematics and class mistress of a sixth form. Her friend and colleague, Dorothy Irving (1939–56), taught senior chemistry and was secretary to the staff. Elaine Brumley, a relative newcomer (1951–55), was an inspirational teacher of classics and warmly welcomed into the group. Olive Herschfeld-Mack (neé Russell) a gentle Quaker friend of all, was one of a group of women who were devoted to Miss Ross, among them, June Epstein of the music staff and Lesley Cunningham of ACER.

Among the senior girls were many who had come up in the school and were moulded in Miss Ross' ways. In 1948 they had endorsed her desire that the wartime decision to give no prizes be continued, and each girl on leaving be given a valedictory book containing a record of her contribution to the school. The ethos of the school was transmitted to newcomers by staff and pupil office bearers. If Miss Ross was not visible as often as before, through her open door, her presence still permeated the school. A student beginning her years in the early 1950s would have seen and heard

Miss Ross at assembly and would have been known to her by name at 'mark readings'. It was still Miss Ross' school, in purpose and organization, and displayed her principles in action.

She had created an institution remarkable in its time. The school had reflected the balance she sought so assiduously in her own life. She had in her report to the School Council in 1940 spoken of 'the apparent contradiction between "disciplined" and "unfettered"'.[94] Self-expression unlimited was totally irresponsible. In her own life she felt the tension between self-realisation and the pragmatic and moral obligation to ensure that she did not transgress the rights of others in the community in which she lived. The organization of her school was designed to educate girls to realize that rules and punishments could not relieve them of the responsibility for self-discipline. Her limited democracy could function only with co-operative understanding of the individuals who formed the community.[95] The children could not intellectually grasp the full significance of her ideal but they could and did (on the whole) respond to the spirit in which she sought to make it real, though during her last years as headmistress the younger girls recognized many layers of authority between themselves and their headmistress.

There were signs that the Anglican hierarchy, some Old Girls and some parents, influenced by the Australian version of McCarthyism, feared that she had gone too far towards 'the left'. Her girls were too thoughtful, too outspoken, not respectful of authority. They were allowed to wear berets instead of hats. In winter, slacks could be worn within the school. Was it deliberate, as hinted by Ivy Brooks in a letter to the headmistress on 30 May 1949, that a 'meagre group of girls had marched on Empire Youth Sunday carrying the school banner and representing my old school . . . I could not help wondering what was the reason for such a miserable showing'.[96] Miss Ross replied: 'We were asked to send our girls straight to the Cathedral Service and we were by far the largest Anglican School group of these schools . . . You may be sure it was a mistake in organisation and not a case of lack of loyalty'.[97] That the question had been raised was significant, as was the generalization from an instance of hoydenish behaviour by girls of the school on a suburban train by 'one very jealous of Anglicana'. 'Putting it bluntly there is the beginning of the ultimate of over-sexed girls . . . As an employer of girl typists in my office I fancy I would hesitate if the applicant stated she came from CEGGS for fear that the Brighton incidents were not mere solitary happenings.'[98] The headmistress allowed herself sarcasm in her drafted reply. She hoped the correspondent 'had written also to the Headmasters of Melbourne Grammar and Wesley College'. She informed him of the steps she would take and added:

> would you give me some advice about how to 'police' a rule with children many miles away from school? We can maintain control of girls while they are within the school grounds. We can endeavour to set standards in school. We can and do remind girls many times about their behaviour in public places.[99]

These letters indicate an undercurrent of unhappiness among conservative Anglicans with the changes in post-war Melbourne which they found reflected in MCEGGS. An Old Grammarian remembers 'the Archbishop in Assembly referring to rumours about the staff at school being involved in communism and asking anyone who heard this to report to him or the School Council'.[100]

The celebration of the Silver Jubilee of the school in 1953 provided an opportunity for drawing together past students, parents, staff, pupils and members of the public who admired the ethos of the school. It was a traditional occasion, with a play, *The Building of the House* written by an Old Girl, Mrs Coppel née Marjorie Jean Service, a back-to-school day, a formal dinner, a church service and the publication of *The Melbourne Church of England Girl's Grammar School Jubilee History*. For the headmistress it was an exhausting time of public appearances and supervision. As it came to a successful conclusion Miss Ross became increasingly aware of the widening generation gap between herself and her pupils. Her contract had been renewed for a further three years in April 1948, and then? She was now sixty-two. She had finally to obey her doctor and give up smoking. The school which had been her joy was becoming a burden in the changing political and educational scene. She was always a fighter and a stayer, but the time to leave was becoming closer. 'Staffing always a problem' was noted in 1952 when there was 'the usual fairly heavy turnover'. She was happy to participate in the making of a film designed to widen interest in the ideas she had institutionalized.

After she had found what she thought the most appropriate moment to announce to the School Council her intention to retire, the film was planned, and at the end of 1955, Mr Geoffrey Thompson spent five days filming the daily life of the school. The film of four girls talking together emphasized three key points of her developed policy: the mix of girls, the use of group work and informal methods of discussing and dramatizing. Miss Ross wrote a leaflet and made a tape-recording for *Living and Learning Together*.[101] The film harvested the success she had achieved and made easier her decision to leave.

5

In the Community

The headmistress had led her school, 'nosing her way' towards designing a remarkable institution. The reputation of her achievement was fostered by word of mouth, in the press and in professional journals. She became known as a force in educational circles, she received invitations to preside over public committees, to speak to many organizations, to present prizes at school speech days and to represent Australian educationalists beyond Australia. Her influence went far beyond the fences of the South Yarra school and the State of Victoria.

Her presence was felt among other formidable headmistresses of her generation. Her contributions to the early conferences of the Association of Heads of Independent Girls' Schools of Australia were notable for their robust down-to-earth tone. At the inaugural meeting in December 1945 at Invergowrie Homecraft Hostel in Kew (a domestic science training institution set up by the Headmistresses Association in 1932), she said: 'she felt that much time was spent discussing the ways in which knowledge of international affairs was given to students but what was necessary was international understanding . . . she wanted her students to read widely, to think, to have opinions and to question'.[1] She incited her colleagues to do likewise:

We are afraid to experiment, and that is one of the things all schools could and should be—laboratories for educational experiment . . . It would be rather a good thing if at some stage next year we all just took a fortnight's holiday to come together really fresh to think out some of these things.[2]

Miss Ross noted that in their own sessions at the conference headmistresses were finally practising what they had preached and were adopting small group discussion as a form of conferring. Miss Ross spoke in 1952 on 'Educational problems today', as a keynote speaker to incite discussion. She spoke to her colleagues of the issues that were concerning them, but in her contributions always exhibited an impatience with the least sign of complacency with current practice. Her gadfly stings won her both friends and detractors: she was never a nonentity in this group.

As we have seen, D. J. had underestimated the effect of her six months' absence from the school in 1947. She likewise did not forsee that her resignation in 1955 would so drastically alter the future of MCEGGS. Her school had been a guided democracy; she exercised her leadership function by inspiring others to adopt her views and to work harder than contractual obligations required. D. J. was not introspective, she mastered herself by acting rather than reflecting. She exercised charisma, she did not pause to analyse this attribute. It is not possible to explain the extent of her influence on her staff and on her pupils without pausing to consider what is meant by saying Miss Ross personified charismatic leadership.

Max Weber's analysis of political leadership provides a way into the discussion. He designated three types of leadership: charismatic, traditional and rational legal. A headmistress of MCEGGS in 1939 inherited a tradition of authoritarian control. She was in a rational/legal, that is, contractual, relationship with the Council —the governing body—and by extension with staff and pupils. The charismatic element came from the process, the manner in which she exercised the powers that tradition and contract conferred. 'Charismatic authority operates informally through human relationships.'[3] Commitment, then, is to a powerful bond with the leader rather than to a set of rules or hierarchical bodies of authority that represent the status quo. Weber saw charismatic authority in direct contradiction to the logic of rational/legal and traditional systems. This does not fit the situation in which Miss Ross operated. His analysis, nevertheless, pin-points the exceptional element in the manner in which Miss Ross exercised her legal/rational and traditional authority. It emphasizes the strength of the loyalty which many of her staff and pupils felt to her personally, and explains how bitterly they continued to resent the modifying or destroying of the structures she had created.

Weber has pointed out that charismatic authority bears the seeds of its own destruction. Once control has been established, devolution of authority follows and becomes routine: 'Charismatic authority then poses a fundamental paradox: the very forms of bureaucracy and tradition that it rises up against ultimately consume it'.[4] As MCEGGS grew bigger, devolution of power to make decisions had to occur. Direct communication had to be replaced by structures, and gradually the emphasis shifted to the structures as significant. Commitment to the forms of authority was seen as commitment to the leader.

In Miss Ross' case, the charismatic leader withdrew and her staff, under the formal leadership of her deputy headmistress, Mrs Sylvia Martin, tried for two years to maintain the structures and the spirit of her rule. They were so intent on the task that they did not take into account the changes that resulted from the loss of her input. They relied on the structures to retain her imprint, and themselves to represent her personal contribution.

Miss Ross had been wiser. By mid-year 1954 when she had notified Council of her intention to resign, she had thought about the future of her creation. Perhaps the school was becoming too expensive, too big for one person to invigorate all sections. Perhaps the small site indicated that it might be more practical to become a grammar school, and leave the preparatory and junior forms to other Anglican schools. Perhaps the educational pendulum was swinging in tune with the political climate. She had observed in England that NEF ideas were regarded there as outmoded. She retained her belief in the practices she had built on them. Perhaps she should have shared her doubts about the future for MCEGGS with her staff and prepared them for a future without her instead of urging them to persist in her ways. She wanted her school to survive although her reason convinced her that change would come. Her distress at abandoning MCEGGS was deepened by her reasoned consideration of possible changes: 'It would be a much easier school to run and probably much less expensive, but I would not be satisfied'.[5] She advised the Council that 'it needed a younger and more vigorous woman and to be clear about the prospective nature of the school before the appointment of a new Head'.[6]

In 1959 when I decided to leave Mercer House, D. J. was to counsel me: 'You count your successes by what you achieved while you were in office', she said, 'then you leave, and when you leave, leave not only formally but emotionally'. It was difficult for her to follow the advice she was later to give. She made the first move when she went abroad in 1956. She and Mary Davis planned a holiday which would reflect their shared concerns in education and music.

The itinerary they had planned was varied and exhausting—they would be tourists, music lovers and educationalists. The sequence of their experiences has had to be pieced together from a travel diary in D. J.'s handwriting. The entries do not always accord with the printed dates. They seem to have been scribbled at odd moments during their journeyings in Europe. D. J. and Mary appear to have sailed from Melbourne on 23 March 1956, stopped in Singapore on 5 April, Colombo on 12 April and then to have disembarked in Italy, and as tourists, threw their coins in the Trevi Fountain in Rome, and heard *Samson and Delilah* at La Scala.[7] D. J. records that on 25 and 26 April she was 'completely intoxicated by Spring in Italy'. Both D. J. and Mary noted a visit they paid to the International Children's Village in Switzerland for children who had become homeless during World War II. Basel, with its network of railways, came to be the centre of their European ventures. By June they were in England where they each had duties for their schools and contacts to resume or to make.

Miss Ross had taken with her a copy of the film *Living and Learning Together*. This, she introduced at Australia House to an audience which included Old Grammarians from Melbourne Grammar and MCEGGS. Her diary records other engagements which tied her to the school. She found relief in the many concerts London offered and in some tourist outings. On Sunday 3 June she 'worked all day until 3.30 then went Jasons Trip on Regents Canal'.

Professional obligations had to have priority while she and Mary were in England. They both attended the Headmistresses' Conference and formal dinner. On 7 and 8 June, Miss Ross alone had a serious commitment to advise the London subcommittee of the Council of MCEGGS on the appointment of her successor. Dr John Foster, Lady Clarke, Lady White and Miss Adams (headmistress of Croydon High School) had, since 14 October 1954, been the delegates appointed to interview and recommend candidates. Miss Ross talked with them individually and went to Putney County School to contact the headmistress of one candidate, Miss Edith Mountain. She met Miss Agnes Catnach several times. Miss Catnach knew the Australian scene and had visited all Australian States in 1955.[8] She was confident her staff member would develop the requisite skills. Miss Mountain's lack of experience as a headmistress was not an insuperable obstacle for Miss Ross who had herself come to that position without previous trial. Miss Catnach confirmed Miss Ross and Miss Davis' favourable impression of Miss Mountain. Miss Ross felt some sympathetic rapport with the younger woman. She had, with Mary, visited Edith Mountain in her flat and showed the film of *Living and Learning Together*. Edith Mountain was no doubt a poised and courteous hostess in speaking of the aims of education. Since the principles underlying the scenes exhibited in the film were couched in the very general terms of current educational discourse, it was possible for the two teachers as they watched together to attribute apparently contradictory practices to identical principles. No specific practices follow logically from slogans. What Miss Mountain would do if she became headmistress might not be clear to Miss Ross from their general agreement on the wording of aims. Procedures, means to the end, may conflict even when there is general agreement on the end that is envisaged. That the interregnum had already been too long had to be considered. Previous applicants had not been satisfactory and invitations to Dr Elwyn Morey and Dr (later Dame) Margaret Blackwood to accept the headmistress position had been refused. Miss Ross endorsed the unanimous recommendation sent to the Council by the London panel.[9] By this action she had further committed herself emotionally to the future of MCEGGS. The odd notes in the diary of 22 June: 'Migraine': 'went to bed exhausted— six days in bed . . . in bed all day with heavy cold', tells of her always troublesome body. But, ill or well, on 23 June she met her Old Girls at 3.30 at the Victoria League in Cromwell Road and went to Chichester to show the film at Bede Grammar School.

This duty done, Mary and D. J. could turn their thoughts towards an adventure they had planned. They then spent 'six weeks from Bergen to Buda by way of Basel . . . full of delights and frustrations, excitement and depression, of amusement and sadness . . . the time was full of interest as is all time that is spent with other people'.[10] D. J. reveals many facets of herself in the glimpses she allows us during these weeks. She is often physically exhausted, has migraines and colds, but these do not detract from her unaffected delight in new places and new people.

The 26th of July found them at the twelve-day NEF Conference in Utrecht, 'both with migraines' and 'feeling like death'. The conference was 'most stimulating' but D. J. gives us more detail of:

> the very simple home of a young Dutch couple with three lovely children in a new housing settlement and in spite of the distance from the city and its austerity (no bath and no hot water) we were very happy there and we were really sorry when the Conference ended.[11]

From 8 to 25 August was tourist time, including Innsbruck, Salzburg and Vienna, but in her letter to the staff Miss Ross focuses on the five days (25 to 30) August spent in Hungary. She wrote:

> Greetings to all the staff and good wishes for third term. How time does fly. I think of you often and hope that the awful winter we hear so much of here has not completely dampened your spirits or quenched your ardour for either holidays or work . . . We are forbidden to read foreign newspapers or books. We cannot get them . . .

This is a rare and revealing letter in which Miss Ross reaches out to old friends on her staff. She writes in simple and telling language of being one of the few Australian tourists to enter Hungary in 1956 before the uprising. She and Mary had to join a Swiss tour with forty people from Basel as 'no tours go from Britain yet'[12] and they had been warned not to travel as individuals. Her insightful observations and the gentleness with which she mentions how, despite her fluency in French and German, people are generally afraid of free conversation with her, reveals a sensitive traveller open to hurt:

> I almost wept at one incident in Pest in the market. The rest of the bus load had gone in, but my foot was being a bit troublesome so I sat in the bus, watching the flower sellers and the passers by. But once they found someone in the bus they were no longer passers by. A crowd of women, some of them very old, one middle-aged German speaking who was the spokeswoman and a number of girls, youths and children stood and questioned me—and I them—in very bad but apparently intelligible German for more than a quarter of an hour. What did we eat in Australia? How far away was it? Had we come all the way in the bus (this from a very old one!). Travel was good—it is good to see other people and know about them. London is a good place (this from a boy of about eleven years). Then just as the others came back and the bus prepared to go off, two of the flower sellers—middle-aged women—each thrust a bunch of carnations into my hands and ran off quickly to the back of the crowd. I obviously could not offer them money and hadn't a personal thing of any sort to give—but with all my heart I wished I could offer them the freedom of my life in Australia.[13]

She tells of still unexploded mines by the roadside, of unrestored shelled buildings in the city of Budapest, and of false claims in brochures that all wartime damage had been restored. There are many incidents in which her charm and outgoing warmth brought questions about Australia and strangers of all ages responded to her. She escaped with Mary from the group to shop and to observe. She writes from the heart. It is not a political treatise but it tells much of the conditions imposed on Budapest by the Stalinist regime in Russia. A group of tourists, shepherded by a tour guide and interpreter, would not have learned of the impending uprising led by Imre Nagy which occurred as the travellers reached London on 4 September after the tour had ended in Basel.[14]

It is not surprising that D. J.'s thoughts turned to MCEGGS on 5 September in London when she endured being 'in bed all day with heavy cold'. Hungary had been a profoundly disturbing experience and the news that was begining to filter through the English media must have brought troublesome thoughts of the friendly simple people who had given her flowers. She noted that 'those not completely withdrawn into a private world seem afflicted with a profound and crippling cynicism'. Could she hold on to her Christian belief 'change humanity and you will be able to change society', opposed as it was, in her view, to 'the Marxist dictum, change society and you will be able to change human nature'?[15]

London in the autumn matched her mood. She went to bed exhausted and spent six more days in bed and pulled herself together to visit the Houses of Parliament, renew acquaintance with Olive Gordon, a colleague from the ATTI days. The days and evenings were filled with a school speech day, a visit to North London Collegiate, the oldest girls' school in England, and to Mary McMillan Training College where she met a man 'who might be suitable for Corio' and a woman for ATTI.[16] Fortunately, there were concerts and 'a nice little dog Popper', to cheer a dinner with Miss Edith Mountain and Miss Gottschalk, who taught modern languages at Putney County School. Her thoughts were turning towards home. She had received a letter I had sent her suggesting that Mercer House would welcome any contribution she felt inclined to make. By the time the *Queen Mary* docked in New York on 13 November she had decided that she could work again among congenial people, training teachers.

Her travels in America are treated briefly in the diary. Notable entries include mention of Baltimore and a polytechnic high school there. She 'disliked' Chicago and met a Mr Yeomans at Shady Hill School 'who might consider a year's exchange with ATTI'. The entries in the diary add little to knowledge of her as a traveller. Entries end in San Francisco where they embarked to cross the Pacific for Sydney and home.

Home for Mary meant the new school year. For D. J., Melbourne was a challenge to rearrange her life. The years she had shared with Mary made comforting domestic arrangements possible but they entailed a period of demanding activity. She had inherited from Ethel Ross, her girlhood friend, the cottage they had shared at Panton Hill. That was sold and, with her pension from MCEGGS and an inheritance from an aunt, she was able to plan and build a modest bungalow-flat attached to the house Mary shared with her mother in the Melbourne suburb of Camberwell, and to share with Mary the purchase of a small cottage at Inverloch on the South Coast.[17] As Mary lived at St Catherine's these arrangements ensured the joint and separate living they had developed over their long relationship. D. J.'s many friends and professional acquaintances offered her a variety of work and pleasures to be pursued from this firm base, yet it was not an easy time. She was still bound to MCEGGS by many threads. Her friends were among the staff and the network of parents, heads of private schools, ACER and Melbourne University's Faculty of Education and the Australian College of Education.[18] Everywhere she went she was greeted by people who recognized her in her capacity as headmistress of her school. She was surprised by the invitation to become a Member of the Order of the British Empire (MBE) in June 1957, but the delight of her friends made her acceptance an added pleasure.

D. J. was no longer 'The Headmistress' but being the head-mistress had led her to assume some appropriate behaviours. She had carried heavy and diverse responsibilities and her life had been lived very much in the public gaze. She might have expected to be freed from the burdens of her success in that role but circumstances in which she was not formally enmeshed kept the spotlight upon her as she sought to develop her new life.

Miss Edith Mountain took up her duties in the third term of 1957. D. J. had asked me, as principal of Mercer House, to support Miss Mountain in what was a transparently difficult position. Our overbred white British bulldog bitch Emma had, as a consequence of a liaison with a Queensland heeler, provided a token of support in Bulfa, one of a dozen improbable pups. This engaging small animal, together with an offer of more professional collaboration, was graciously accepted. The impact of Miss Mountain on the school and 'the crisis' that beset her early years as headmistress is primarily of concern in this book as they affected D. J. then and in her later life, and in so far as her response at the time reveals her to us. We have already considered in Chapter 1 how the crisis cast a rosy glow over the Ross years for progressive educationalists. In telling this story the author cannot be entirely ignored. Miss Ross had, in the early 1950s, invited me to discuss policy and practice with her middle school staff. She had encouraged me to accept the headship of Mercer House and more recently I had suggested that she might find some satisfaction in returning to teach there as a member of my staff. It is clear that our educational ideas and ideals were compatible; I believe that I was sufficiently hard-headed to take a relatively detached stance in the troubled times. I sought an interview with the newly arrived Archbishop Dr Woods and offered to give him a professional appraisal of the situation from a perspective to which he might not otherwise have access. At Bishopscourt he chose to see me in the presence of Dr Darling, headmaster of Geelong Grammar School, and though it was a courteous three-way discussion it did not succeed as an attempt at mediation.

D. J. was in an unenviable situation. She had anticipated that there would be some structural changes in the fabric of administration and in the content of the education she had devised. She had not allowed, in supporting Miss Mountain's appointment, for the character and social conditioning of the new headmistress which would make the process of change intolerable to thirty-six of the sixty-one staff members of the school. She had herself dismissed all the preparatory school staff after one year in office and encouraged each of them to apply for the advertised positions. Having done that, she was prepared to wait and make piecemeal changes until she could carry staff, parents and girls with her. It took her years before her plans for the school came to fruition. Miss Mountain came from a tradition of autocratic school principals; she was probably not prepared for the democratic Australian suspicion of 'Poms' and their expected patronizing approach. Well-qualified teachers at the school in a handwritten letter which 'never saw the light of day' commented:

> She seemed to conceive of headship as completely autocratic, as involving unquestionable authority for making decisions which she felt should be accepted without reasonable discussion or explanation . . . we do feel that any change should be essentially related to our own past development rather than arbitrarily arranged according to an English pattern.[19]

The letter was written three terms after Miss Mountain had taken up her post. On the same day, 8 October 1958, there were 'notices on all Common Room boards saying there was a letter in the boardroom for staff to sign before 1.45 pm. It affirmed loyalty to Miss Mountain and the school and expressed complete confidence in Miss Mountain's administration'.[20] The letter also appeared on boards read by pupils. Fifteen senior mistresses were affronted and delivered resignations. The resignations were delayed pending a policy speech to be delivered by Miss Mountain on 15 October. The speech did not produce 'complete confidence in Miss Mountain's administration' and the fifteen members of staff confirmed their resignations and additional names were added.

D. J. was beset on all sides. She had returned from seeing the horrific damage human beings had done to each other in the name of ideologies to find turmoil erupting in what she had expected to be a reasoned process of change in her school. She had made a mistake in her estimate of Miss Mountain's suitability to be her successor. There is a resemblance to her earlier appointments of underqualified younger women to posts of responsibility. Mary Davis and Alison Winfield had her as their mentor while they grew into their new roles. In her sixties D. J. may have responded favourably to Edith Mountain's potentiality and person and not realized that she would not have the opportunity to develop the new appointee as Miss Remington and Miss Gilman Jones had restrained and guided her. She had schooled Mary in a closer emotional relationship and had planned and developed a career for Alison Winfield. She had also underestimated an Australian reaction to any perceived sign of Pommy superiority. These were decisions that increased her anguish as her staff resigned and parents who had agreed with her principles removed their daughters.

The school Miss Mountain inherited was not the school Miss Ross had created in her time. The previous chapter records the effect of social and political developments on the support of some parents and Old Girls for the ethos of the school. For these groups and for some members of staff a more conservative policy had been anticipated. The acting headmistress, Mrs Sylvia Martin, had envisaged her task as maintaining the school as Miss Ross had left it. During 1956 and for two terms in 1957 she had appointed only two new members of staff. Both staff and girls missed the charismatic leadership which had preserved the school against change. In a letter dated 13 November 1958 to Miss Valentine Leeper, a longtime supporter of Christian democracy as the basis for schooling at MCEGGS, D. J. reaffirmed basic principles:

Dear Valentine,

Thank you very much for your letter of understanding and distress about the school, and for your efforts on its behalf. It is a calamity indeed both for the school and for the Church, which has, I feel, mismanaged the whole thing from every point of view. I am afraid I was not very hopeful once other issues were dragged in than the original purely educational one.

I know that very many of the Old Girls of the school are deeply concerned, and like you, have made individual efforts, but apparently with little effect.

I have tried to keep out as well as I can, as I am well aware that by entering in in any way I might add fuel to flames already fairly high. Gwenda [Lloyd] wrote a splendid letter to the Archbishop, but it only roused ill-feelings unfortunately.

I fear that the school must inevitably suffer a bad decline for a time, but I firmly believe that there is a pattern in all things and that it may even emerge a better place even though that may take a long time. I am sincerely sure that what I and many of the more thoughtful members of staff stood for is good both educationally and in a Christian way of life.

Thank you for thinking of me. Let us hope that the next two months will turn events.[21]

By being there she could not but add fuel to the flames. The teachers who resigned had almost all been appointed by her: they had been the companions who had enabled her programme for her school to become a reality. She had shared lunch and morning tea at school and been a guest and received them as guests in the cottage by the sea. They had weathered the evacuation as a team and most had returned to rebuild the post-war school. She had to surmount her personal conflict. She knew change must come but her love for her creation and loyalty to individuals fought with her rational decision.

As the resignations mounted, these colleagues showed her their letters and asked her advice. She identified herself with their problems and blamed the Church for mismanaging the situation. She felt the Council, with its weighting of clergy, had listened to rumours other than the original purely educational issues.

D. J. considered that there was 'an original purely educational issue'. She had underestimated the popular association of progressive education with left-wing politics and she had not fully realized the extent to which her own reputation had restrained overt comment from the political right wing of the MCEGGS school community. Miss Ross had on her staff women whose politics were to the left of her own and, in a broadcast talk on 29 October, Mrs Jessie Clarke summarized the views of those past students and parents who saw a sinister communist influence in the methods of administration and ways of teaching in the school. They assumed that Miss Ross who had appointed these members of staff shared their politics.

D. J.'s response is understandable. Though she had confirmed the appointment of a successor whom she expected to introduce changes which must antagonize some of her devoted staff, she could not have anticipated Miss Mountain's retreat from contact with the staff as a group and the way she built barriers by writing notes to avoid contact with individuals. Nor could she have anticipated that the secretary, Miss Betty Murray, whom Miss Mountain had inherited from Sylvia Martin, would become Miss Mountain's close friend and would protect her from the senior women whom the headmistress found formidable.

D. J. faced an insoluble dilemma. She wrote glowing references for the staff who had resigned and rejoiced when they were appointed to posts worthy of their experience. It was hard to watch the educational middle ground disappear. Authoritarian discipline reappeared in some schools while in others, extremes of individualism and emphasis on process was pursued at the expense of content. D. J. had maintained a hope for the future of Australian education in which a balance would be preserved between the NEF emphasis on self-discipline and motivated study and the inherited belief that knowledge and content of curriculum was of central importance. She saw these aims presented in schools as conflicting and she turned with relief to an institution in which her hope was preserved.

Miss Ross took up part-time work at Mercer House in 1958. Though language in psychology and in techniques had changed, Mercer House courses still emphasized that personal relationships, patient listening to people and compassionate understanding were the key issues. The preparation of adults for teaching children of various ages and abilities was organized on lines familiar to Miss Ross, though larger numbers had required more formal organization. A governing student staff council, self and peer assessment as elements in marking, and team teaching were approved by Miss Ross. She could adopt the policy of inculcating responsibility to pupils and their schools by offering student services in times when illness or an other emergency left a class without a teacher. She recognized that her ways of coping were still acceptable. Her students were nearer her age than her pupils at MCEGGS.

With the changes in the status of courses at Mercer House had come changes in the student body. The part-time students were older men and women turning to teaching from careers which entailed early retirement. The younger men and women came mainly straight from school to undertake full-time courses which allowed them to teach either in independent or State Schools. A Junior Secondary Registration had been added to Primary and Sub-Primary certification. There were refresher courses for practising teachers and a Centre for Remedial Teaching was projected.

Miss Ross first taught the mature part-time students and her strength returned as she enjoyed the respectful appreciation of both students and colleagues on the staff. She found she could annotate existing course outlines to add her particular flavour to her lectures and seminars and—she still drove her car to supervise students in their schools—Miss Ross was not too old to supervise and delight a 'mature age' student. A teacher interviewed in 1998 remembered a supervision conducted by Miss Ross. She had prudently given her St Catherine's pupils written work for her 'crit' and was conversing with Miss Ross at the back of the classroom while her pupils worked. 'Have you thought of doing something different?' asked her supervisor, 'Like coming in through the window?' It tickled her fancy, as no condemnation of being boring could have done.[22]

Unexpected burdens were laid on her shoulders when I found it necessary to announce my resignation in 1959; I left in March 1960. Miss Ross presented the certificates at the final garden gathering and spoke generously of her dreams for ATTI and my achievements for Mercer House. She agreed to share the duties of acting principal with the vice-principal, Mr Fred Katz, a psychologist, a *Dunera* boy, who was about half her age. Miss Ross would take responsibility for female and mature age students, leaving the men and internal management to Mr Katz.[23] He would report to the Council. This interim period was short: by September 1960 a new principal had been appointed, Mr Harry Traynor, the Mercer House specialist in speech and drama, with whom Miss Ross continued to act amicably. After his death on 5 July 1961, she acted as principal until Mr McWilliam was appointed in January 1962. She continued her formal role of Dean of Women and wise consultant until she retired once more in 1967.

The institution was fortunate that her confidence and unpretentiousness enabled her to move in and out of prime responsibility with ease during a period of uncertainty. For almost nine years Mercer House had given Miss Ross a place from which she could continue to be an influential figure in education in Victoria despite periods of ill health. Some decline in her physical powers can be traced in the increasing wavering of her once firm handwriting. During her Indian summer there is evidence which shows how she embodied sane, progressive educational programmes, as one faction in education moved to extreme notions of freedom and others reacted to these views by emphasizing the need for discipline and a traditional curriculum.

Miss Ross made an impressive number of contributions to public discussion. Her association with the NEF continued. In 1957 she refused an invitation to be president of the Victorian section; she became Federal President in May 1958.[24] Presumably, she had not wished to take a prominent position in Victoria at the moment when her successor was establishing herself at MCEGGS. When she gave the 1960 President's Report to the WEF Victorian section, she spoke about the possible dilution of WEF ideals:

> ... We need to make quite clear to prospective new members that we have certain educational principles and that the fellowship is not just another educational body which we must join but a group of people who believe certain things and attempt to put what we believe into practice.[25]

Miss Ross, as always, had no patience with teachers who adopted fashionable slogans or joined organizations to further their own professional careers. The passionate beliefs that had launched the NEF were in danger of becoming the stale commonplaces of educational discourse. She continued her practical concern with Preshil as a school implementing WEF principles.

The 1958 Conference of the Assistant Mistresses' Association of Victoria, 'Education for Australia's Future' was held in October at MCEGGS. Miss Mountain had been invited to chair Professor Fredericks' opening address and Miss Ross was to lead a discussion group and to sum up the proceedings. She challenged the participants with typical throw-away sentences: 'These things have been said before. So they have, but have they been acted upon, questioned, rethought and accepted or rejected, as the case may be?' Her distress shines through more questions she asked of the teachers: 'Does more knowledge both in science and in the humanities mean more understanding? Does not the ability to read lead us down as well as up?'[26]

Her presence at this conference was a generous response to yet another heavy demand made upon her. She was concerned, as always, for the future of the school. She did refuse an invitation to go as Australian delegate to the International Conference of the WEF in Delhi, India, in 1961 and was glad Dr Norman Curry was prepared to relieve her of the journey. However, she could not in conscience refuse to attend the Australian and New Zealand Congress for International Co-operation and Disarmament.

She was much in demand as a speaker in her so-called retirement. On 24 November 1962 she delivered a paper, 'The needs of the community and the education of women and girls', sponsored by the University Women's College Council. She also accepted commitments as a member of many educational governing bodies:

> Council of Public Education with its sub-committee the Registration Comittee; Soldiers' Children's Education Board with its two sub-committees—Matriculation Committee and Interviewing Committee; Committee of Management of the Royal Melbourne Hospital and Associated Hospitals' School of Nursing, with its two sub-committees—Executive Committee and Education Committee; University Women's College Council; Preshil, the Margaret Lyttle Memorial School Council; Christ Church Grammar School, South Yarra; St Christopher's College, Australia (and the) Y.W.C.A. Training Committee, for both of these she does training work; Soroptimists' Club of Melbourne Executive Committee with its sub-committee, the long-term project committee; Science and Technology Careers Bureau sub-committee for Scholarships; Faculty of Education, Melbourne University; Schools Board Executive; Council of the Incorporated Association of Registered Teachers of Victoria .[27]

Her experience at MCEGGS was called upon in 1964 when, with T. R. Garnett of Geelong Grammar School and Mr Alan Ingham, she was a keynote speaker at a seminar held at Mercer House entitled 'The problem of the non-academic child'. She was one among a number of members of the Lyceum Club elected to form 'The Catalysts'. They met regularly for a simple meal and to hear each other read short papers to open discussion. Among the papers D. J. read to this group were: 'What makes them tick?' in May 1960, in August 1963, 'Is anybody listening? and, of particular interest is a late paper, dated 14 November 1966, entitled, 'Cats and curiosity'. She reminded fellow members that in 1953 she had read them a paper with the same title, but since then she had learned much from their papers and from others. Among friends D. J. could speak freely. She dared in this paper to read her poem to them. 'Hell', she warned, 'in my poem means to be driven by one's own ignorance'.

Curiosity

Curiosity may have killed a cat;
More likely the cat was just unlucky
or else curious
to see what death was like, having no cause
to go on licking paws
or fathering litter upon litter of kittens
Predictably.

Nevertheless to be curious
is dangerous enough. To distrust
what is always said, what seems,
To ask odd questions, interfere in dreams,
Leave home, smell rats, have hunches,
does not endear him to those doggy circles
where well-made baskets, suitable wives, good lunches,
are the order of things and where prevails
much wagging of incurious heads and tails.

Face it. Curiosity
will not cause him to die
only lack of it will.

Never to want to see
the other side of the hill
or that improbable country
where living is an idyll
although a probable hell
would kill us all.
Only the curious have, if they live, a tale
worth telling at all.

Dogs say cat loves too much, is irresponsible
is changeable, marries too many wives,
deserts his children, chills all dinner tables
with tales of his nine lives.

Well, he's lucky. Let him be
nine-lived and contradictory
curious enough to change, prepared to pay
the cat-price, which is to die and die again and again,
each time with no less pain.
A cat minority of one
is all that can be counted on
to tell the truth. And what he has to tell
on each return from hell
is this: That dying is what the living do
that dying is what the loving do
and that dead dogs are those that do not know
that hell is where—to live—they had to go.[28]

She remarked that in 1953 the paper she had read to them had been about genetics. That paper had been called 'What will the uncoil be?' In the later paper, she stated the problem of genetics:

Is the new born child the product of his inheritance, of his genes, his glands, his chassis? Is he a bundle of reflexes conditioned by his culture? Is he the sport of heredity or the robot of circumstances? In a laboratory we can produce a formula for the exact combination of genes we want. In our culture we can effect such changes as we think desirable. We know this, and it is this very awareness that differentiates us from the animals and plants, which serve us so often with false analogies. Along with this self awareness goes hand in hand our most human and most uncomfortable characterisitic—the perilous right to choose.

But we cannot flout the recognised needs of our animal nature. We have recently come to understand the intricate connections by which a broken heart becomes a blocked nerve-track, or a hyper-extended artery, or by which an unpaid grocery bill becomes something an x-ray can reveal in the stomach.[29]

She spoke passionately against a state using genetic manipulation as a substitute for warfare with weaponry:

. . . No doubt sperm banks will be common but surely not as instruments of the State. Geneticists can produce better cattle for our human betterment and better strains of wheat for our dietary improvement. But cattle and wheat are not self conscious creatures. Three qualities differentiate us from them. Our conscious understanding however imperfect, of our own possibilities, our sense of the dignity and worth of ourselves as persons.

. . . Ever since I became a cat consumed with curiosity I have been trying not only to deal with human diversity but to unearth some of its secrets . . .

She comes to a pessimistic conclusion: 'Perhaps on the whole, it would be better if we continued to fumble along in our usual and perennial scholastic mist . . . my 1953 and 1966 revision are both inconclusive and questing, seeking answers not yet available'.

Among these women, each distinguished in her field, she felt free to voice her uncertainty, but what shines through is her unshakeable conviction that each human being is individual and therefore must be observed and treated appropriately. However minute the categories into which persons are placed there is no precise fit, no label can explain the complexity of a child in the class or the adult who teaches them. It is remarkable that Miss Ross managed to fulfill the obligations which she incurred when she became a Charter Foundation Member of the Soroptimists' Melbourne Club in June 1948. That she did so was confirmed when the Club conferred Honorary Membership on her in April 1964, together with her fellow member, Dr Lucy Bryce CBE, 'both of whom have given outstanding services to Soroptimism and the community'.

Soroptimist Clubs had sprung up in developed Western countries in the aftermath of World War I. In Great Britain in 1920, the local Rotary Club had fostered a Venture Club for women on principles similar to their own, and in 1921 in California, the first Soroptimist Club gave the name to what was to become an international sorority modelled on international Rotary: 'Soroptimism comes from the words soro—a sister, optima—best'.[30] 'An acceptable explanation is "Women at their best, helping others to be their best."'[31] It is an international organization of professional

and business women, selected from responsible figures representing various vocations. It is designed, as is Rotary, to promote a
kinder face of capitalism in which high ethical standards in business and professional work will lead to international understanding and friendship. Soroptimists believe that their organization
advances the status of women in particular and, in general,
advances human rights for all people.

It is not surprising that the Soroptimists recognized the leadership qualities and administrative skills of their representative
principal of a private girls' school. Miss Ross became president of
the Melbourne Club and also president of the Divisional Union
(now region) of Victoria. In 1955 she represented Victoria on the
Co-ordinating Committee to act as liaison between all Divisional
Unions in Australia and to make contact with clubs in New
Zealand.

Among the Melbourne Soroptimists, Miss Ross found congenial
members: Dame Margaret Blackwood (botanist), Dr Elizabeth
Turner (paediatrician), Miss Thelma Jarrett (a prominent public
figure), Miss Gracemary MacKinnon (Wool Board), Miss Meredith
McComas (president of the Council of University Women's College), Miss Margareta Webber (bookseller), Dr Jean Littlejohn
(medicine, the first president).

Over the years this organization of distinguished women has
fostered charitable and civic action projects, while individual members accepted an obligation to succour needy, disabled or distressed
persons. For Miss Ross it was one more obligation in an already
burdened life. An example of her activity as a member was given
by Ms Rosalind Martin who became involved in a joint project
with the headmistress. They undertook the rehabilitation of young
female prisoners who had only one black mark against their names.
Ms Martin and Miss Ross together met each girl as she was freed
from Fairlea Womens' Prison, housed them, counselled and used
their networks to find jobs. Ms Martin writes: 'I just drove the
car and listened to Miss Ross gently talking to her and exploring

possibilities without apparent effort or superiority . . . Excellent. This girl was one of our great successes'.[32]

Miss Ross was leading a fruitful life, writing and taking social action. She had yet another task, to record the story of her work as headmistress of MCEGGS. She began with the help of intimate friends, who had been her staff members, to prepare a lengthy statement 'An Australian school at work'. Correspondence with Dr K. S. Cunningham tells the story.[33] The ACER had begun a monograph series with a volume *Foundations of Secondary Education* by Professor W. F. Connell (first published in 1961 and to be revised in 1967). Dr W. C. Radford records:

> I believe that the work done by Miss Dorothy Ross during the period when she was Headmistress of Melbourne Church of England Girls' Grammar School deserves wider notice than it has had, both for the theory behind it and for the constant experimental nature of her schools organisation and administration. I therefore asked Miss Ross if she would set out for use in the monograph series, an account of her work at the school.[34]

Dr Cunningham was asked 'to deal with' the lengthy manuscript Miss Ross provided and he responded in a letter dated 23 June 1964: 'It seems desirable to provide a kind of rationale for the publication and links with other ACER publications in the series'.[35] To ensure this, Dr Cunningham wrote two introductory chapters explaining 'The scope and purpose of the present monograph' and 'General principles and problems in secondary education'.[36] He then adapted Miss Ross' account of the structure and functioning of the school. He notes in a letter of 30 October 1964 to Miss Ross: 'You will realize that I have picked up ideas and passages of yours and then often interpolated ideas that have occurred to me as I have written . . . You must be quite frank if you do not agree with them or if you think they are irrelevant'.[37] It was not until D. J. was in Camberlea Nursing Home reflecting on her past that she became 'quite frank' about this book that bore her name as second author. Dr Cunningham in a later letter feels:

that our view points on fundamentals are so close that there is very little to iron out . . . the central value or philosophy, if you prefer the word, is the concept that every pupil should be treated fully as a 'person' with all that this implies (*Mutatis Mutandis* this applies, I take it, to members of staff as well). Pastoral care, induction of new pupils, participation in group activities, self government in defined areas, consultation at all levels—all these would appear to spring from such a concept. Perhaps we could include the idea that equal status should be granted to all studies provided they were the ones best suited to the individuals concerned.[38]

D. J. may well have felt that this somewhat dry statement did not fully represent her view for she annotated the paragraph 'Gwenda', as if Mrs Gwenda Lloyd could help her resolve her doubt. If she felt at the time of publication that somehow an essential element was lacking in the account, a Canadian reviewer expressed it for her:

The monograph becomes a splendidly practical manual as it details the organization of timetables and curricula, specifies procedures for assessment and guidance, and elaborates techniques for achieving self-government among staff and pupils. Lengthy appendices provide illustrative supporting material. Further, in each chapter, pithy theoretical discussions introduce the descriptions of procedures at MCEGGS. These chapters contribute a brisk and precious portrayal of a remarkable school. Further, they at once attest to the non-government school's capacity to innovate, and afford a testimonial to an unusual, forward-thinking headmistress.

But the monograph is incomplete, for the descriptions derive from Miss Ross's viewpoint, and with Miss Ross comprehensivism is an attitude of mind. The reader wonders about characteristics of pupils and staff. Particularly of staff, for Miss Ross demands 'teachers who are masters of their craft', who employ 'different teaching methods . . . in the different sets' while, in whole class groups of mixed ability, they use 'different methods of accommodating individual differences'. None of these statements is elaborated. In essence, the monograph gives an excellent description of a formal structure, of the manner in which a comprehensive static organization can function, but it is not entirely convincing.[39]

It needed Miss Ross' 'mud and dust' and more. The practical examples drawn from the living school and the spirit with which she taught that procedures must be carried out with tactful consideration for the sensibilities of each member of the community if the structures were to function smoothly would have carried conviction.[40] Dr Cunningham does not stress her fundamental religious conviction.

The publication in June 1967 of *An Australian School at Work* did not mark the end of Miss Ross' contribution to education. She was ill during 1967 but when she had resigned from Mercer House, as always, leaving a post triggered plans for travel. A trip to Canada and the United States is recorded, but no details of her itinerary or correspondence have come to light.

The following year, back in Melbourne, she resumed her attachment to Mercer House. She assisted Enid Shann (whom she had taught at ATTI) in teaching a correspondence course for country students which occupied her for two or three days a week: she drove as far as Frankston, Geelong and Ballarat to visit the students. In 1969 she finally retired.

The years 1955 to 1969 were important ones in the story of D. J.'s life. They were the last in which she exercised her skills as a professional teacher and charismatic leader. She had grown in stature as she tested her religious belief and educational practice in the aftermath of World War II. She clung fast to her ideals, to the firm belief in the educative function of personal relationships as she worked in the familiar ambience of Mercer House. She spoke publicly and wrote of her ideas. The times were changing and an ageing body called a halt to her public career. The pain of detaching herself affirmed her wholehearted commitment in an unusually long professional life. D. J. had lived those years in a stable relationship with Mary Davis. The support Mary would now give her and the care and devotion of her many friends added warmth to the years of her physical decline. Sometime in 1969 I read her the Dylan Thomas poem 'Do not go gentle into that good night'. The verse which spoke most directly to her mood is the following:

Though wise men at their end know dark is right,
Because their words had forked no lightning they
Do not go gentle into that good night.[41]

And it cut her then as Kathleen Ferrier's song had when she had resigned as headmistress of MCEGGS in 1955. The world she had to watch as her powers failed offered little comfort and her vitality made it difficult for her to let go. It was the relationships which she had considered the essential element in her professional life that mellowed her unwilling decline into old age.

6

Relationships

'Teaching and learning still remain as they have always been a matter primarily of human relations.'[1] Miss Ross told this to her audience when she gave the John Smythe Memorial Lecture on 17 August 1954. As we have seen, she repeated the idea many times during her professional career, before and after that date. She was extrapolating from her own experience. When she taught, she felt the process: the affective bridge between her students and herself. She knew that this feeling would not flow unless she accepted as equally worthy of respect and consideration the clever and stupid, those who were physically attractive or physically repulsive to her, and the hard workers and the lazy. She knew that each one must be stimulated to make a theory or a fact their own and their curiosity and imagination must be whetted. Miss Ross used the word 'relationship' to mean the necessary connective between teacher and pupil. The term is a generalization which does not specify to which of many forms of interaction it refers. The relationship may be the power of one person over another, it may be one of love, or hate, or contempt, or limited to erotic exchanges.

Semantic problems had little appeal for Miss Ross; she was apparently satisfied to convey an impression of a positive bond essential to one person learning from another. Her generalization encompassed the changes in the form and content of relationships between pupil and teacher during her teaching life. These mirrored changes in the language in which parents and children spoke to, and of, each other. Social interaction between men and women was expressed in words which changed in the cluster of meanings they conveyed. Miss Ross was in advance of contemporary Australian thinking. The stress she placed on relationships as the key to good teaching mollified the then current stress on discipline, to implement authority in hierarchically organized schools.

Obedience, rote learning and promotion by age were still considered essential in many Australian schools. Punishment as a consequence of failure to learn, and prizes as incentives, were to be found in both government and independent schools. The prevailing form of teacher–pupil relationships conformed to the norm of the parent–child nexus. The parent or teacher was the authority. The notion of a reciprocal relationship modified the absolute authority of the adult. In a reciprocal relationship a pupil could say, 'Not so, Miss Ross', at a mark reading and not be dismissed as impertinent. It is clear, that for Miss Ross, 'relationship' referred to a type or mode of interaction between teacher and pupil which she characterized as 'democratic'.

The description of her school as 'democratic' does not stress sufficiently the affective cement which produces *Gemeinschaft*—a community, rather then *Gesellschaft*—a legally constituted organization.[2] The emphasis that Miss Ross placed on the *quality* of the teacher–pupil relationship was the essential element in her concept of a good school. It is a very demanding notion. Reliance on relationships as an organizing principle requires adults confident in their capacity to love their pupils, and children and adolescents capable of responding, and co-operating in management and willing to make the effort to learn.

It was, as Miss Ross knew, an ideal, not without its dangers. She sought to exemplify the manner of living which was needed to make the system work. The open door to her study was a symbol of her accessibility; of a willlingness to listen to any member of staff or any pupil who chose to enter. The boundary between a strictly professional and a private responsive relationship is as difficult for a teacher to determine as it is for psychiatrist, doctor, priest or lawyer. The difficulty is magnified when the teaching-learning relationship is defined as an affectionate interchange.

The feeling tone of the evidence given in interviews by many past students, their parents, and the women on the staff as they speak of Miss Ross, tell how much she gave freely in professional relationships. She did exemplify for them the principle that she advocated. She did not abrogate her constitutional authority, she modified it in use by love and respect for teachers and pupils. This was her ideal, and this is the icon.

D. J. was a vital living woman in her late forties when she became principal of her school. She was not immune to likes and dislikes. She had been a receiver as well as a giver in the teacher–learner experience when she worked with Susan Isaacs. She had learned from a teacher who combined practice of Freudian psychoanalysis with a down-to-earth practicality and a warmth in relationships. From Susan Isaacs she had learned how affection could be combined with restrained involvement which was a necessary ingredient in the ideal relationships she wished to practise herself, and wished her teachers to emulate.

Susan Isaacs was one of the people who shaped her adult personality. The ways in which D. J. reinvented herself during her lifetime need to be considered if her own reflections on her past life considered in chapter 7, are to be fully appreciated. We have seen the only child of middle-aged parents and have noted how her happy relationship with her father in her childhood was truncated as she was, at various times and in different ways, removed from his influence, as he turned more to alcoholism. Her emotional life was thereafter lived largely with women. Without attributing precise weight to various contributing factors, it is clear that lack of brothers and male first cousins, single-sex schooling, the absence of Australian able-bodied men during the five years of World War I, and the conventions of university life, restricted her close acquaintance with men. In her first years as a student, she was a very attractive young woman and had casual male admirers. She spoke of a fellow student who carried her books from the tram stop to the university. It is difficult today to realize how separately men and women, married and single, lived their lives when D. J. was young, before professional sharing was commonplace and mixed bathing permitted.

Social distance was preserved by gendered forms of address, even children were accorded Miss Marian or Master Andrew by servants. Miss Winfield did not address either of her headmistresses by their first names even when she was their guest at the holiday home Miss Ross shared with Miss Davis. Miss Ross' male colleagues and friends normally used the prefix when speaking to or of her.[3]

Social distance between men and women was also preserved by regulations and by conventions. Marriage was a bar to employment in the State Education Service of Victoria and married women were as rare as men on the staffs of the independent schools for girls. This conventional distance between persons accentuated the limited contact with men that teachers in the independent girls' schools experienced. Girls growing up in the first decade of the twentieth century who had no brothers searched the Bible and text books for information about male bodies and the process of pro-creation. A letter from Miss Ross to parents of her sixth form pupils reveals her understanding of the prevailing taboo and her own robust attitude to the importance of knowledge of anatomy and physiology. She was no prude, but she understood the Victorian reticence of many parents of her pupils. She wrote to them on 2 April 1943:

> It has come to my notice that senior girls are asking questions among themselves on the subject of sex, and some girls have come to me with a request for a clearer knowledge than they get by desultory talk. I think that parents of senior girls could help considerably by talking freely to their daughters, who should not be left in ignorance especially in these difficult times. For this reason it is my intention

to deal with the matter from a social and biological point of view with all sixth forms. I shall take the classes myself and the instruction given will be along objective biological lines.

I can recommend the following book to all parents who would like to place some simple reading matter in the hands of their daughters, though I do not intend to lend it to any girl without her parent's permission.

Plain Words. A Guide to Sex Education by W. J. Thomas. With a foreword by Dr H. E. Burgmann, Bishop of Goulburn.

Your cooperation is asked in this difficult matter.[4]

It is significant that some girls came to her, rather than to their mothers for help. What they sensed was a liberal understanding of the physical world from which sex was not excluded. Though it will become clear that D. J.'s erotic image was female,[5] her all-encompassing humanity enabled her to have many friendships throughout her life with persons of all ages and both genders in which sexual orientation was not central. Her standpoint became that of 'a gender neutral humanist'.[6] In that context, it is a distinguishing mark of our humanity that we do not regard each sexually desirable person as an object for a sexual relationship. Customary guidelines in all societies lay down who are permissable objects for a sexual relationship, and normally personal choice decides within those limits. In different chronological times in various cultural enclaves the conventions change, and persons adapt desires and performance accordingly.

D. J.'s lifetime saw changes in the laws in England relating to publication of fiction and to practice relating to the sexual behaviour of consenting adults. These new laws reflected shifts in the opinion of those members of the public who had sufficient influence to promote legalizing their own acceptance of hitherto criminal behaviour.

It is not possible in these pages to trace the part played by the different sectors of society, the media, the legal profession, the churches, literati, professional and working-class groups in this story. Here, I will relate what affected D. J.'s changing perception of herself as the years of her long life passed. It has already been noted that she possessed high intelligence, acute sensitivity and the habit of seeking to understand the changing society in which she lived. Her upbringing had ensured that she would test her thoughts, feelings and actions by her criteria of good and evil. Her moral stance was no merely introjected superego, that is, she critically examined the rules her parents and society had instilled in her and accepted or rejected what her intelligence and belief told her was right or wrong for her. She grew a conscience. Her practical intelligence focused on persons and situations in each day; it was this commitment to individuals, not a policy but following her nose, to which others responded. D. J. did not reflect on her relationships as she acted. Conceptualization followed action. The persons she encountered as a child included two father figures: her natural parent, and George Morrison, then headmaster of Geelong College. She spent holiday time with his family but as a teenager, her first close relationships were with Ethel Ross and with Nell Ross (no relation to either of them), who completed the trio. Ethel Ross has appeared in chapter 2. A music teacher, she helped Dorothy find a position at Oberwyl; Ethel's father found Dorothy a suitable companion for his motherless daughter. This was, then and is now, a normal situation. Chance remarks indicate that it was an emotionally charged and close relationship with Ethel Ross. Together they bought land at Panton Hill, and built a primitive two-room cottage for weekend retreats and holidays, which they shared with friends and pupils. The relationship faded as their lives took different paths and Ethel Ross died and willed her share of the cottage to Dorothy J. Ross.

D. J.'s teenage years and her early young womanhood were shaped in this way. Like many women of her generation, the late 1920s and early 1930s were decisive in building a concept of identity for her middle years. The publication of the writings of Krafft-Ebing and Havelock Ellis, and the setting up in Norman

Haire's rooms in Harley Street of the World League for Sexual Reform, brought public debate about female sexual identity openly into the English-speaking world. When D. J. was in England in 1929, as we have seen in chapter 3, she was gaining a teaching qualification, and brought back a copy of Radclyffe Hall's *The Well of Loneliness*, with her to Melbourne.[7]

This fictional plea for understanding of the life of a 'genetic invert' gave many women a framework in which they could explain the passionate friendships they experienced with other women. The belief in the balance between inherited factors and psychosocial conditioning have varied over time, and with it, the words used to describe a range of psychological and physical interactions between women. Whether it be invert, lesbian or gyn-affection 'the very diversity and complexity of womens' relationships is lost in too simple categorisation',[8] and in a too simple use of the term 'time'. In linear time, 1929–30, D. J. as a biologist, was open to the story told by Radclyffe Hall and to the censorship and trial that followed its publication. In biological time, D. J. was thirty-seven years old; in her vigorous, physical years her thoughts and feelings were in a moment of upheaval. She, at that stage, applied to herself some of the attributes with which Radclyffe Hall had endowed her fictional heroine, Stephen Gordon. D. J.'s physical constitution, asthmatic and prone to migraine, was always at war with her physical vigour, powered by a strong will. Photographs of her have revealed how her body responded to her changing concept of herself. Gone was the roundness and softness of her university years. She seemed to have grown smaller, leaner, stripped of flesh.

D. J. moulded herself always with patience and dignity. Her passion for her profession steadied her as she took up her post at ATTI in 1930. She knew who she was, and what she had to offer her students. Their testimony leaves no doubt of her essential self-confidence and her ability to relate professionally to young men and women. Among her students was Mary Davis who was to become her life-long partner. Neither she nor Mary have left a record of the ripening of their lecturer–student relationship into an intimate friendship. It is clear that mutual erotic attraction at first cemented their friendship. D. J., the older experienced woman, defined the early relationship. Mary was then twenty-nine and had been directed by Miss Gilman Jones to continue her education as a teacher at the ATTI. The younger woman responded to the loving attention of a powerful personality. Someone who knew them both well described them as 'chalk and cheese'.[9] Mary Davis had the social aplomb and the well-groomed appearance of her Western District background. The golf course and Flemington racecourse were her natural playgrounds.

Through the vicissitudes of their long shared life, the balance between them shifted many times. The parameters were set by their unequal education and intellectual preoccupations. D. J. remained the mentor in the professional sphere. She promoted and schooled Mary, first at MCEGGS, when she appointed her head of the junior school and later, when on her recommendation, Mary was appointed headmistress of St Catherine's in 1950. It was Miss Ross who negotiated Mary's salary with the appointing committee.[10]

The importance of Mary's career to D. J. can be gauged by the amount of time she devoted to it in the first year of Mary's headmistresship. One whole day a week, every Thursday, she spent at St Catherine's. This was a weekday she could ill afford away from her own school. How did the talks between them go during the hours they spent in professional conclave? There are no records of the topics they discussed. The evidence to be relied on is the changes that Mary brought to St Catherine's. They are Miss Ross' programmes for MCEGGS modified to meet the possibilities of a smaller single-sex school which drew on a wealthy social group for pupils. The temper of the establishment was nearer to the school Miss Ross had inherited from Miss Gilman Jones than the contemporary MCEGGS from which Mary had moved.

D. J. and Mary were alike in their understanding of the practical possibilities of the situation at St Catherine's. From their different perspectives they could agree on the order in which shared goals could be approached. D. J.'s tutelage was concealed at St

Catherine's, though it did not go unnoticed in either school, or in the educational community. Mary gradually became her own professional self. Her sharpened intuitions enabled her to become a respected headmistress, admired by her Council and her pupils. D. J. and Mary shared a profession which involved them in many activities that kept them in regular contact. Mary resided at St Catherine's after 1950 and shared a home with her mother in suburban Mont Albert. D. J. had her quarters at MCEGGS and the responsibility for Mrs Ross, with whom she stayed occasionally. Together they were regular subscribers to Musica Viva concerts and took pleasure in theatre-going when busy schedules allowed. Mary had her golf and her bridge and could be seen occasionally at the races. Their relationship became the stable background from which each reached out in friendship to other people in their worlds. Mary had her family, brothers, and their children, and a sister. D. J. was emotionally involved with her female friends. Mary and D. J. shared some social occasions, but, on Sundays, D. J. frequently visited a married couple who were *her* friends. D. J.'s appointment diary records that she shared Christmas dinner with the Falk's in 1953; Mary was with her family. As D. J.'s strength waned, Mary became the caring, younger partner, providing home and devotion to the ageing woman. Mutual love had taken many forms of caring. What further needs to be said about a relationship of such duration?

Perhaps the nature of their relationship will become clearer, if described, as one of a number of such partnerships between headmistresses and their female colleagues of D. J.'s generation. In Victoria the list is a long one, and the social circumstances that fostered the personalities of women teachers in independent schools at that time, provide convincing explanations. The women who became headmistresses in the independent girls' schools of Victoria during the first half of the twentieth century had, amid their differences, some discernible shared characteristics. Those who had inherited family schools taken over by the Christian denominations or transformed into company schools were ladies of middle-class upbringing. They had grown up and shared in the reticences of their extended families. They had not learned the words to explain to themselves why father and mother were unusually distant or unusually affectionate at family breakfast on Sunday morning. The discipline of 'good manners' created a facade which prevented the expression of sexual longings in adolescence, even to oneself in private. Money and sex were not appropriate topics for ladies to consider or to discuss. The erotogenic zones of a woman's body were familiar and could be imagined as lovingly shared. The male and his body was an unknown world. The fixation on objects of passion became labile. Girl children who had no siblings grew up in half a world, fear and fantasy inhabited the unknown half. The Australian male of that generation did not readily use a vocabulary of loving words to his children. Convention ordered different clothes for boys and girls and different permitted actions. The male world had been sealed off for many of the generation of head-mistresses who led their schools in the mid 1920s and 1930s.

It is not surprising that they found love objects among their professional colleagues. In many circumstances, in the army in war-time, in prisons, in nunneries and presbyteries, in boarding schools, the longing for closeness to other human minds and bodies decrees that we love the available. It has been pointed out earlier in this text that facile categorization does not fully explain the nuances of inter-action between persons. The phrase, 'her erotic image was female', does not necessarily entail a statement that all, or any, erotic zones were mutually pleasured in a close relationship between persons of a shared gender. There are variations in the recorded relationships of headmistresses and their colleagues. They had created relation-ships to mitigate the burdens of their professional calling. Miss Constance Tisdall OBE, MA, a respected headmistress and edu-cator, reacted differently to a situation similar to that experienced by Miss Ross.

In 1961 Miss Ross had said, in part, at the launch of Miss Constance Tisdall's book *Forerunners* which tells the story of her family's contribution to education at Rosbercon in Victoria: 'I don't belong to the Old Rosberconians but I'd have been a nicer person if I had been'.[11] She was the speaker introducing Miss Tisdall, who had been for twenty-seven years headmistress of Rosbercon and, when that school was forced to close in 1933, she had become for ten years headmistress of St Anne's School in Sale. Miss Ross had made clear her affinity with Miss Tisdall by adopting for the Council of MCEGGS the substance of the prayer Miss Tisdall used for the very first Conference of the Association of Headmistresses of Independent Girls' Schools: 'May we have Thy Presence in our minds. Thy Peace in our hearts, and Thy Power in our lives . . . Give us serenity to accept what cannot be changed; courage to change what should be changed; the wisdom to know one from the other'.[12]

The difference between Miss Ross and Miss Tisdall is clarified by the ordering of the elements of this prayer. Miss Ross placed first Courage to change what ought to be changed. Serenity to accept what cannot be changed, was for her the second alternative, and wisdom to know the unalterable from that which can be changed, was the agreed conclusion.[13]

Like Miss Ross, Miss Tisdall brought back to Australia in 1929 a copy of Radclyffe Hall's *The Well of Loneliness*. Her first reaction to reading it was: 'I didn't finish it. Can see why it was banned. The association with perversions. I have not finished it'. She did finish it the next day[14] but she did not identify herself with the heroine and had no doubts about the innocence of her long-term loving relationship with a married woman, Mrs Frances Thorn. She wrote in her diary: 'A true friend is the best thing in the world. Perfect happiness and rest. Growing happiness, growing serenity'.[15] The strength of this reciprocal relationship sustained Miss Tisdall while she was headmistress of Rosbercon until the school closed and subsequently when she was headmistress of St Anne's.

Her diary is written in romantic language and speaks with assurance of the God-given gift of such love. In *Forerunners* Miss Tisdall had written that she had 'no desire to marry . . . no inkling that way ever'.[16] The confidence with which she found refuge from the demands of her work in the relationship with Mrs Thorn is seen in the calm of her professional life. 'There was an atmosphere at Rosbercom', commented Miss Ross 'in which personal relations can grow and flourish at ease . . . now in an atmosphere like this experiments can take place like the Dalton Plan which was put into practice at Rosbercon'.[17] Miss Tisdall commented in a diary entry:

> Personal relationships are always difficult and most important—To be head of any establishment is not easy. Difficulties of a nice balance of Freedom and Discipline. To have a home and get the routine and ritual of a college. And each person's trouble is important: especially that of loneliness.[18]

The serenity of Miss Tisdall's life was disturbed for a time when, in her late sixties, she questioned the relationship she had formed with a younger widowed student at St Christopher's College in Melbourne, which had been established in 1945 to train females for full-time service in the Church of England. Miss Tisdall had become founding principal. Being Josie's 'Dear little precious' interfered with her work. She considered there was an erotic element in the relationship. She thought it was not a sin to love Josie but to let her love stand between her love of God and her work for Him was: 'What have I learnt? . . . That there can be a true equal and right friendship with disparity of age . . . I have learnt the true meaning of body and mind'.[19]

Constance and Josie shared the principal's house in the grounds of the college. Constance had appointed Josie her assistant:

> I may be wrong but I have a growing conviction that Josie is the right person. But it may not be best for her. God help me to see clearly—or to leave my private feelings out of it. Indeed I think I do. What should the Principal of this college have ideally?[20]

Miss Tisdall lists twelve qualities and concludes that Josie has all 'but the thing that hinders her is the lack of "push"'. To get Council to support an appropriate salary for Josie, Miss Tisdall decides to write a 'carefully thought out letter to Dorothy Ross', who is a member of the Council.[21] This decision led to short-lived difficulties with the Dean and Council and hurtful gossip in the college. Her appointment of Josie was endorsed by the Council, and the friendship endured until Josie died of a heart attack in 1966. Frances Thorn's life had ended earlier after an incapacitating illness. Constance outlived them both. She died, aged ninety-one, in 1968. The way in which Miss Tisdall responded to the challenges of changing times also differed from that of some contemporary headmistresses. Some had relationships that were widely accepted as uncontroversial.

'Miss Cunningham of Fintona and Miss Chilvers quickly recognised an affinity with each other, a steady friendship developed which remains to this day.'[22] They kept separate houses in term time but liked to spend their holidays together and when they retired, shared a house. Miss Margaret Cunningham owned her school, and when she bought it from Miss Hughston in 1935 Miss Chilvers had already been a staff member since 1919. 'Margie has all the ideas', records Miss Chilvers, 'I just put them into action'.[23] 'From the beginning, Miss Chilvers supplemented and complemented everything I proposed to do', said Miss Cunningham. 'It was a complete partnership of work and endeavour.'[24] 'Cun' and 'Chil' to the girls, they were their headmistress and her deputy. Their roles encompassed their being; personal and professional were merged for those who speak of them.

Not all such relationships were accepted as uncomplicated. Miss Catherine Wood a Scott, educated in South Australia and in 1951, 'newly appointed Chief of Staff and heir apparent to Miss Daniell, principal of Ruyton Girls' School since 1913'[25] undertook a difficult task. Miss Daniell returned to teach part-time and became president of the Old Ruytonians' Association in 1953. Miss Wood sought refuge from her professional problems in a cottage in the grounds which she shared with her close friend on the staff, Doreen Young, the senior English teacher.[26] Parents and Council voiced their 'personal objections which could not readily be put down on paper'[27] in a string of complaints about her actions as principal. Miss Wood, accompanied by Miss Young, took promised long service leave in England in 1960 and resigned from there. Miss Wood subsequently, in 1962, became a successful headmistress of a small English girls' boarding school, St Ronan's in Derbyshire. 'She died as the result of an accident in 1970 while still in office at St Ronan's.'[28]

No such objections were voiced of Miss Dora Gipson (founding headmistress of St Margaret's) and 'her dear friend of many years',[29] Miss Constance Farmer. 'The school was her family, the girls, like the boys at Glamorgan were the children she never had.'[30]

Among these colleagues, the relationship between Miss Ross and Miss Davis appears as one among a number of partnerships common in this generation of headmistresses. The demands made on headmistresses of independent girls' schools were heavy. The school council had to be managed. It was usually chaired by a man, and if it was a church school, there was a substantial proportion of male clergy among members. Representatives of an old girls' association and the parents' association were often included. Parents of individual pupils had to be considered, for the school was largely dependent on the fees they paid. If the daughter was unhappy or rebellious, unsatisfactory schooling provided a ready explanation. Teaching and support staff were constant in their demands for encouragement and stimulation.

A headmistress was expected to play a leading role in conferences, and in State and federal educational bodies. Each day brought its schedule of duties and decisions. There was little time for recreation, especially if an unmarried daughter had obligations to an elderly parent and salaries were low. 'What I need is a wife.' This wry comment is attributed to a business woman. A headmistress would understand immediately the need for a close supportive relationship in her social life; restricted by a heavy work load, she often found the object of her search for love and consolation in a colleague. The broad lines for understanding her situation are clear.

The subtle variations of each relationship are not clarified by creating rigid defining categories. Each individual life history is needed in order to understand whether a relationship included an overt erotic component and whether emotions and conditions permitted its physical expression. The term 'physical expression' is vague. It covers a range of movements and their accompanying sensations, from embraces, kissing, anal, oral and genital contact. There is seldom written evidence to determine the precise nature of the bodily exchanges in a close friendship between an individual headmistress and her female colleague. Nor, in the 1990s, are contemporaries aware of the precise erotic exchanges between the heterosexual partners with whom they socialize. What is important to a biographer is not the physical detail, but how a person experienced her friendships and how the language of the time allowed the feelings to be verbalized, and what part the friendship played in the development of character. The loving presence of another female supported a headmistress as she functioned in a patriarchal society.

There is no logical relationship between social categories and people's sense of self and identity. The fragile borderlines that define what is 'normal' in human relationships curved in and out in D. J.'s ninety years in ways that led her to always seek an underlying truth with which she could live in peace.

She came to adult understanding at a moment when sex, homosexuality, lesbianism were overtly discussed, and so in constructing her self, her sexuality was important to her. She had friendships with the men she met in her professional life. One, when asked how he perceived her as a woman, replied: 'Well, she did not thrust it at you'.[31] Other men speak of her ease in heterosexual contact. An informal approach was characterized by warmth and plain speaking, convivial smoking and drinking, and mutual respect for intelligence and grasp of educational and political issues. A feminist was outraged when a male colleague praised Miss Ross for 'having a man's mind'.[32] Her life was rich in friendships with both partners among her married friends and in appreciation of their young children.

She was on friendly terms with many of her fellow teachers. Though D. J. claimed in a letter to a staff member that she kept professional and personal relationships quite separate, the warm relationships she cultivated with some mothers of her pupils and with unmarried women on her staff show how this claim should be understood. Among her close friends on the staff she nominated Miss Elizabeth Lothian and Mrs Gwenda Lloyd as persons with whom as headmistress, she had close personal relationships, and still when necessary, could, if they disagreed, exercise her authority. She claimed it was compatible to maintain valued personal relationships while her position in professional argument could be maintained. When there was no erotic attraction the boundary was preserved. The two women she chose to mention as her close friends on the staff made very different contributions to the school. Gwenda Lloyd has not always received the proportion of praise to which she is entitled for what she gave to MCEGGS during the Ross years. Mrs Lloyd and Miss Ross shared a plan for the school and the differences between their views did not undermine friendship.

With Miss Lothian, Miss Ross enjoyed a relationship based on mutual respect. Elizabeth Inglis Lothian was an English woman who was ten years older than Miss Ross. She was a distinguished classical scholar who was a member of the staff of MCEGGS from 1914 to 1946. She was a fellow Catalyst[33] and a member of the Fabian Society of Victoria from 1908. She had also been a tutor at Queen's and Ormond Colleges at the University of Melbourne. When D. J. was no longer 'the headmistress', she experienced changes in her relationships with her contemporaries. Grief at leaving MCEGGS was balanced by freedom from the constraints of her position in the institution. For her staff, she retained her status in relation to themselves; for her self, she no longer had the responsibility entailed in selecting and employing, in judging their worth for achieving her ends for the school. The hierarchy of her 'democratic' school was in the past. What remained were inter-personal relationships and the shadows cast by the past. Charisma remained, when D. J. was no longer personally responsible to the Council for administration of the school, nor to parents for the education of their daughters, 'having favourites' was no longer an appropriate description for choosing like-minded friends and avoiding the incompatible.

Her retirement marked a significant break in the behaviour others expected of her. A retired headmistress had a new role to be learned. The vitality which enabled D. J. to overcome her frail physique also expressed itself in her emotional life. She had many relationships, some short and some prolonged, with friends inside and outside her world of schools. She interpreted for herself the nature of these friendships as the language and the freedom to express feelings changed over time. Her stature as a mature human being was in her conscious decision to pursue those relationships with women which were, as she expressed it, 'right for me' and 'right' for the recipient of her love. The question of 'right for me' and right for the recipient of her love should be seen in the context of Christian doctrine relating to relationships between women. Radclyffe Hall and her long-time lover, Lady Una Troubridge, were devout practising Catholics. Female 'inverts' were not at that time condemned for overt physical relationships as were homosexuals. Christian doctrine defined sinful exchanges by penile penetration and strictly speaking a woman could not so sin. The extension of sin to all erotic feelings and to physical exchanges between women was made in some cultures. In this grey area, individual women made conscientious choices. The moral imperative that mutual understanding of the rightness of acts was mandatory allowed pleasure in caresses to be acknowledged by believing Christian women. D. J. outlived the effect Radclyffe Hall and the sexologists had on her life and, as discussed in the next chapter, finally understood her past life in a different discourse.

Her friendship was valued by a number of married couples. She lived long enough to enjoy the company of those she had taught after they married and had children and she knew some grandchildren of her colleagues. As she grew older, her genius for understanding the very young was expressed in a gentleness of voice and gesture and a certain tentativeness which allowed young children to respond to her in their own time. She had complained that she did not know what it was to be an aunt. She became a welcome great-aunt in many households.

An account of headmistresses and their relationships would be incomplete without mention of their dogs. The icon had a dog in the car beside her, a dog followed her about the school. She was photographed with 'Tony' in the 1930s, the first of a sequence of cocker spaniels. By 1952 it was fat, pampered 'Geordie', and 'Beau', born in 1969, wrote for himself on the back of a snap when he was boarded with a friend while D. J. went away in the 1970s: 'with my good wishes for my favourite food fancier. I wonder if there's a recipe here for Dogs Ambrosia. If there is I am sure you will be able to produce it. My tongue is hanging out drooling already. Your Gourmand Beau'.

Miss Davis is pictured with her matriculation class in 1956; she has her black cocker spaniel 'Boodle' at her feet. He was so much part of St Catherine's that when he died the school collected money for 'Lockie', a black poodle, to replace him.[34] And Miss Mountain's 'Bulfa' was infamous for his theft of sandwiches at lunchtime.[35]

> the higher and domesticated animal is, so to speak, a 'bridge' between us and the rest of nature. We all at times feel somewhat painfully our isolation from the sub-human world—the atrophy of instinct which our intelligence entails, our excessive self consciousness, the innumerable complexities of our situation, our inability to live in the present . . . Man with dog closes a gap in the universe.[36]

The headmistress with her dog was recognized by her pupils as human. She loved her pet, as the girls loved their own. There was a living, 'pattable' bridge between them. For the headmistress herself, she could be playful, childish in this relationship as she could not in the adult persona she must convey to council, parents, staff and students. She could assume in her affection for her pet whatever emotions she felt she lacked in interpersonal relationships. Her dog could be her fantasy other.

With Miss Ross there was a deeper affinity with her pupils. She retained always a child-like curiosity, a wish to understand and to know which could never be satisfied. Her pupils recognized in her a perpetual seeking which was akin to their own curiosity.

Reference has been made briefly to the changes in adult–child–adolescent relationships during the years when D. J. first began to teach one little girl in 1913 and her retirement from MCEGGS in 1955. She had become aware herself of the two generations that by then separated her from her youngest pupils. That she retained sufficient flexibility to win the confidence of her captain of the school and members of the Council she had created, can be understood as an outcome of the way in which she lived in the particular. Each meeting was here and now and might have a surprising outcome. The lively interest Miss Ross retained in each school girl she met enabled her to maintain some contact despite rapid and substantial generational changes in the way girls grew up in Victoria.

The market had discovered adolescence as an opportunity for sale of teenage merchandise. The widened range of 'suitable' entertainment, possibilities of travel, public knowledge of contraception, dress codes and standards of behaviour for adolescent girls and boys, challenged school teachers who had been educated before World War II. The few, like Miss Ross, who had begun their study of education just before World War I faced a new social world. Miss Ross occasionally made pleas through the Parents' Association for restraint in planning entertainment for birthdays or boat race, and end of schooldays celebrations. Much as she regretted commercialization and vulgarity of reporting of schoolday events, her openness to those pupils she still met in the too-large school retained the quality of much earlier encounters.

In this chapter, relationships between adults have been stressed. Comment should be made about Miss Ross' professional relationships with her pupils and, despite her own doubts, how warmly and easily she socialized with the boys and girls of her friends.

It is a rich emotional life which has been written of, without such human breadth the educator could not have so enriched the lives of her pupils and students. As we turn the pages to listen to D. J. herself, it seems she did not realize how many lives had been quickened by contact with her. She had given more than she knew in the diverse circles in which her professional life had engaged her.

Such a rich emotional life was not lived without tensions and problems. Some subordinates resented criticism if Miss Ross found their dedication to the school or ATTI did not equal her own. Her tone could be abrasive when her usual control failed. Some school girls rejected her mannish appearance and the abruptness which concealed her shyness. She had a devoted following among fellow headmistresses; for those who clung to the old ways she was a threat to their self-confidence. Response to her was never neutral. The legendary Miss Ross is enshrined in the recollections of the many who admired her.

7

The Icon Revisited

Once I wrote a book—
About how in a school,
I thought the *Why* would be obvious
In retrospect I do not think it was.
How is about Doing.
Why is about Being.[1]

D. J. introduced the two notebooks she kept in the nursing homes
in which she spent her last years with these words. She continued:

There are as many Hows as there are people Doing: for no two people
do exactly the same thing in exactly the same way. It is easy to
describe the How, but almost impossible to describe the Why in
words. But it is the Why that matters most when we begin to think
about schools and education . . . If the Why is the same, the Doing,
no matter how different, will achieve the same end. It is the Why
that matters. If the Why is different the end result will be different,
even if superficially the How is the same.

. . . This book [K. S. Cunningham & D. J. Ross, *An Australian
School at Work*] was of benefit to Administrators and Heads perhaps,
but probably did more harm than good, because the character of a
school depends not on the How but on the Why. If the first principle, human relations—the being of the actors in relation to one

another, is not based on the fundamental principle of love—then no amount of How can achieve the same end. Superficially, it may look the same. Fundamentally, it is world's apart. The How of making relationships among Head, staff, parents and girls can be learnt superficially from a simple book on school relations, but person to person relationships can't. I have not such an elevated idea of human nature as to imagine that the personal relations between staff and staff or staff and girls was on a high scale and was always perfect but there was an overall 'feel' that people mattered.

. . . Teaching is exacting enough to cause tempers to rise, and irritations to make for bad moments all round, but there was also a 'feel' that these people—adults, adolescents and children—were really human, and not brainy robots who took bad moments as a personal affront.

. . . I am venturing to write an Apologia for that book—topsy turvey as it were—to show the Why in every piece of How.[2]

To show the Why in every piece of How was the task D. J. set herself for the last years of her life. She began her task in the familiar surroundings of her garden flat, but the indignities of her failing body exasperated her. She felt her dependence increased with each failing capacity. First, she could no longer drive her car. Her decreased hearing deprived her of pleasure in the Musica Viva concerts she had shared with Mary. She found she could no longer read to her blind musician friend Margaret Sutherland,[3] but required large print books herself. Weariness of the flesh did not decrease her pleasure in sharing the lives of the friends who visited her. She became her old self in listening, advising and supporting. She was helped to fill in any empty hours, one friend provided a loom and taught her to weave,[4] another was eager to type for her. June Epstein began to write her memoir. There was a friend to drive her when she ventured out. This was still the good time, but she did not like the world she read about:

In my childhood and in my own retrospect the world moved on slowly but with dignity and deliberation. In my later years—in my seventies and eighties, the world moved along with neither deliberation nor dignity. This discovery was partly brought about by an [effort] undertaken with help of an energetic friend when I was 87 —the cataloguing of my books collected over many years of my life.[5]

She began to look back to reconsider, to assess. She began, as does this chapter, with the Apologia for her work as an educationalist. It was too late for D. J. in her eighty-fifth year to draw together the theories in which her practice had been grounded. The thoughts which she scribbled down, sometimes during a sleepless episode during the night: 'This is what I wrote in the middle of the night —so you can see it will be a little difficult to read',[6] or just before the television news interrupted a train of thought, are echoes of what she had said or written during her working life. She had given her writing to a devoted friend to type for her, but her insights are not drawn together into a coherent whole. In retrospect, she saw that in her articles she had been concerned to state prescriptions for practice assuming that readers shared, or at least, would be aware of, the 'Why' on which she relied. In her active years, she had spoken to, and written for, parents who had sent their daughters to MCEGGS, fellow members of the NEF, colleagues, and student teachers. Melbourne, Australia, was her constituency. What could she have assumed her audience would expect when she first addressed them as supervisor of the ATTI in 1930, as headmistress of her school eight years later, and then, at various moments in her career?

She could not suppose that in 1930 there were many who were aware of the emergence of psychology as a discipline distinct from philosophy. At the University of Melbourne, Psychology, Logic and Ethics were taught as a single subject in the late 1920s. Jean Piaget's study, *The Child's Conception of the World* had been published in English, in London, only the year before. R. S. Woodworth's *Psychology. A Study of Mental Life* had appeared in 1922. There were copies in Melbourne by 1930, but it was not a popular work by that date. Some among her general audience might have heard of

Alfred Binet. There had been an English edition as early as 1912. Intelligence testing was in vogue.

Eight years later, Koffka's *Principles of Gestalt Psychology* had not yet appeared in English. William McDougall was lecturing in the University of London and publicly disputing with Professor C. M. Joad whether methods of science were applicable to the study of mind. The words of Freud and Jung were appearing in English translation, Susan Isaacs was publishing. *Love, Hate and Reparation*, two lectures by Melanie Klein and Joan Riviere, appeared in print in 1937.[7] The Australian market for psychological works was small, and there was a time lag before bookshops in Melbourne carried the latest works. D. J. could not suppose that her audiences would understand even if she was herself conversant with the most recent books in a rapidly growing field.

By the time D. J. moved to Camberlea Nursing Home, psychology had become a popular discipline with many different approaches to the study of human personality. Controlled animal behaviour and various post-Freudian therapies were discussed in the media. It is against this backdrop that Miss Ross' publicly stated ideas must be read. In Camberlea, she was aware of the rapid development of this field basic to education, but it was too late for her to read and evaluate current trends.

Her writings in Camberlea do not suggest that she had come to terms with old age and dying. The image that emerges is of a person fretting and struggling to justify her educational policies as right for her and right for the circumstances in which she had applied them. She was not at ease with the outcome of her working life. She still had to prove to herself the value of what she had done.

Imagine her propped up with pillows, papers scattered over the counterpane, pen on the cluttered bedside locker, and shawl draped over her shoulders—bony arms and thin wrists and urgent hands scrabbling among the papers to find the one that would encourage her to continue to write in the waiting notebook. She is not ruminating gently about the past, she is fighting, with death as her enemy, to make sense—to answer her own questions 'Why was it that I did this rather than that? Was there a better alternative?' D. J. characteristically begins her jottings with thoughts about persons:[8]

> one must not disregard the infinite complexity of human beings— teachers and taught and the resulting necessity for flexibility in group relations . . . The first thing you've got—must [sic] to think of is the genes. The next is the home and the school and the family . . . see Community as Community of persons or school Living and Learning together . . . Do we develop a philosphy or just a way of life that is comfortable for us? . . . Should there be a differentiation in home and school or should there be many schools?[9]

She answered that there ought to be far more schools than there are now and they all ought to be much smaller than they are now. There should be some that are highly academic, some that are comprehensive, and others that have reputations for doing very well in certain areas, such as music and art. She goes on to discuss at what age a choice of secondary school should be made. After an interval, she tried again: 'I don't know where we were up to. This doesn't fit in but I'll read it . . . a discipline is a method of finding out, of learning and of knowing—it's a research method'. She then writes of the disciplines that should make up the curriculum of the school. But then an awkward thought surfaces: 'Do boys and girls really enjoy learning?' She is now not so confident that failure to learn is the result of inadequate teaching. As always, she reverts to the particular and then she writes clearly and vividly, she emphasizes: 'it is important that the teacher's attitude of caring for each child does not give him the impression of prying into the private life'.[10]

From her reservoir of memories, particular incidents pop out of the generalizations and she is, for a brief moment, the headmistress, knowing her scholars. Later, she remembers the problems at ATTI when what she taught students in training was negated by the supervising teacher in the practice school. She muses about some organizations which seem devised for the convenience of teachers rather than the welfare of the pupils. She is ranging over her years of experience, still searching her past for certainties.

These notes in her old age are about what had been done, and the reasons that she gave for choosing, for example, letter grades rather than numerical assessment, and ongoing assessment rather than examinations, are 'common sense' reasons. There is no attempt to state a theory of personality from which the reasons would arise. The sometimes contradictory aphorisms she penned at this time do reveal some of the unreconciled elements of Progressive Education, for example, 'joy in learning is really joy in achieving a form of independence'. This is a discounting of *content*, of achieving understanding of some geometrical puzzle, or some explanation of apparently unconnected happenings, and it is also seen in a throwaway suggestion that: 'the less bright children who are nearly always given the least bright teachers, whereas, they should be given the brightest teachers, because their job is much more effective if you put a good teacher with a poor class'.[11]

In practice, Miss Ross had maintained a balance between emphasis on 'process' which would have excluded the methods of some learned teachers who enthused intelligent pupils to exercise their minds on *content*. She institutionalized this balance in hiving off highly intelligent girls for more demanding work and socializing them by joining them for some studies with a broad spectrum of less academically able pupils.

In her reflections in her old age, she could sometimes state that *process* was all important, a view that some contemporary teachers advocated with passion. To a friend who put the question: 'What made you develop your school practice as philosophy?' She replied:

> The 'feel' of what was right for me. I was just 'being me'. I did not argue 'This is right', but 'This is my way'. There are other ways but I came to *feel* that the main function of schools is to pave a way for boys and girls who are, as U.N.E.S.C.O. put it, 'learning to be'.[12]

It would not do her justice to treat these jottings as her mature statement of her intellectual position. Her achievement was the institutions she inspired and the manner in which her pragmatic programmes assimilated what was of value from both sides of contemporary argument. What she called her 'philosophy' of education has been considered in previous chapters. What we now observe is a tired mind and a sometimes trembling hand seeking to record what she now thinks of her life as a devoted educator. She writes: 'And I started hindsight [*sic*], looking back thirty-five years to conventional schooling, organisations, curriculums, prospectuses and so on. Whether that's attempting too much I don't know'.[13] Probably it was, but what tenacity!

Her mature position is best understood in her reasons for leaving MCEGGS when she did. She had acted in the best interests of her school. 'We are getting too big for our methods', she had said in the 1950s and the political and educational pendulum was swinging in a more conservative direction. The women who were on the staff of MCEGGS and were to her educational and political left, were influencing procedures and the curriculum beyond the limits of tolerance of Council and of some parents. D. J. knew that the spirit and the organization which embodied that spirit had been right for the time, and unequivocally right in essence. As we have seen, a gentle swing of the pendulum was what she hoped for, keeping the ideals—some brake perhaps, some modification of curricula—perhaps a disciplinary check which would not endanger the free spirit, the unselfish contribution made by the girls to the governing of their school.

Her Grammar, she then had considered, could learn something from the English high schools, something perhaps about the patient hard work that studying the content of a subject required. Her senior girls had learned this. Their Matriculation results testified to the success of her methods, but it was time to consider if these results could be maintained as numbers of students increased and new staff came to teach them. The staff was getting too big for her personal influence to ensure that the balance she believed to be right for the time was kept. This was her mature position.

Here spoke the Icon. What followed gives insight into her painful searching for the spirit that animated, that gave life to the structures she had created. She was reflecting on what she had in some sense always known, but now, looking back, needed to reassure herself. She had seen her Grammar and her ATTI disappear in subsequent changes to both institutions. It was too early for her to consider her practical achievements in perspective. She had never formulated a philosophically coherent theory of education. Her tortured search for the 'Why' acknowledged and revealed that her genius was in her practice. Her theorising was not profound. Her public addresses had been successful because many in her audiences shared this limitation.

During 1979 she had decided that the practicalities of caring for her were becoming too burdensome for Mary, the busy headmistress of St Catherine's Girls School. It was not at the time easy to find a congenial nursing home and D. J. first moved herself into Aylesford House, 157 Wattle Tree Road, Malvern. This was an adapted single-storey private house, light and airy with linoleum-covered passages. Friends who visited her there found her pathetic in an inappropriate environment.[14] Her room was bare of familiar belongings, and there was no companionable cocker spaniel. The gusto with which she had lived was extinguished by antiseptic conditions suitable for the hypothetical 'old lady'. Aylesford House had provided temporary refuge until a place was found for D. J. at Camberlea Private Nursing Home, Camberwell. There she was one among a number of well-known elderly citizens. Camberlea was careful of the dignity of the residents. If someone telephoned to enquire about a visit, a voice replied: 'I will ask Miss Ross if she is receiving'. A second glass of sherry was proffered. Yet, D. J. complained in her notes: 'They do not understand old people'.[15] She was not 'old people'. She was herself, still striving to live in understanding her past. She had always realized herself in doing; contemplation did not come easily as a replacement for what her failing powers denied her. She wrote:

I wish I were forty again and could have some finger in some educational pie. But even if it were possible, it would be wishful thinking. The mills of God politically, and the educational systems grind slowly—and life is very short . . . If I were given back my forty springs I'd like to have a go.[16]

D. J. turned from her professional story to ask: 'What makes us what we are?' Here, she was unencumbered by a coherent theory into which she must fit the episodes of her life as she remembered them. Filtered through the opacity of old age, she surveyed her own road to maturity, 'groping to maturity'. She made a wry comment: 'Well we all have our childish points, but some people are almost all these points. It is a useful thing to do, to take our immature spots and contemplate them now and then'.[17] She wrote: 'Because of being [an] only grandchild I was deprived of contemporary company and of feeling of family. In spite of my mother's efforts I was starved of people of my own age, so people mattered'.[18]

I was a disadvantaged child and this definitely influenced the course of my development—only child, only grandchild, no sisters or brothers, or first cousins—therefore a total lack of understanding of what it takes to be a sister or to have a sister . . . As you grow up you can be told about or see or listen to family (conversation) from your friends but you can't feel these . . . you can hear about having babies but you can't feel what it is like. You can enjoy your friends' babies and children as an outsider . . . You can rejoice when they become grandparents but you can't even be an aunt let alone a grand aunt. So you adopt the children of the world and become a teacher.[19]

She remembers the early years and her joy in learning and in the fostering care of her musical father and her mother. Holiday trips—Sydney, Adelaide, Cowes, Gippsland Lakes, Warburton and Geelong, a second home. Fourteen to eighteen, the boarding school years are noted. 'Work, games, holidays, pets, Peggy the goat, bicycles.'[20] She has not much recollection of her late childhood and early teens. The years eleven to fourteen before she went to boarding school were probably blocked out. They were the turmoil of early adolescence, and an unacknowledged perception of her father's problems to which she does not refer in her notebooks. Perhaps it was then, before boarding school enveloped her, that she began to realize how closely she identified with her father. At school she had the sisters for whom she craved, and the intellectual and sporting challenges in which she delighted. These she remembered in Camberlea.

We have read how the publications of Radclyffe Hall and Richard Von Krafft-Ebing gave words and form to her perception of herself at that time. Attraction to other women was attributed to genetic factors by biologists and psychologists. When D. J. was in her late thirties she had longed for relationships with sisters, not brothers, as she recalled her youth, and so, when a scientific explanation was offered for this wish, it was to sisters that she turned for close friendship and for loving. In her later years she had moved with the times and attributed the shape her life had taken, at least in part, to the social circumstances which made women her 'natural' companions. Together they enjoyed music, discussing books and taking journeys. The mutual devotion she shared with Mary passed her test of 'right for me', and right for her and survived the development and change of her views of herself for more than fifty years.

She had demanded of her other close relationships that they be 'right' for both partners. Her female 'children', the pupils in her schools and the children of her friends, of both genders, were loved as parents love their children. There is no need of technical terms to understand the generous giving of which she was capable. It was her joy in close relationships which she had stated as a principle of teaching. 'The feel of what was right for me', as she put it. 'Right' for her was a thought or action which produced no sense of guilt and was compatible with her interpretation of the religious canon in which she believed. Her spiritual life was always consistent. It can be built up from the organized groups she chose to join, and from the religious instruction and addresses she gave to the school assemblies. She, like some of her contemporaries, at some time, found reassurance of Divine Love in intimate same-sex relationships.

Brief reference has been made in an earlier chapter to her reading of Ian D. Suttie and her rejection of Freudian theory. Suttie was first published in 1935 and *The Future of an Illusion* had been first published in an English translation in 1928.[21] There is no evidence that D. J. had studied the works of Sigmund Freud in such detail that she was conversant with the intricacies of his argument about the origin of religious belief. She was a scientist—botanist biologist. She did not seek wisdom by way of words, a core of meaning sometimes imprecisely conceptualized, ignored the nuances of adherent meanings.

She said she found Suttie more convincing than Freud, but like Freud, she was clinically wiser than her formulated theories. Suttie criticized Freud for his theoretical errors, and praised his 'therapy by love', as he saw it, but he underestimated Freud's pioneering vision. In 1933 Suttie was too close in time to the publication dates of Freud's major works to see them in the perspective that is now possible.

What Freud was seeking in the clinical papers was the enlargement of the function of conscious purpose in the life of each individual. 'Therapy by love' was a means to this end. If his patient understood the origins of his/her irrational acts they could become controllable by reasoning. To attack Freud's description of the origins of irrational acting does not diminish the importance of the part he has played in the way men and women seek for a life during which the passions can be directed through thinking.[22]

In April 1949 Miss Ross wrote a paper 'Christ in education', read by Charles Murray, at a conference on Religion and Life in Geelong, 'as I was ill in bed'. She begins by explaining:

> If Christ is *explicitly* in the culture, Christ will be in Education. I stress the word explicitly for reasons which must be obvious . . . In short, as the sociologist Linton puts it: 'The old conservative culture had many universals and few alternatives, whereas the new highly secularised cultures have few universals and many alternatives'. An education can only be built up if certain values have either a tacit or an explicit consensus of acceptance.[23]

She quoted Karl Mannheim: '. . . Our task must be to discover how far the same spirit can permeate situations entirely different from those in which it originally emerged. We must develop new methods in which persuasion, free discussion and consciously accepted example will play a role'.[24] She then states:

> There may be no limit to an efficiently run institution but there may be definitely a limit to the size of a 'school family' or Fellowship under God. There is also a limit to school groups, and once that limit is passed, education loses its pastoral character and becomes a machine and not a worshipping fellowship . . . Can we give our pupils what they are obviously groping for, inner grace. They are searching for a heart not a head. Their revolution is of the spirit.[25]

It seems here we come to the heart of the matter. The school as 'a worshipping fellowship' was to be Christianity in the 'mud and dust'. After 1943 D. J. had relied on a book, *What is Christian Education?: A Piece of Group Thinking* which she had annotated, used and reused. It is falling to pieces and covered in brown paper. Her notes indicate how carefully she had analysed and studied the 102 pages. Here we find underlined 'Education is inevitably a relationship between persons',[26] and heavily accented in red pencil 'That one can teach a child little or nothing unless one respects him as a person'.[27] She notes, 'both Christian and Humanist believe that no one should exploit or dominate him'.[28] Part Two of this work, entitled Educational Techniques, examined in the light of Christian assumptions, had been closely studied. The size of school, classes and school and community attracted her attention. There is no reference to ritual, the language is straightforward and to the point. It is easy to see why it appealed to D. J.[29]

It was the simplicity of D. J.'s faith which was the light that pupils and staff recognized, but could not name. It lay at the core of her personal disregard of forms of worship, and was intensely private. Respect for individuals, each unique, was basic in her concept of a school. It is not always overtly acknowledged that this concept was based on a belief that each individual, as a moral agent, is ultimately responsible to the Deity. This belief was the basic element in Miss Ross' formulation of an educational plan. It justified her practical habit of attending with respect to what a member of staff, a pupil, or her parents might say to her. It is apparent in her insistence on the importance of each girl acquiring habits of self-discipline in contrast to learning to conform to rules, either from fear of punishment or in deference to group pressure.

Her talks at morning assemblies and her religious instruction classes were consistent with this approach. She spoke of moral problems, of day-to-day dilemmas of doing 'what you believe to be right'. She might quote from the Sermon on the Mount or the Beatitudes or the Old Testament. She might equally speak of comparative religion. She spoke of the variety of religious practices. She appealed to minds. One Jewish student who chose to attend her assemblies found the breadth of her reference to non-Christian religions challenging. A letter to mothers of Jewish students expresses Miss Ross' concern for the spiritual welfare of each one of her students:

> For some time I have been concerned that the Jewish children at school here have not been able to receive any religious instruction or attend church services. I have now found that it is possible for me to obtain the voluntary services of an instructor in Jewish history, Hebrew and Jewish religious teaching. Classes could be held either on Saturday or Sunday. Would you let me know if you are willing to let your daughter join such a class and if you are willing to contribute something towards the travelling expenses for such an instructor. This would not exceed 2/- a week. I should be glad to know as soon as possible as I will not make arrangements until I know how many parents would like this arrangement made.[30]

'The Diocese of Melbourne was less concerned than others in Australia to impose uniformity of either doctrine or practice and had accepted theological diversity as a fact of life and had acclaimed this as a source of strength.'[31] MCEGGS was within the parish of Christ Church, South Yarra. The ex-officio chairman of the School Council, Archbishop Head 1929 to 1941 and then Archbishop

Booth 1942 to 1956, appointed chaplains to the school. In Miss Ross' day these were Charles Murray (1938 to 1943), John McKie (1944 to 1946), John Housden (October 1946 to December 1946), James Schofield (December 1947 to 1953), and in 1953 Sydney Ball.[32] Among the diverse Church of England parishes, Christ Church followed a conservative ritual. Miss Ross, together with the Church of England boarders, was a regular communicant. The preparation of girls for confirmation and the instruction in the festivals of the Christian year were the province of the chaplain. D. J. admitted that sometimes she experienced a conflict of values.[33] There is no evidence that rituals and ceremonials were essential in her own religious life. The Constitution of the school set out the legal requirements for religious education of the pupils 'according to the syllabus for religious education for the time being of the Diocesan Board of Education'.[34] There was no problem for Miss Ross in fulfilling her obligations, as she infused her own broad Christianity into the formal observances.

There is no evidence to suggest that D. J.'s turning to the Society of Friends, Quakers, in her middle sixties was the consequence of the events that followed her resignation as headmistress of MCEGGS though in the dark days, she saw the Anglican hierarchy 'mismanaging the whole thing from every point of view'.[35] We have followed her from the conventional Church of England of her childhood: 'mother's mother deeply traditionally Anglican, in spite of being Irish. Father, traditionally and very strongly Anglican', through Low Church affiliation in her student days. As an adult, she pursued her own path distinguishing between the forms that situations required and her own private religious life. In the fellowship of silent worship of the Society of Friends she was, in her later years, simply relinquishing the forms which had not since her adolescence been the essence of her spiritual life. She writes of herself:

> On self-analysis I find myself neither a saint nor a socialist (of the political variety) but I have a human conscience and I want to *know*, though knowledge is often uncomfortable. My Protestant upbringing

stirs my conscience to make me seek more knowledge about the human condition and *do* something about it. One lifetime is not enough and we have but one.[36]

She realized that 'the system' had somehow defeated her. Plagued as she was by the bodily infirmities of old age, and the frustration that she could no longer act, she expressed the disillusion and confusion of the society in which she was old. It was not easy for her, she had always planned and acted for the future; her girls would grow into the women who would bring about a better world. Now she regretted 'the children I never had' who would have been her future. It is significant that it was her own children, not Mary's, that she lamented.[37]

Since the entries in the notebooks are not dated it is not possible to decide on a sequence of her thoughts. At one time she is preoccupied with herself, her development in a spiritual or psychological sense. For several successive days she would be thinking of her principles and practices as an educator.

There are pithy sentences that illuminate her long ago practice: 'Always address people by name not their office . . . "Go to Miss Miller" one must tell a pupil not, "go to the Bursar"'. Concerning members of staff, she reflects:

> There are among them conformists, never puts a foot wrong. Ritualists, takes line of least resistance (willing to pay price). Retreatist, understand, unopposed but not committed to system neither accepts nor rejects. Innovators, accepts while disapproving and trying to do something. Rebels, anti both ends and means violently.[38]

'For some people like myself', she writes: 'have tended to rebel against this mechanical and conscienceless social stratification only to find with horror that one is rebelling against everything, so we have nothing to feel proud of. So whatever you do, the system can impinge on you'.[39]

There were still moments when the much younger woman came alive in her. A sudden warm smile would say more than words; then a visitor might remember the deep spontaneous chuckle, the whiff of a cigarette and the glass in hand or an uncontrollable burst of anger or the angular movement as she stooped to pat fat Geordie or Beau. Perhaps, the visitor might, for a moment, share her rage against the tyranny of a failing body and the frustration that she could no longer change 'the system'. She could not, even then, accept that her own life was, as are all lives, unfinished business. Of the friends who visited her in Camberlea, some cared for her physical necessities and by devoted regular services mitigated the reliance on professional help which her proud independence found difficult to bear. Some brought with them their knowledge of Miss Ross/D. J. in her prime and loved her for what she had been. Among them were those who realized that she had changed. She did not find it easy to live beyond the period in which her ideas and practices were praised and emulated as forward-looking. 'Old age is very exasperating', she wrote, in her notebook, 'maybe death'll be a release from exasperation and still is an opening to a future free from it . . . death another door through which one gropes'.[40]

Her will, drawn on 1 May 1981 at Aylesford House, contains a clause which can be read as a last effort to influence 'that system', the man-made world. Subject to provision for Mary during her lifetime, 'my residuary estate shall be held upon Trust as to capital and income for the Apex Foundation for research into Mental Retardation . . . for the purpose of promoting and furthering medical and scientific research within Victoria in any way related to the prevention of mental and physical defects in children at birth'.[41] Here we find the Icon, her last directive is given, we must act to give as good a life as genetic endowment permits to all children. Scientific knowledge must grow, and finance to this end must be provided.

The educator was a superb administrator, she knew that money and facilities for learning and teaching were necessary. Her ends, she said, she could not put into words. The 'How', she could and did describe, plan and contrive. She spent her last years trying to find the words to explain 'Why' she had worked, as she did in hope of social progress. She could not take comfort in the belief that her own brave journey through two world wars and cataclysmic changes in technology, social mores and organization exemplified the 'Why' she sought to formulate. She had grown up in a sheltered corner of the world at a time when the 'tyranny of distance' insulated many young people in Victoria from the tensions generated by European politics. She was rooted in the certainties of her early years until she journeyed into the problematic world outside Australia. The years of hope between the wars, the New Education and the better world that would evolve, sustained her as a working teacher. Then came catastrophe, a testing time for a 'gender neutral humanist'. The Depression leading up to World War II; the realization that bestiality existed in human form could not be ignored. It is no wonder that the final decade of her ninety years was troubled and anxious.

One institution she had fostered, Mercer House, had vanished. Her school was growing again but, as she had forseen, with modifications of her ideal. The optimism that had promoted the NEF had been extinguished in the gas chambers of the Holocaust: yet, in her notebooks D. J. reiterates many times her conviction that the answers to the post-war confusions must be sought in so organizing educational institutions that positive relationships between all members of the school community are cultivated. Women educated in such institutions will contribute to a better world. She never quite gave way to cosmic despair. Her death certificate tells of her declining health: General debility—1 month, Bronchopneumonia—1 week, Chronic asthma, Anaemia—months.[42] The illnesses that she had fought throughout her ninety years dictated the manner of her death.

The obituaries in the *Age* newspaper over several days reframe the Icon after two generations of school teachers had been influenced by her work. The expected entries are contributed by the Council, headmistress, staff and students of MCEGGS, the Old Grammarians and the Sydney Old Grammarians, the WEF and

Preshil School. Several of her students record their indebtedness to her. The feeling tone of affection shines through the formal phrases. A memorial service held in Melbourne Girls' Grammar School chapel was attended by the few contemporaries who had survived her, and by many for whom she had become a legendary figure. Dr Davis McCaughey in his address said:

> we are met to give thanks to God for one whose life and work was focussed not on the transient, the merely conventional or the fashionable, but on seeking out the worthwhile, that of lasting worth . . . A distinction is sometimes made between a reformer, a revolutionary and a radical. The reformer looks at society, be it the society in which we live, the school in which we work, or the whole educational enterprise, and asks 'How can I get rid of this in the interests of something new and better?' The radical asks 'What is the purpose for which this exists at all?' 'Why do we do what we do?' The radical goes on to the root of the matter. Miss Ross was, I think, in that sense, a true radical. She asked the question which others would sometimes have preferred should be left unspoken. Like many radicals she was sometimes accused of being a revolutionary. She certainly stirred up controversy. How could she avoid doing so, if she insisted on the questions 'Why?' and 'What are we doing?'
>
> She herself said that her task at this school was not that of destroying and remaking an unsympathetic tradition, but one of remoulding and redirecting it. She was not a revolutionary, but she was more than a reformer. She asked the searching question.[43]

The woman who emerges from this study of her life had driven herself hard in pursuit of an education for a privileged few. The task that she had set herself was, in a sense, narrow; in both teacher training and in schooling. The demands of administering and teaching the few were so demanding that she paid less attention to the problems of the economically disadvantaged than a later generation would expect. 'So we have nothing to feel proud of' she wrote in Camberlea. She underestimated the worth of her life. She had begun to work when psychology was emerging from philosophy as a field of study. Her intuitive rapport with people enabled her to work in education in a manner which later scientific and humane studies would justify. Her administrative skills were formidable and so she could create institutions which reflected her personal stance, the conclusions that she drew from study and observation and from her spiritual life.

She was a woman of her times. During her long professional life the pace of change in technology and social and political organization was so rapid, her life of action so full, that there were no intervals when she could (if she had had the taste) systematize her thoughts in the words of successive discourses. Her stature is not diminished by seeking to understand her life as struggle and by noting the contribution to her lasting reputation of circumstances which she could not control. Her legacy is still to be seen in the number of persons who are willing to testify to the profound influence she had upon their lives and their professional work. She is quoted, when educators in the 1990s turn to schooling and teacher training, as one hope for the creation of fully democratic societies. D. J. tried to the end to retain this hope as she observed the chaotic disintegration of her certainties. The one certainty she never surrendered was her belief in 'that of God in every Man'[44] to be cultivated in the educational institutions in which the guiding principle was loving relationships between individuals.

D. J.'s mind moved back and forth in time in Camberlea as this narrative has moved back and forth. She was seeking to recover the basis on which she had taught and lived. I have been seeking to discover who she 'really was'. It is fitting that her own words should finally tell of her self:

> One always wears a mask—a camouflage—panache—call it what you will. And one always wants yet fears release from one's mask— loss of self gain of life—for I wear armour though it may be very brittle.
>
> Happiness is the flaunting honey flower of the soul—but the root is pain and the twin fruits knowledge and strength.[45]

Time Line — Dorothy J. Ross, MBE, MA, BSc (Melbourne), DipEd (London), FACE

1891	Born 3 November in Melbourne. Only child of Alfred George Ross and Charlotte (Lottie) née Walden.
1894	Attends Geelong kindergarten and nursery school during a year-long visit to grandmother Walden.
1895	Attends Miss Alice Corr's private sub-primary school in Williams Road, Toorak.
1899	Attends Miss Adderly's private school, Appin Ladies' College, Windsor.
1905	Attends The Priory, Alma Road, St Kilda, as a boarder.
1908	Passes senior public examination.
1909	Completes matriculation examination and wins a non-resident Exhibition to Trinity College, University of Melbourne.
1910	Death of Alfred George Ross. Dorothy enrols in first year of a law course at the University of Melbourne.
1911	Transfers to Bachelor of Arts course.
1914	Graduates BA (with Honours) in Modern Languages and Literature. Captain of tennis team, Princess Ida Club. Enrols in Diploma of Education at the University of Melbourne. Abandons course after second term. Temporary Assistant, 17 September to 31 December, at Coburg Higher Elementary School, Coburg.
1915	Teaches part of the year at Trinity Grammar School, Kew. Resident Mistress at Oberwyl Girls' School, St

Kilda. Buys land at Panton Hill with her friend Ethel Ross, a music teacher at Presbyterian Ladies' College.

1918   Enrols in Botany I at the University of Melbourne. Receives marks equivalent to a first class. Awarded a Master of Arts.

1919   Resigns from Oberwyl. Begins study at the University of Melbourne for a Bachelor of Science degree. Achieves first-class Honours, Exhibition and Brunning Prize in Botany I, and passes in Zoology I and Chemistry I.

1920   Achieves first-class Honours in Botany II and third-class Honours in Physiology I.

1921   Teaches at KTC and St Catherine's, Toorak.

1922   Completes Bachelor of Science degree with second-class Honours and Exhibition in Botany III, second-class Honours and Exhibition in Physiology II. Serves on the Botany Standing Committee of the Schools' Board of the University of Melbourne.

1923   Teaches at KTC and IARTV.

1924   Joint Editor of the *Australian Educational Quarterly* with F. E. Grieve, a Master at Wesley College until April 1929.

1925   Teaching position at MCEGGS as senior botany mistress, housemistress of St Cecilia's until 1928.

1927   Bachelor of Science conferred 9 April.

1928   Accepts appointment as supervisor of ATTI and Mistress of Method (designate).

1929   First trip to London and Europe. Attends a teacher-training course for teachers of experience at the London Day Training College. Attends the Second International Conference of the New Education Fellowship at Elsinore, Denmark. Visits Cizek School of Art in Vienna. Attends a short course in London taught by Maria Montessori.

1930–35 Supervisor and Mistress of Method at the ATTI to 1935. Edits R. H. Yapp, *Botany: A Junior Book for*

Schools. Becomes a member of the executive committee of the ATTI. Mary Davis becomes a student teacher at MCEGGS and a student at the ATTI in 1930.

1935   Three months leave from the ATTI. Goes to London to attend a ten-week course by Susan Isaacs at the University of London, Institute of Education.

1937   NEF conference ('Education for complete living') in Melbourne and other capital cities.

1938   Miss Gilman Jones retires. Miss Ross appointed headmistress of MCEGGS.

1939   Takes up headmistress position aged forty-seven. 3 November 1939, circular to parents portending changes. Dismissal of preparatory junior school staff.

1940   Miss Mary Davis appointed Head of the junior school. Sports Day becomes a Field Day.

1941   An outdoor nursery school opens in the garden of Phelia Grimwade House. The Student Advisory Council has a written constitution.

1942   The school buildings are offered for use by the RAAF. 5 and 6 March evacuation of junior and middle school forms to Marysville and senior forms to Doncaster. First election of prefects.

1944   School becomes an A class school reunited in South Yarra. On Sunday 15 August, last group returns.

1946   June Epstein joins MCEGGS staff.

1947   Miss Ross and Miss Davis take six months leave of absence from MCEGGS. Mary meets D. J. in Europe. Miss Ross attends UNESCO conference at Sevres, Paris, with Professor William Connell. Visits schools in England.

1948   Death of Mrs Ross.

1950   Mary Davis resigns from MCEGGS junior school to become headmistress of St Catherine's, Toorak.

1951   Mrs Sylvia Martin appointed assistant headmistress at MCEGGS.

1953	MCEGGS Silver Jubilee.
1954	Miss Ross gives the John Smythe Memorial Lecture.
1955	The film *Living and Learning Together* is made. Miss Ross retires from MCEGGS, aged sixty-four.
1956	D. J. and Mary holiday in Europe. Miss Edith Mountain is interviewed in England and educational institutions are visited. Sells Panton Hills property and builds the flat at the back of Mrs Davis' house in Mont Albert. Builds a cottage at Inverloch. Joins the Society of Friends.
1957	Moves into the flat at Mont Albert. Accepts an MBE.
1958	Takes a part-time position in charge of mature age students at Mercer House.
1959	Becomes Federal President of the NEF in Australia. Attends the Australian and New Zealand Congress for International Co-operation and Disarmament as president of the education section of the NEF. MBE conferred.
1960	Fellowship of the Australian College of Education conferred.
1964	Death of Mrs Caroline Davis née Garde.
1967	Miss Ross retires from Mercer House. *An Australian School at Work* is published.
1968	Returns to Mercer House part-time to assist Enid Shann with the correspondence course.
1969	Finally retires from Mercer House.
1972	Mercer House absorbed into Toorak Teachers College. D. J. becomes a resident at Aylesford House, Malvern.
1980	Moves into Camberlea Nursing House, Camberwell (no records of exact date of entry).
1982	Dies 11 April aged ninety years in Camberlea.
1991	29 August. Mary Davis dies in a car accident aged eighty years.

Notes

Introduction

1. Jane Welch Carlyle quoted in J. A. Froude, 'Letters and memorials', in Ronald Blythe (ed.), *Penguin Book of Diaries*, p. 342.
2. Michael Ignatieff, *A Life: Isaiah Berlin*, p. 301.

1 The Making of an Icon

1. Professor R. J. Selleck in conversation with the author.
2. John Berger, Jean Mohr & Nicholas Philibert, *Another Way of Telling*, pp. 89, 96, 100.
3. Berger et al., pp. 111, 228–9.
4. June Epstein, *A Golden String: The Story of Dorothy J. Ross*, p. 75.
5. See chapter 4.
6. Epstein, *A Golden String*, pp. 77, 93.
7. Dorothy Jean's ancestry is carefully described by June Epstein, ibid.
8. She was unhandy until in her old age someone purchased a loom for her and taught her to weave. Was she her mother's daughter after all?
9. I visited D. J. in the winter of 1930.
10. Epstein, *A Golden String*, p. 92.
11. No. 6017 in Melbourne University Records, University of Melbourne Archives.
12. Farley Kelly, *Degrees of Liberation: A Short History of Women in The University of Melbourne*, Women Graduates Centenary Committee of the University of Melbourne, Parkville, 1985, p. 21. Greek was not an entry requirement for Law so it was possible to transfer to Arts and pass Greek I at a later stage.

13 Kelly, *Degrees of Liberation*, p. 69.
14 Geoffrey Blainey, *A Centenary History of The University of Melbourne*, p. 141:
15 Epstein, *A Golden String*, pp. 22–3.
16 R. McCarthy & M. Theobald (eds), *Melbourne Girls' Grammar School: Centenary Essays 1893–1993*, p. 55.
17 IARTV Papers.
18 Isaiah Berlin, *The Sense of Reality: Studies in Ideas and their History*, pp. 45–9.
19 W. Connell, 'Innovative headmistress—D. J. Ross', in C. Turney (ed.), *Pioneers of Australian Education. Vol. 3. Studies of the Development of Education in Australia 1900–50*, pp. 227–8.
20 A. Sandell, *A Forum for the Sharing of Educational Thinking: A History of Nearly Sixty Years of the World Education Fellowship in Victoria*, p. 272.
21 Sandell, p. 267.
22 Transcript of interview with Margaret Connell, December 1970, Dorothy Ross Papers, University of Melbourne Archives.
23 Chapter heading of W. F. Connell's contribution to C. Turney (ed.), *Pioneers of Australian Education, vol. 3*.
24 Interview with Nina Crone, 19 November 1998.
25 Interview between Cecile Trioli and Dr Gwyn Dow, 12 May 1996.
26 Letter to Lyndsay Gardiner, n.d., Lyndsay Gardiner Papers.
27 Interview between Wilga Rivers and Lyndsay Gardiner, 2 May 1991, Dorothy J. Ross Papers, L55/13/17, box 3, University of Melbourne Archives.
28 Interview Rivers and Gardiner, 2 May 1991.
29 Letter by G. Lloyd, n.d. in possession of Barbara Falk.
30 June Epstein, February 1981.
31 See chapters 6 and 7.
32 Letter to D. Ross, 31 January 1945, Series 10, unit 7, box 71; Series 10, unit 9, box 70, Melbourne Girls' Grammar School Archives.
33 Letter to J. Epstein, 28 February 1945, Series 10, unit 7, box 71; Series 10, unit 9, box 70, Melbourne Girls' Grammar School Archives.
34 Letter to D. Ross, 29 July 1945, Series 10, unit 7, box 71; Series 10, unit 9, Melbourne Girls' Grammar School Archives.
35 Letter to J. Epstein, 28 February 1945, Series 10, unit 7, box 71; Series 10, unit 9, Melbourne Girls' Grammar School Archives.
36 Interview between Elizabeth Pownall and Desma McDonald, 16 October 1985, cited in McCarthy & Theobald (eds), p. 194.
37 'The crisis', an episode in the history of MCEGGS, is discussed in chapter 5.
38 She was half-time teacher at MCEGGS in 1952 and full-time from 1953 to 1956.
39 Interview with Blanche Merz, 17 September 1997.

40 Interview with Noeleen Ward, 23 October 1996.

41 Interview with Noeleen Ward, 23 October 1996.

42 See, B. Falk, 'I was there: design for memory', in M. Baker (ed.), *History on the Edge: Essays in Memory of John Foster (1944–1994)*, pp. 244–54.

43 McCarthy & Theobald (eds.), p. 152.

44 *Age*, 21 August 1981.

2 'Nosing My Way' Towards a Theory of Education

1 From a letter written by Froebel in 1834 in S. J. Curtis & M. E. A. Boultwood, *A Short History of Educational Ideas*, p. 378.

2 June Epstein, *A Golden String: The Story of Dorothy Jean Ross*, p. 27.

3 Epstein, *A Golden String*, p. 26.

4 Inspector's Report, Coburg Higher Elementary School, 14 October 1914. Victorian Education Department Register of Appointments and Removals of Teachers. No. 16499. See also, School Correspondence Files VPRS 640.

5 Epstein, *A Golden String*, pp. 22, 23.

6 Interview with V. Leeper, November 1997. Question from V. Leeper: 'Were they relatives? They were always together'. They were not. Ethel Ross was then a music teacher at Presbyterian Ladies' College.

7 Epstein, *A Golden String*, p. 28.

8 Interview with Dr David Cohen, 1 July 1998. See also, *Age*, 8 December 1997.

9 D. J.'s phrase.

10 F. Tate, *The Education Record of War Service 1914–1919*, p. 4.

11 'The Headmaster of Perth Boys' School directed his staff to refrain from discussing the war with students. He believed it had disturbing effects on the pupils' emotional and educational progress.' See, Andrew Spaull, *Australian Education in the Second World War*, p. 57.

12 E. Hobsbawm, *Age of Extremes: The Short Twentieth Century, 1914–1991*.

13 Hobsbawm, p. 7.

14 Tate, p. 4.

15 Tate, p. 4.

16 L. Gardiner, *The Free Kindergarten Union of Victoria 1908–80*, pp. 53–5.

17 The school opened in Heyington Place, Toorak, in September 1922.

18 'The Lord Bishop' was used by Miss Langley to add tone to her report of Speech Night 1917. See, Margaret Fendley, 'Of new woman and true women', in D. E. & I. V. Hansen (eds), *St Catherine's: A Centenary Celebration 1896–1996*, p. 14.

19 Quoted in Sylvia Black, 'Leafy Toorak', in D. E. & I. V. Hansen (eds), *St Catherine's*, p. 22.

20. E. Smithers, 'Gather ye rosebuds', in D. E. Hansen & I. V. Hansen (eds), *St Catherine's*, p. 42.

21. Black, in D. E. & I. V. Hansen (eds), *St Catherine's* p. 34.

22. Quoted in F. Kelly, *Degrees of Liberation*, p. 68.

23. Entry by L. M. M. Mitchell in B. Nairn & G. Serle (eds), *Australian Dictionary of Biography, Vol. 9, 1891–1939, Gil–Las*, p. 517.

24. Private discussion with the late Diana Dyason.

25. A founding principal of MCEGGS.

26. 1938 Headmistress Report.

27. Curtis & Boultwood, *A Short History of Educational Ideas*, p. 524.

28. 'The man of theory is not a dreamer, he is the man who understands and evaluates facts, the man of insight, the man who sees life clearly and sees it whole.' 'Theory is not active, it is the satisfied contemplation of results achieved. To be wisely theoretical we must be intelligently practical.' Quoted in John Adams, *The Evolution of Educational Theory*, p. 4.

29. *Australian Educational Quarterly*, September 1924, editorial.

30. Caldwell Cook, *The Play Way: An Essay in Educational Method*. Cook dedicated his book to W. H. Rouse, headmaster of The Perse School who implemented his educational method. Cook advocated play and acting as avenues to learning. See also, Cecil Shrinkfield, 'The Perse School', in *Australian Educational Quarterly*, vol. 3, no. 1, first term, 1927, pp. 10–12.

31. Tisdall letter to family and friends, 31 May 1929, Ms 8592 1013/3 La Trobe Library.

32. See William Boyd (ed.), *Towards a New Education*.

33. D. J. Ross, 'Some impressions of the Elsinore Conference', in *Australian Educational Quarterly*, vol. 5, no. 2, October 1929, pp. 20–3.

34. Ross, 'Some impressions', pp. 21, 22, 23.

35. The work of Franz Cizek, begun in the teaching of art in schools, was institutionalized in Vienna and spread to England, America and Australia. The freeing of the creative impulse in very young children changed the atmosphere of kindergartens and sub-primary schools in those countries. See also, *Australian Educational Quarterly*, vol. 1, no. 1, September, 1924, pp. 36–40.

36. W. F. Connell, 'Innovative headmistress—D. J. Ross', in C. Turney (ed.), *Pioneers of Australian Education*, pp. 209–10.

37. Norman H. Dobson, *Mercer House: The Story of the First 50 Years 1921–1971*.

38. Adams, *The Evolution of Educational Theory*, p. 349.

39. Adams, *The Evolution of Educational Theory*, p. 349.

40. D. J. Ross, 'Dr. Montessori's Elsinore address', in *Australian Educational Quarterly*, vol. 6, no. 1, May 1930, pp. 29–30.

41 D. J. Ross in *Australian Educational Quarterly*, vol. 7, no. 1, April 1931, p. 17.

42 For a discussion of their theories see chapter three.

43 Editorial, 'An experiment', in *Australian Educational Quarterly*, vol. 6, no. 2, October 1930, p. 8.

44 C. Turney, (ed.), *Pioneers of Australian Education*, vol. 3, p. 7.

45 Box 20, 23/6, Mercer House Archive.

46 Box 20, 23/6, Mercer House Archive.

47 Quoted in Dobson, p. 4.

48 IARTV Executive Council Minutes, 5 October 1932, IARTV Papers, L54/2/14, University of Melbourne Archives.

49 IARTV Minutes, August 1933, IARTV Papers, L54/2/14.

50 ATTI Executive Council Minutes, 5 October 1932, IARTV Papers, L54/2/14.

51 My emphasis. 1934 Conference.

52 1934 Conference.

53 D. J. on teaching rounds.

54 In 1931 the author accompanied D. J. on several occasions when she made her teaching rounds and sat in the back of the classroom with her, and often the school supervisor, while the student demonstrated the five Herbartian Steps in an ever-so carefully prepared lesson.

55 See J. McCalman, *Journeyings: The Biography of a Middle-Class Generation 1920–1990*, pp. 147, 149, 150.

3 A Step Forward

1 Anne Macky, a Melbourne musician and founder of the New Conservatorium, and her husband Stewart, were living in England and had rented Castle Hill cottage at Kingston in Herefordshire which they often shared with Dorothy Ross. The New Conservatorium founded by Anne Macky in 1917 was located at 31 Spring Street, Melbourne. The aim of the New Consrevatorium was to provide music education and to encourage the study of art, literature, architecture, and later, also speech. It promoted Australian drama by Louis Esson, Vance Palmer, Henry Lawson and Stewart Macky. See, Anne Macky biographical file, arranged and edited by Henry Bak, published by Mark Neill, Melbourne, 1996 (A. Macky file, Percy Grainger Museum, University of Melbourne).

2 'The mental hygiene of the pre-school child', paper read at the joint meeting of educational sections of the British Psychological Society, 27 June 1928, published in Susan Isaacs, *Childhood and After: Some Essays and Clinical Studies*, p. 3.

3 See R. Wollheim, *Freud*, chapter 4.

4 Ian D. Suttie, *The Origins of Love and Hate*.

5 Suttie, p. 6.

6 'His ideas were amongst the first victims of their success and a generation brought up on him would be unable to say with any great precision what they were.' Wollheim, *Freud*, p. 234.

7 Suttie, p. 242.

8 A colleague of Havelock Ellis, Dr Norman Haire was a fashionable psychiatrist-sexologist with rooms in Harley Street. He gathered around him medical men and women, including homeopaths, psychologists and educationalists, who had reacted to the works of Freud, Jung and Adler. Dora Russell was the second wife of Bertrand Russell and with him was to found a progressive school for their own children and those who shared in these psychological interests.

9 D. J. gave the author a copy early in 1929, see chapter 6.

10 See C. S. Lewis, *The Four Loves*.

11 Lewis, pp. 38, 40, 56, 117.

12 John Adams, *Modern Developments in Educational Practice*, pp. 272, 276.

13 Lewis, p. 14.

14 Wollheim, p. 234.

15 The author visited Alice Crowther at the Goetheanum in 1934.

16 A. S. Neill, *Summerhill: A Radical Approach to Education*, p. 40.

17 Neill, p. 40.

18 Neill, pp. 206, 245, 316.

19 Leslie Weatherhead, *Psychology, Religion and Healing*, p. 408.

20 Weatherhead, *Psychology, Religion and Healing*, section 4, 'Modern methods of healing through psychology', pp. 255–301.

21 Neill, p. 25.

22 Victor Bonham-Carter, *Dartington Hall: The History of an Experiment*.

23 Bonham-Carter, pp. 195 and 196.

24 Roy Wake & Pennie Denton, *Bedales School: The First Hundred Years*.

25 Wake & Denton, p. 244.

26 Wake & Denton, p. 48.

27 Wake & Denton, pp. 215, 217–18. Arnold Dolmetsch founded a movement in Southern England for the revival of playing of early music on copies of contemporary early instruments. He taught by what he considered eighteenth-century pedagogical methods. Dunhurst was the first school in England to teach the recorder.

28 J. Dewey, *Democracy and Education*, 1916. Theodor Brameld was to visit Australia in 1947. Harold Rugg & Ann Shumaker, *The Child-Centered School: An Appraisal of the New Education*. George S. Counts, *Dare the School Build A New Social Order?*

29 K. S. Cunningham & Dorothy J. Ross, *An Australian School at Work*, p. 84.
30 D. E. & I. V. Hansen (eds), 'A wider world', in Hansen & Hansen (eds), *St Catherine's: A Centenary Celebration 1896–1966*, p. 81.
31 D. E. & I. V. Hansen (eds), *St Catherine's*, p. 81.
32 J. McCalman, *Journeyings*, p. 118.
33 McCalman, pp. 93–4.
34 A. Zainu'ddin, *They Dreamt of a School: A Centenary History of the Methodist Ladies' College, 1882–1982*, p. 271.
35 C. Turney (ed.), *Pioneers of Australian Education, vol. 3*, p. 7.
36 W. Bate, *Light Blue Downunder: The History of Geelong Grammar School*, Speech Day Report 1930, p. 205.
37 Hershfeld-Mack was a Quaker. He married a Friend, Olive Russell, a loved middle school teacher at MCEGGS and a friend of her headmistress, Miss Ross.
38 K. S. Cunningham & W. C. Radford, *Education for Complete Living: The Challenge of Today.*
39 Cunningham & Radford, pp. 3–13.
40 Cunningham & Radford, pp. 10, 11.
41 I did not see D. J. between 1935 and 1950 (when I returned to Australia), nor did we correspond, so, for this period, I am dependent on publicly available sources for information and later discussions with her.
42 ATTI Executive Committe Minutes, 23 November 1936, IARTV Papers.
43 Epstein, *A Golden String: The Story of Dorothy Jean Ross*, p. 54.

4 Challenge and Response

1 See *Nisi Dominus Frustra*, for Council composition in 1953, p. 168.
2 Gwenda Lloyd rejoined the staff in 1940.
3 1938 Headmistress report. Series 10, unit 1, box 49, Melbourne Girls' Grammar School Archives.
4 Minute of Appreciation, IARTV Papers.
5 IECD box LS/5/7/21 4. University of Melbourne Archives.
6 MCEGGS Council Minutes 1939.
7 Ailsa G. Thomson Zainu'ddin in R. McCarthy & M. Theobald (eds), *Melbourne Girls' Grammar School: Centenary Essays 1893–1993*, p. 65.
8 See various acts, quoted in *Nisi Dominus Frustra*, pp. 26–178.
9 Thomson Zainu'ddin in McCarthy & Theobald (eds), p. 63.
10 June Epstein, *A Golden String: The Story of Dorothy J Ross*, p. 59.
11 Letter (anonymity preserved).
12 ATTI Executive Committee Minutes, 4 November 1946, 26 November 1946.

13 In her first annual report Miss Davis acknowledged Miss Ross' 'interest and help throughout the year. She always makes us feel that her interest lies just as much in the Junior as in the Senior School'. Series 26, unit 1, box 41, Melbourne Girls' Grammar School Archives.

14 For example, Lauriston Girls School. The Misses Irving, their nieces, Misses Kay and Pippa Irving, a cousin Miss Beecher.

15 Council Minutes, 25 October 1939. Series 26, unit 1, box 41, Melbourne Girls' Grammar School Archives.

16 *Nisi Dominus Frustra*, p. 152.

17 Interview with Alison Winfield, 9 July 1998.

18 Interview with Alison Winfield, 9 July 1998.

19 From the Headmistress' report to Council 1939. Speech Day and Distribution of Prizes. Series 26, unit 1, box 41, Melbourne Girls' Grammar School Archives.

20 *Nisi Dominus Frustra*. p. 113.

21 *Nisi Dominus Frustra*. p. 112.

22 Speech Day Report 1948. Series 26, unit 1, box 41, Melbourne Girls' Grammar School Archives.

23 MCEGGS Newsletter. 12 May 1954, p. 7, Dorothy Ross Papers, L55/13/17, box 2, University of Melbourne Archives.

24 K. S. Cunningham & D. J. Ross, *An Australian School*, p. 68.

25 Cunningham & Ross, p. 103.

26 Epstein, *A Golden String*, p. 62.

27 15 April 1942. Report to Council, series 26, unit 1, box 41, Melbourne Girls' Grammar School Archives.

28 Interview with Louise Baker, 27 May 1998.

29 Report to Council, 15 April 1942, series 26, unit 1, box 41, Melbourne Girls' Grammar School Archives.

30 These letters were shown to me with the proviso that the name of the recipient was not included in the text.

31 Letter to a member of staff (anonymity preserved).

32 Letter to a member of staff (anonymity preserved).

33 Letter 26 October 1943, School Administration, series 7, unit 3, box 68, Melbourne Girls' Grammar School Archives.

34 'Evacuation 1942', Melbourne Girls' Grammar Archives. See also, paper delivered to World Education Fellowship. Victorian Section, 19 June 1942, MS. 10915, box 11. State Library of Victoria.

35 See, D. McDonald, 'The war years, 1939–45: an oral history', in McCarthy & Theobald (eds); J. Epstein, *A Golden String*; W. F. Connell, 'The school as a democratic community: the educational ideas of D. J. Ross', in McCarthy & Theobald (eds).

36 Alison Winfield, 'An untold tale', undated, courtesy of Alison Winfield.

37 The bombing of Dresden, 13 February 1945, VE Day was 8 May 1945, the bombing of Hiroshima was 5 August 1945, VJ Day was 15 August 1945.

38 See B. Falk, *No Other Home: An Anglo Jewish Story*, for a fuller development of this theme.

39 Epstein, *A Golden String*, p. 56.

40 An 'A' class school was regularly inspected by the School Board and on satisfactory results was free to conduct its own examination and to vary published courses of study.

41 Staff Meeting Book, November 1941–December 1944, series 10, unit 8, box 48, Melbourne Girls' Grammar School Archives.

42 *Nisi Dominus Frustra*, p. 172.

43 Schonell was away but there were good people there: interview with Alison Winfield, 9 July 1998.

44 After MCEGGS Alison Winfield worked part-time at St Leonard's and St Catherine's. Then, 'I replaced myself at St Leonard's and went full-time to St Catherine's. Miss Davis was not well that year and I was needed there'.

45 Interview 15 January 1994 (anonymity preserved).

46 Interview January 1998.

47 Interview January 1998.

48 *Nisi Dominus Frustra*. pp. 171–2.

49 See W. F. Connell in McCarthy & Theobald (eds).

50 My emphasis.

51 *Nisi Dominus Frustra*, p. 115. Authorship is generally attributed to Mrs Gwenda Lloyd. The short-lived magazine *Brick*, 29 November 1957 states: 'Mrs Lloyd had much to do with the writing of the school play the *Building of the House* which was first performed in the Jubilee year 1952 and wrote the history book *Nisi Dominus Frustra*'. See, Gwenda Lloyd Papers, 2/8/14, University of Melbourne Archives. See also, Staff Meeting Book, November 1941–December 1944, series 10, unit 8, box 48, Melbourne Girls' Grammar School Archives.

52 Staff Meetings Book, November 1941–December 1944.

53 In private conversation with the author in the late 1950s.

54 W. F. Connell in C. Turney (ed.), *Pioneers of Australian Education, vol. 3*, p. 221.

55 It is curious that in Cunningham & Ross, *An Australian School at Work*, that the religious basis for the described techniques is omitted.

56 *Nisi Dominus Frustra*, p. 173.

57 Cunningham & Ross, p. 138.

58 In 1953, for example, '40 girls sat for martriculation and 38 gained full passes, with 11 first-class honours and 38 second class honours. The special

Cromarty Prize for English Literature was won by a girl from the school. There were also 6 University College Scholarships and 17 Comonwealth Scholarships. In 1954, 42 girls sat for matriculation and 37 gained passes, with 10 first-class honours and 44 second-class honours. There were 23 Government Scholarships and 2 College Scholarships, as well as 2 Junior Government Scholarships, 4 Education Department Scholarships and 3 Kindergarten Training College Scholarships. The results of Old Grammarians at the University were also good, and in a great variety of courses, and an Old Grammarian topped the final honours list in the Law School, being only the third woman to do so. There were also a number of Old Grammarians elected to the Students' Representative Council, showing that they continue to take an interest in helping to run student affairs in the way in which they were encouraged to do at school.' See MCEGGS Parents Newsletter, 6 December 1955, no. 18, pp. 7–9, Dorothy Ross Papers, L55/13/17, box 2, University of Melbourne Archives.

[59] For full text, see Dorothy Ross Papers, L55/13/17, box 1, University of Melbourne Archives.

[60] John Smythe Memorial Lecture, University of Melbourne 1954, series 8, unit 2, box 47, Melbourne Girls' Grammar School Archives.

[61] *Nisi Dominus Frustra*, p. 160.

[62] The name was adopted in 1908.

[63] *Nisi Dominus Frustra*, p. 162.

[64] *Nisi Dominus Frustra*, p. 167.

[65] W. F. Connell in McCarthy & Theobald (eds), p. 97.

[66] A note from a parent in 1953, 'The welcome mat is certainly laid out for parents at MCEGGS. Parents are helped to feel that the school needs their side of the story, and teachers give the impression that the childrens welfare is of very real concern to them'.

[67] In England in the late 1930s and early 1940s the author was engaged in a research project which was designed to isolate the emotional factors in IQ tests.

[68] Interviews with the late Dr G. Dow.

[69] Miss Cunningham at Fintona placed more reliance on test results than Miss Ross. Miss Ross retained her sharp perceptual observation of behaviour and could detect signs of inhibited strengths and was not afraid to sometimes act on intuitions that defied results of tests.

[70] Interview, 18 August 1998 (anonymity preserved).

[71] Cunningham & Ross, p. 39.

[72] Cunningham & Ross, p. 148.

[73] Lyndsay Gardiner Papers.

[74] MCEGGS Magazine, December 1965, p. 94. See, Gwenda Lloyd entry in *Australian Dictionary of Biography* by Barbara Falk, forthcoming.

75 W. F. Connell in McCarthy & Theobald (eds), p. 102.

76 W. F. Connell in McCarthy & Theobald (eds), p. 101.

77 Cunningham & Ross. p. 71.

78 MCEGGS Newsletter, 6 December 1955, no. 1, vol. 8, pp. 7–9, Dorothy Ross Papers, L55/13/17, box 2, University of Melbourne Archives.

79 Discussion with D. J. and the late Diana Dyason.

80 Letter to Miss M. Bage, 14 November 1952, series 34, unit 5, box 48, Melbourne Girls' Grammar School Archives.

81 Headmistress Report, July 1954, p. 1, series 26, unit 1, box 41, Melbourne Girls' Grammar School Archives.

82 MCEGGS Magazine, no. 138, December 1955, p. 68. Council Report, in Gwenda Lloyd Papers, boxes 2/7, 2/8, University of Melbourne Archives.

83 W. F. Connell in McCarthy and Theobald (eds), p. 107.

84 Gwenda Lloyd Papers, box 2/7, University of Melbourne Archives.

85 Finance Committee Minutes, Series 59, unit 1, box 100, Melbourne Girls' Grammar School Archives.

86 See snapshot reproduced in Turney (ed.), p. 203.

87 Correspondence 1925–55, series 10, unit 3, box 49, Melbourne Girls' Grammar School Archives.

88 Ann Curthoys & John Merritt (eds), *Australia's First Cold War: 1945–1953, Vol. 1, Society, Communism and Culture*, p. 8.

89 Curthoys & Merritt (eds), ch. 5.

90 Between 1947 and 1963, 819 000 immigrants from Southern, Northern and Eastern Europe came to Australia. See Curthoys & Merritt (eds), p. 9.

91 Fay Woodhouse, *Anti-Communism and Civil Liberties: The 1951 Communist Party Dissolution Referendum Debate at the University of Melbourne*.

92 See following chapter.

93 This relationship is considered in Chapter 6.

94 W. F. Connell in McCarthy & Theobald (eds), p. 95.

95 Max Weber developed this point in distinguishing between *Gesellschaft* and *Gemeinschaft*, roughly translated as legal state and community.

96 Letter 30 May 1949, series 7, unit 11, box 68, Melbourne Girls' Grammar School Archives.

97 Letter 31 May 1949, series 7, unit 11, box 68, Melbourne Girls' Grammar School Archives.

98 Letter 10 May 1955, series 7, unit 12, box 69, Melbourne Girls' Grammar School Archives.

99 Letter 10 May 1955, series 7, unit 12, box 69, Melbourne Girls' Grammar School Archives.

100 Interview, 1 April 1998 (anonymity preserved).

[101] The film is in the Melbourne Girls' Grammar School Library, see also, series 38, unit 8, box 66, Melbourne Girls' Grammar School Archives.

5 In the Community

[1] D. E. & I. V. Hansen (eds), *Feminine Singular: A History of the Association of Heads of Independent Schools of Australia*, p. 32.

[2] Hansen (eds), *Feminine Singular*, p. 14.

[3] Jay A. Conger (ed.), *Charismatic Leadership: The Elusive Factor in Organizational Effectiveness*, pp. 16–17.

[4] Weber quoted in Conger (ed.), p. 16.

[5] Headmistress Report, 14 July and 12 October 1955, quoted by R. McCarthy in R. McCarthy & M. Theobald (eds), *Melbourne Girls' Grammar School: Centenary Essays 1893–1993*, p. 151.

[6] Quoted in McCarthy & Theobald (eds), p. 151.

[7] Diary entry, Dorothy Ross Papers, L55/13/17, box 4, University of Melbourne Archives.

[8] R. McCarthy, in McCarthy & Theobald (eds), p. 148.

[9] The Council of MCEGGS minuted its thanks to Miss Ross with their gratitude to the London Committee: Council Minutes, 22 January 1957, series 10, unit 3, box 49, Melbourne Girls' Grammar School Archives.

[10] Diary entry, Dorothy Ross Papers, L55/13/17, box 4, University of Melbourne Archives.

[11] Letter to the staff, Dorothy Ross Papers, L55/13/17, box 4, University of Melbourne Archives.

[12] Letter to the staff, Dorothy Ross Papers, L55/13/17, box 4, University of Melbourne Archives.

[13] Letter to the staff, Dorothy Ross Papers, L55/13/17, box 4, University of Melbourne Archives.

[14] The uprising in Hungary, led by Imre Nagy, a moderate nationalist communist, was one of a number of movements which attempted to relieve Russia's central European Empire of the heaviest of yokes after the death of Stalin in 1953. Nagy advocated withdrawal from the Warsaw Pact, recognition of Hungary as a neutral country and the establishment of a multi-party political system. The Russian army invaded Hungary in November 1956 and the uprising was brutally suppressed.

[15] Diary entry, Dorothy Ross Papers, L55/13/17, box 4, University of Melbourne Archives.

[16] Diary entry, Dorothy Ross Papers, L55/13/17, box 4, University of Melbourne Archives.

[17] June Epstein, *A Golden String: The Story of Dorothy Jean Ross*, p. 93.

[18] Fellowship conferred May 1960.

19   Dorothy Ross Papers, LS 55/13/17, box 2, Miss Mountain file, University
     of Melbourne Archives. Letter written by E. Pownall, Lyndsay Gardiner
     Papers—unsigned.
20   Letter, Lyndsay Gardiner Papers.
21   Letter, D. J. to Valentine Leeper, 13 November 1958, series 8, unit 3,
     box 34, Melbourne Girls' Grammar School Archives.
22   Interview with Miss Doris Winter-Irving, 12 August 1998. Miss Doris
     Winter-Irving first taught at St Catherine's, then briefly, at St Leonard's
     before returning to St Catherine's in 1956; she retired in 1985. She became
     head of humanities at St Catherine's and acted as principal in 1956 when
     Miss Davis took six months' leave to accompany Miss Ross on the journey
     described in this chapter.
23   Norman H. Dobson, *Mercer House: The Story of the First 50 Years
     1921–1971*. Fred Katz went on to the Psychology Department of the
     University of New South Wales in 1961 and subsequently to a post in
     medical education in Geneva, where he died.
24   WEF Papers (Victorian section), MS 10915, box 1, State Library of Victoria.
25   1960 President's Report, WEF papers (Victorian section), MS 10915,
     box 2, State Library of Victoria.
26   Dorothy Ross Papers, L55/13/17, box 3, University of Melbourne Archives.
27   *New Horizons in Education*, no. 20, Spring, 1958, p. 35.
28   Poem, 'Curiosity', Dorothy Ross Papers, L55/13/17, box 3, University of
     Melbourne Archives.
29   Paper, 'Cats and curiosity', Dorothy Ross Papers, L55/13/17, box 3,
     University of Melbourne Archives.
30   Gertrude F. Kentish, *The Story of Soroptimist International of The South West
     Pacific for the Golden Jubilee 1937–1987*, p. 1.
31   Paper, 'Soroptimist International' by Elizabeth Hyde, Lyndsay Gardiner
     Papers.
32   Letter written by Rosalind Martin, 31 March 1990, Melbourne Girls'
     Grammar Archives.
33   Dorothy Ross Papers, L55/13/17, box 3, University of Melbourne Archives.
34   Foreword by Dr W. C. Radford, in K. S. Cunnningham & Dorothy J. Ross,
     An Australian School at Work.
35   Letter written by Dr K. S. Cunningham, 23 June 1964, Dorothy Ross
     Papers, L55/13/17, box 3, University of Melbourne Archives.
36   Chapters 1 and 2, Cunnningham & Ross.
37   Letter written by Dr K. S. Cunningham, 30 October 1964, Dorothy Ross
     Papers, L55/13/17, box 3, University of Melbourne Archives.
38   Letter written by Dr K. S. Cunningham, 3 January 1965, Dorothy Ross
     Papers, L55/13/17, box 3, University of Melbourne Archives.

[39] Ian W. Paterson, *The Alberta Journal of Educational Research*, Edmonton, Canada, in Dorothy Ross Papers, L55/13/17, box 3, University of Melbourne Archives.

[40] The lone case history detailed the procedures that helped one pupil. It revealed an efficient machinery.

[41] Dylan Thomas, *Collected Poems 1934–1952*, p. 116.

6 Relationships

[1] 'The trend towards the comprehensive school', John Smythe Memorial Lecture, in Dorothy Ross Papers, L55/13/17, box 1, University of Melbourne Archives.

[2] For a discussion of these distinctions, see Ferdinand Toennies, *Community and Association (Gemeinschaft and Gesellschaft)*; Max Weber, *The Theory of Social and Economic Organization*.

[3] Even married couples might address their spouse with the gendered prefix.

[4] Letter to parents, 2 April 1943, Melbourne Girls' Grammar School Archives.

[5] To consider this formulation consult Sigmund Freud, *Three Essays on the Theory of Sexuality*; see also, Sigmund Freud, *Collected Papers vol. 11*, pp. 202–32; Richard Wollheim, *Freud*, pp. 107–26; Alison Mackinnon, *Love and Freedom: Professional Women and the Reshaping of Personal Life*.

[6] Rosemary Tong, *Feminist Thought: A Comprehensive Introduction*.

[7] She lent her copy to me in 1930.

[8] Janice Raymond, *A Passion for Friends: Towards a Philosophy of Female Affection*, p. 193. 'To be a lesbian means to extend what has been called a sexual preference beyond the realm of reality of a sexual category to a state of social and political existence' (p. 14). See also Elizabeth Grosz, *Volatile Bodies: Towards a Corporeal Feminism*: 'Bodies are not fixed, inert purely genetically or biologically programmed entities that function in their particular ways and in their determinate form independent of their cultural milieu and value' (p. 190). Catherine Gallagher & Thomas Lacquer (eds), *The Making of the Modern Body: Sexuality and Society in the Nineteenth Century*, note: 'the language of naturalistic description does not exist in a cultural vacuum but is itself deeply embedded in the culture from which it comes' (p. 1).

[9] Interview (anonymity preserved) 1998.

[10] St Catherine's Council Minute Book, 1949, St Catherine's School Archives.

[11] Address given by Dorothy Ross at the launching of Constance Tisdall's book, 10 November 1961, series 8, unit 3, box 34, Melbourne Girls' Grammar School Archives.

12 From D. E. & I. V. Hansen (eds), *Feminine Singular: A History of the Association of Heads of Independent Girls' Schools of Australia*, p. 244.
13 See chapter 4, p. 147.
14 Constance Tisdall Diary, 11 November, 12 November 1929, La Trobe Library.
15 Constance Tisdall Diary, 4 January 1923, La Trobe Library.
16 Constance Tisdall, *Forerunners*, p. 32.
17 Launch of Tisdall, *Forerunners*.
18 Constance Tisdall Diary, 5 July 1947, La Trobe Library.
19 Constance Tisdall Diary, 1 March 1946, La Trobe Library.
20 Constance Tisdall Diary, 12 July 1947, La Trobe Library.
21 Constance Tisdall Diary, 22 January 1955, La Trobe Library.
22 Joan Gillison, *Margaret Cunningham of Fintona: A Biography*, p. 61.
23 Gillison, *Margaret Cunningham of Fintona: A Biography*, p. 61.
24 Gillison, *Margaret Cunningham of Fintona: A Biography*, p. 72.
25 Marjorie Theobald, *Ruyton Remembers 1878–1978*, p. 89.
26 Theobald, *Ruyton Remembers 1878–1978*, p. 183.
27 Theobald, *Ruyton Remembers 1878–1978*, p. 183.
28 Theobald, *Ruyton Remembers 1878–1978*, p. 184–5.
29 D. E. & I. V. Hansen (eds), *St Margaret's Berwick: Castle-in-the-Air*, p. 89.
30 Hansen & Hansen (eds), *St Margaret's Berwick*, p. 89.
31 Interview, 20 November 1998 (anonymity preserved).
32 Interview, 20 November 1998 (anonymity preserved).
33 The Catalysts is a group of professional women who meet monthly for a meal and the exchange of ideas on subjects introduced in short papers by a member. Some members are also members of the Lyceum Club which is the venue for the meetings. 'Dorothy Ross was elected a member in 1936 and remained one till she died, though in her last years she rarely attended.' Letter to author from Helen Ferber, 19 February 1997.
34 D. E. & I. V. Hansen (eds), *St Catherine's: A Centenary Celebration*, p. 132.
35 Personal information.
36 C. S. Lewis, *The Four Loves*, p. 51.

7 The Icon Revisited

1 D. J. Ross notebook, Dorothy Ross Papers, L55/13/17, box 4, University of Melbourne Archives.
2 Dorothy Ross Papers, L55/13/17, box 4, Notebooks. Apologia was used by Cardinal Newman to mean explanation and justification. It does not in his context indicate apology.
3 Margaret Sutherland had taught Ethel Ross.

4   June Epstein, *A Golden String*, p. 95.

5   D. J. Ross notebook, Dorothy Ross Papers, L55/13/17, box 4, University of Melbourne Archives.

6   D. J. Ross notebook, Dorothy Ross Papers, L55/13/17, box 4, University of Melbourne Archives.

7   William McDougall, *Psycho-Analysis and Social Psychology*; the lectures were published in Melanie Klein & Joan Riviere, *Psychoanalytical Epitomes*.

8   The following quotation is taken from her notebook and is typed as she wrote it with cross-outs and inclusions.

9   D. J. Ross notebook, Dorothy Ross Papers, L55/13/17, box 4, University of Melbourne Archives.

10 D. J. Ross notebook, Dorothy Ross Papers, L55/13/17, box 4, University of Melbourne Archives.

11 D. J. Ross notebook, Dorothy Ross Papers, L55/13/17, box 4, University of Melbourne Archives.

12 D. J. Ross notebook, Dorothy Ross Papers, L55/13/17, box 4, University of Melbourne Archives.

13 D. J. Ross notebook, Dorothy Ross Papers, L55/13/17, box 4, University of Melbourne Archives.

14 Interview (anonymity preserved), 2 October 1998. The author, among others, visited her.

15 D. J. Ross notebook, Dorothy Ross Papers, L55/13/17, box 4, University of Melbourne Archives.

16 D. J. Ross notebook, Dorothy Ross Papers, L55/13/17, box 4, University of Melbourne Archives. She had read A. E. Housman, *Collected Poems*, Grant Richards, London (1896), 1908, p. 15:

>   And since to look at things in bloom
>   Fifty springs is little room,
>   About the woodlands I will go
>   To see the cherry hung with snow.

17 D. J. Ross notebook, Dorothy Ross Papers, L55/13/17, box 4, University of Melbourne Archives.

18 D. J. Ross notebook, Dorothy Ross Papers, L55/13/17, box 4, University of Melbourne Archives.

19 D. J. Ross notebook, Dorothy Ross Papers, L55/13/17, box 4, University of Melbourne Archives.

20 D. J. Ross notebook, Dorothy Ross Papers, L55/13/17, box 4, University of Melbourne Archives.

21 S. Freud, *The Future of an Illusion*.

22 For a discussion of this point see W. D. Falk, *Ought, Reasons and Morality: The Collected Papers of W. D. Falk*, Cornell University Press, 1986.

23 D. J. Ross, 'Christ in education', 1949, unpublished paper, Dorothy Ross Papers, L55/13/17, box 3, University of Melbourne Archives.

24 Ross, 'Christ in education', Dorothy Ross Papers, L55/13/17, box 3, University of Melbourne Archives.

25 Ross, 'Christ in education', Dorothy Ross Papers, L55/13/17, box 3, University of Melbourne Archives.

26 Marjorie Reeves & John Drewett, *What is Christian Education?: A Piece of Group Thinking*, p. 3

27 Reeves & Drewett, p. 4.

28 Reeves & Drewett, p. 8.

29 The author is indebted to Mr Arthur Sandell for the loan of Miss Ross' copy of Reeves & Drewett, *What is Christian Education?: A Piece of Group Thinking*.

30 Dorothy Ross, letter to parents, 3 August 1942, Melbourne Girls' Grammar School Archives.

31 David Hilliard, 'Intellectual life in the diocese of Melbourne', in B. Porter (ed.), *Melbourne Anglicans: The Diocese of Melbourne 1847–1997*, p. 43.

32 David Cuthbert, *Christ Church in South Yarra: A Social History, 1850–1990.*

33 Private conversation with the author.

34 *Nisi Dominus Frustra.*

35 Letter, D. J. to Valentine Leeper, 13 November 1958, series 8, unit 3, box 34, Melbourne Girls' Grammar School Archives.

36 D. J. Ross notebook, Dorothy Ross Papers, L55/13/17, box 4, University of Melbourne Archives.

37 Radclyffe Hall wrote to her last lover, Souline: 'If I had been a man I would have given you a child', quoted in Sally Cline, *Radclyffe Hall: A Woman called John*, p. 287.

38 D. J. Ross notebook, Dorothy Ross Papers, L55/13/17, box 4, University of Melbourne Archives.

39 D. J. Ross notebook, Dorothy Ross Papers, L55/13/17, box 4, University of Melbourne Archives.

40 D. J. Ross notebook, Dorothy Ross Papers, L55/13/17, box 4, University of Melbourne Archives.

41 Will no. 8786/82.

42 Death Certificate no. 08786/82.

43 Dr D. McCaughey, Eulogy for Dorothy Ross, Service of Thanksgiving for the Life of Dorothy Jean Ross, Tuesday 20 April 1982.

44 The Friends (Quakers) often speak of 'that of God in every man'; the phrase is quoted from Hugh Doncaster, *Personal Relationships Between Men and Women*, The Friends Home Service Committee, London, 1950.

45 This is D. J.'s punctuation. The words are in a letter written to an intimate friend during World War II (anonymity preserved).

Bibliography

Archival and Manuscript Material

Select Writings and Speeches of Dorothy Ross

In Dorothy Ross Papers, L55/13/17, box 1, University of Melbourne Archives

'The trend towards the comprehensive school', John Smythe Memorial Lecture, University of Melbourne, 17 August 1954.

Dorothy Ross Notebooks, Camberlea.

Dorothy Ross Papers, L55/13/17, box 2, University of Melbourne Archives

'The problems of the non-academic child in our school', April 1964, seminar at Mercer House.

Dorothy Ross Papers, L55/13/17, box 3 University of Melbourne Archives

Magic black and white (typescript), 17 April 1937.

Why work? (typescript), 15 June 1940.

Some hard facts and serious speculations (typescript), 21 August 1942.

An untold tale (with illustrations from school examinations 1942) (typescript), 17 August 1946.

What will the uncoil be? (typescript), September 1953.

What makes them tick? (typescript), 9 May 1960.

Is anybody listening? (typescript), 12 August 1963.

Cats and curiosity (typescript), 14 November 1966.

Human relationships in education, Friend's Summer School, 1953.

Apologia—nosing my way to a philosophy of education, *c.* 1975.

Percy Grainger Museum, University of Melbourne

Anne Macky file.

The University of Melbourne Archives

The Dorothy Ross Papers, L55/13/17, boxes 1–4.
IARTV Papers, L54/2/14.
Gwenda Lloyd Papers, box 2/13/15–18.
IECD Papers, box LSS/7/22. 36, LS/5/7/21. 4.
Princes Ida Club, 1/2/15, box 1/1.

Deakin University, Stonnington Campus

Mercer House Archive, box 20, 23/6.

Melbourne Girls' Grammar School Archives, South Yarra

D. J. Ross

Series 7, School Administration, unit 1, boxes 69, 72; unit 10, box 69; unit 11, box 68; unit 12, boxes 68, 70; unit 2, boxes 68, 69, 70, 72; unit 3, boxes 68, 69; unit 4, boxes 58, 69, 70, 73; unit 5, boxes 57, 69, 70; unit 6, boxes 68, 70; unit 7, boxes 69, 70, 73, 95; unit 8, boxes 69, 70, 72; unit 9, box 69.
Series 8, Miss Dorothy J. (D. J.) Ross, unit 1, boxes 29, 45, 67, 76; unit 2, boxes 27, 45, 47, 67, 73; unit 3, boxes 34, 45; unit 11, box 70.
Series 10, Staff Administration, unit 1, box 70; unit 10, boxes 68, 70; unit 3, boxes 49, 50, 70, 72; unit 6, boxes 33, 69, 72; unit 7, boxes 71, 72, unit 9, box 70.
Series 12, Chapel of Saint Luke the Evangelist, unit 4, box 55, unit 6, box 62.
Series 16, MGGS Parents' Association, unit 13, box 68.

Series 21, MGGS Buildings and Landscape, unit 14, box 44.
Series 26, School Council, unit 1, box 41; unit 8, box 40.
Series 27, Executive Council, unit 5, box 88.
Series 34, School History—General, unit 4, box 57; unit 5, box 48; unit 7, box 82.
Series 35, The MGGS Boarding School, unit 10, box 66.
Series 38, Video Collection, unit 8, box 54, including notes on the film *Living and Learning Together*, MCEGGS Newsletter, 22 March 1956, pp. 3–7, series 38, unit 8, box 54, Melbourne Girls' Grammar School Archives.
Series 57, Memorabilia, unit 1, box 96; unit 3, box 96.

Correspondence 1925–1955

Series 3, Student Publications, unit 1, box 15.
Series 5, Miss Kathleen Gilman Jones, unit 2, box 46.
Series 7, School Administration, unit 2, box 69; unit 5, boxes 55, 57, 69.

Headmistress' Reports 1925–1956

Series 10, Staff Administration, unit 3, box 49.
Series 26, School Council, unit 1, box 41; unit 8, box 40.
Series 59, Melbourne Girls' Grammar School Council, unit 1, box 100.
Series 9, Headmistress' Reports to Council 1923–1938, unit 5, box 27.

La Trobe Library

The World Education Fellowship Papers, MS. no. 10915, boxes 1, 2, 10, 11.

Tisdall Family Papers, MS. no. 8592, boxes 1013/3, 1017, 1018, 1019.

Lyndsay Gardiner Papers

Unsorted (in possession of Barbara Falk).

Inspector's Report, Coburg Higher Elementary School, 14 October 1914. Victorian Education Department Register of Appointments and Removals of Teachers. No. 16499. See also, School Correspondence Files VPRS 640.

'Soroptimist International', and Soroptimist Papers (in possession of Miss Elizabeth Hyde, Melbourne).

St Catherine's School Archives

School Council Minute Book, 1949.

Unpublished Works

Holmes, K., 'Spaces in her day: Australian women's diaries, 1919–1945', PhD thesis, Department of History, University of Melbourne, 1992.

Meabank, Jullann, 'The influence of the ideas of progressive education on teacher training in Victoria *c.* 1920 to *c.* 1950', PhD thesis, Education, University of Melbourne, 1996.

Muir, N., 'Images of D. J. Ross: the public construction of an educational icon', MEd research essay, University of Melbourne, 1993.

Interviews

The late Ruth Alexander, Louise Baker, Dr David Cohen, Lynette Cooke, Nina Crone, the late

Dr Gwyn Dow, June Epstein, Dr Ian Hansen, Dorothy Hansen, Professor Molly Holman, Betty Hotchin, Elizabeth Hyde, Helen Johnson, Valentine Leeper, Robyn Levi, Margaret Lyttle, Dr Desma McDonald, Joan McPhee, Elizabeth Meredith, Blanche Merz, Judith Moore, Joy Morgan, Jessie Nicholson, Mrs Payne, the late Dr Jean Plenderleith, Marian Poynter, Elizabeth Retallick, Arthur Sandell, Dr Barbara Sawyer, Professor R. Selleck, Dr Judith Tisdall, Noelleen Ward, Alison Winfield, Doris Winter-Irving, Brenda Wirth and Don Wirth.

Published Works

Books

Adams, J., *The Evolution of Educational Theory*, Thoemmes Press, Bristol, (1912) 1994.
—— *Modern Developments in Educational Practice*, University of London Press, London, 1922.

Archambault, R. D. (ed.), *Philosophical Analysis and Education*, Routledge and Kegan Paul, London, 1965.

Archdale, Betty, *Indiscretions of a Headmistress*, Angus & Robertson, Sydney, 1972.

Baker, Mark (ed.), *History on the Edge: Essays in Memory of John Foster (1944–1994)*, History Department Monograph Series, University of Melbourne, Melbourne, 1997.

Bate, Weston, *Light Blue Down Under: The History of Geelong Grammar School*, Oxford University Press, Melbourne, 1990.

Berger, John, Mohr, Jean & Philibert, Nicholas, *Another Way of Telling*, Pantheon, New York, 1982.

Berger, John, *Ways of Seeing*, BBC and Penguin Books, London, 1972.

Berlin, Isaiah, *The Sense of Reality: Studies in Ideas and their History*, edited by Henry Hardy, Chatto & Windus, London, 1996.

Black, Alan W. (ed.), *Religion in Australia: Sociological Perspectives*, Allen & Unwin, Sydney, 1991.

Blainey, Geoffrey, *A Centenary History of The University of Melbourne*, Melbourne University Press, Carlton, 1957.

Blythe, Ronald (ed.), *Penguin Book of Diaries*, Penguin, Harmondsworth, 1991.

Bonham-Carter, Victor, *Dartington Hall: The History of an Experiment*, Phoenix House, London, 1958.

Boyd, William (ed.), *Towards a New Education*, a record and synthesis of the discussions on the New Psychology and the Curriculum at the Fifth World Conference of the New Education Fellowship held at Elsinore, Denmark, in August 1929, Alfred A. Knopf, London, 1930.

Boyd, William & Rawson, Wyatt, *The Story of the New Education*, William Heinemann, London, 1965.

Brameld, Theodore, *Education for the Emerging Age: Newer Ends and Stronger Means*, Harper & Row, New York, 1965.

Brennan, N., *Village School*, Hawthorn Press, Melbourne, 1973.

Campbell, Ruth, *History of the Melbourne Law School*, Faculty of Law, University of Melbourne, 1977.

Carr-Saunders, A. M. & Wilson, P. A., *The Professions*, Oxford University Press, Oxford, 1993.

Cline, Sally, *Radclyffe Hall: A Woman called John*, John Murray, London, 1977.

Conger, J. A. (ed.), *Charismatic Leadership: The Elusive Factor in Organizational Effectiveness*, Jossey-Bass, San Francisco, 1988.

Connell, W. F., *The Australian Council for Educational Research 1930–80*, ACER, Hawthorn, 1980.

—— *A History of Education in the Twentieth Century*, Curriculum Development Centre, Canberra, 1980.

—— 'Innovative headmistress— D. J. Ross', in C. Turney (ed.), *Pioneers of Australian Education, Vol. 3, Studies in the Development of Education in Australia 1900–1950*, Sydney University Press, Sydney, 1983.

——*The Foundations of Secondary Education*, ACER, Hawthorn, 1961.

Cook, C., *The Play Way: An Essay in Educational Method*, William Heinemann, London, 1919.

Counts, George S., *Dare the School Build A New Social Order?* Arno Press, New York, 1969.

Cunningham, K. S. & Radford, W. C., *Education for Complete Living: The Challenge of Today*, Melbourne University Press, Carlton, 1938.

Cunningham, K. S. & Ross, Dorothy J., *An Australian School at Work*, ACER, Hawthorn, 1967.

Curthoys, Ann & Merritt, John (eds), *Australia's First Cold War:*

1945–1953, Vol. 1, Society, Communism and Culture, Allen & Unwin, Sydney, 1984.

Curtis, S. J. & Boultwood, M. E. A., *A Short History of Educational Ideas*, University Tutorial Press, London (1953), 1961.

Cuthbert, David, *Christ Church in South Yarra: A Social History 1850–1990*, Christ Church South Yarra Vestry, South Yarra, 1996.

Dewey, John, *Democracy and Education: An Introduction to the Philosophy of Education*, Macmillan, New York (1916), 1959.

Dobson, Norman, H., *Mercer House: The Story of the First 50 Years 1921–1971*, Dobson, Melbourne, 1971.

Doncaster, Hugh, *Personal Relationships Between Men and Women*, The Friends Home Service Committee, London, 1950.

Dow, Gwyneth (ed.), *Learning to Teach: Teaching to Learn*, Routledge and Kegan Paul, London, 1979.

—— *Teacher Learning*, Routledge and Kegan Paul, London, 1982.

Dow, Hume (ed.), *More Memories of Melbourne University: Undergraduate Life in the Years Since 1919*, Hutchinson of Australia, Hawthorn, 1985.

Epstein, June, *A Golden String: The Story of Dorothy Jean Ross*, Greenhouse, Melbourne, 1981.

—— *Woman with Two Hats: An Autobiography*, Hyland House, South Yarra, 1988.

Faderman, L., *Surpassing the Love of Men: Romantic Friendship and Love between Women from the Renaissance to the Present*, William Morrow, New York, 1981.

Falk, Barbara, *No Other Home: An Anglo Jewish Story*, Penguin, Ringwood, 1988.

Fendley, Margaret, *A School on a Hill: Strathcona 1924–1984*, Hyland House, South Yarra, 1986.

Fitzpatrick, Kathleen, *PLC Melbourne: The First Century 1875–1975*, PLC, Burwood, 1975.

Freud, Sigmund, *The Future of an Illusion*, translated by W. D. Robson-Scott, International Psychoanalytical Library, no. 15, Hogarth Press, London (1928), 1943.

—— *Collected Papers*, vol. II, Hogarth Press, London, 1942.

—— *Three Essays on the Theory of Sexuality*, translated by James Strachey, Image Publishing, London, 1942.

Gallagher, C. & Lacquer, Thomas (eds), *The Making of the Modern Body: Sexuality and Society in the Nineteenth Century*, University of California Press, Berkeley, 1987.

Gardiner, Lyndsay, *Tintern School and Anglican Girls' Education 1877–1977*, Tintern Church of England Girls Grammar School, East Ringwood, 1977.

—— *The Free Kindergarten Union of Victoria 1908–80*, ACER, Hawthorn, 1982.

—— *Janet Clarke Hall*, Hyland House, South Yarra, 1986.

Gillison, Joan, *A History of The Lyceum Club Melbourne*, McKellar Press, Melbourne, 1975.

—— *Margaret Cunningham of Fintona: A Biography*, Fintona Girls School and Globe Press, Melbourne, 1982.

Gregory, J. S., *Church and State*,
Cassell Australia, North
Melbourne, 1973.

Grosz, Elizabeth, *Volatile Bodies:
Towards a Corporeal Feminism*, Allen
& Unwin, St Leonards, 1994.

Hall, Radclyffe, *The Well of Loneliness*,
Falcon Press, London (1928), 1949.

Hansen, D. E. & I. V. (eds), *Feminine
Singular: A History of the Association
of Heads of Independent Girls' Schools
of Australia*, Hyland House,
Melbourne, 1989.

—— *St. Catherine's: A Centenary
Celebration 1896–1996*, Helicon
Press, East Ivanhoe, 1996.

—— *St Margaret's, Berwick: Castle-in-
the-Air. The First Sixty Years 1926–
1986*, Hyland House, Melbourne,
1996.

Hobsbawm, Eric, *Age of Extremes: The
Short Twentieth Century 1914–1991*,
Abacus, London, 1995.

Houseman, A. E., *Collected Poems*,
Grant Richards, London (1896),
1908.

Ignatieff, Michael, *A Life: Isaiah
Berlin*, Chatto & Windus, London,
1998.

Isaacs, Susan, *Childhood and After:
Some Essays and Clinical Studies*,
Routledge and Kegan Paul,
London (1948), 1950.

Kelly, Farley, *Degrees of Liberation: A
Short History of Women in The
University of Melbourne*, Women
Graduates Centenary Committee of
the University of Melbourne,
Parkville, 1985.

Kelly, Farley (ed.), *On the Edge of
Discovery: Australian Women in
Science*, Text Publishing,
Melbourne, 1993.

Kentish, Gertrude F., *The Story of
Soroptimist International of The South
West Pacific for the Golden Jubilee
1937–1987*, G. F. Kentish,
Frankston, Victoria, 1987.

Klein, Melanie, *Love, Hate and
Reparation*, Kegan Paul, London,
1933.

—— *Contributions to Psychoanalysis
1921–1945*, Hogarth Press,
London, 1948.

Klein, Melanie & Riviere, Joan,
Psychoanalytical Epitomes, no. 2,
Hogarth Press, London, 1937.

Koffka, K., *Principles of Gestalt
Psychology*, Kegan Paul, London,
1940.

Krafft-Ebing, R. von, *Psychopathia
Sexualis: A Medico-Forensic Study*,
with an introduction by Ernest van
den Haag, Putnam, New York,
1965.

Laquer, Thomas, *Making Sex: Body
and Gender from the Greeks to Freud*,
Harvard University Press,
Cambridge Massachusetts, 1990.

Lawson, M. D. & Petersen, R. C.,
*Progressive Education: An
Introduction*, Angus & Robertson,
Sydney, 1972.

Lewis, C. S., *The Four Loves*, Fontana
Books, London, 1960.

Mackinnon, Alison, *Love and Freedom:
Professional Women and the Reshaping
of Personal Life*, Cambridge
University Press, Cambridge,
1997.

McCalman, Janet, *Journeyings: The
Biography of a Middle-Class
Generation 1920–1990*, Melbourne
University Press, Carlton, 1993.

McCarthy, R. & Theobald, M. (eds),
Melbourne Girls' Grammar School:

Centenary Essays 1893–1993,
Hyland House, Melbourne, 1993.

McDougall, William, *Psycho-Analysis and Social Psychology*, Metheun, London, 1936.

Nairn, B. & Serle, G. (eds), *Australian Dictionary of Biography, Vol. 9, 1891–1939*, Melbourne University Press, Carlton, 1983.

Neill, A. S., *Summerhill: A Radical Approach to Education*, Victor Gollancz, London, 1962.

Nisi Dominus Frustra: The Melbourne Church of England Girls' Grammar School Jubilee History, Arbuckle & Waddell, Melbourne, 1953.

Olney, James (ed.), *Autobiography: Essays Theoretical and Critical*, Princeton University Press, New Jersey, 1980.

Overstreet, H. A., *The Mature Mind*, W. W. Norton, New York, 1949.

Pesman, Ros, *Duty Free: Australian Women Abroad*, Oxford University Press, Melbourne, 1996.

Piaget, Jean, *The Child's Conception of the World*, Kegan Paul, London, 1929.

Porter, Brian (ed.), *Melbourne Anglicans: The Diocese of Melbourne 1847–1997*, Mitre Books, Melbourne, 1997.

Raymond, Janice, *A Passion for Friends?: Towards a Philosophy of Female Affection*, Women's Press, London, 1986.

Reeves, Marjorie & Drewett, John, *What is Christian Education?: A Piece of Group Thinking*, Christian News Letter Books, no. 13, Sheldon Press, London (1942), 1943.

Rorty, Amélie Oksenberg (ed.), *The Identities of Persons*, University of California Press, Berkeley, Los Angeles, 1976.

Rugg, Harold and Shumaker, Ann, *The Child-Centered School: An Appraisal of the New Education*, Harrap, London, c. 1928.

Sandell, A., *A Forum for the Sharing of Educational Thinking: A History of Nearly Sixty Years of the World Education Fellowship in Victoria*, Fast Books, Wild & Woolley, Glebe, 1995.

Scheffler, Israel, *Of Human Potential*, Routledge and Kegan Paul, Boston, 1985.

Scheffler, Israel (ed.), *Philosophy and Education Modern Readings*, Allyn and Bacon, Boston, 1966.

Scott, Ernest, *A History of the University of Melbourne*, Melbourne University Press, Carlton, 1936.

Selleck, R. J. W., *The New Education: The English Background 1870–1914*, Pitman & Sons, Melbourne, 1968.

Shoemaker, Robert & Vincent, Mary (eds), *Gender and History in Western Europe*, Arnold, London, 1998.

Simons, Patricia, 'Alert and erect: masculinity in some Italian Renaissance portraits of fathers and sons', in Richard Trexler, *Gender Rhetorics: Postures of Dominance and Submission in History, Medieval and Renaissance Texts and Studies*, Binghamton, New York, 1994, pp. 163–75.

Southall, I., *The Story of the Hermitage: The First Fifty Years of the Geelong Church of England Girls' Grammar*

School, F. W. Cheshire, Melbourne, 1956.

Spaull, A., *Australian Education in the Second World War*, University of Queensland Press, St Lucia, 1982.

Spence, Jo & Holland, Patricia (eds), *Family Snaps: The Meaning of Domestic Photography*, Virago Press, London, 1991.

Suttie, Ian D., *The Origins of Love and Hate*, Kegan Paul Trench, London (1935), 1948.

Tate, F., *The Education Record of War Service 1914–1919*, Executive Committee of the Education Department's War Relief Fund, Melbourne, 1921.

Theobald, Marjorie, *Ruyton Remembers 1878–1978*, Hawthorn Press, Melbourne, 1979.

—— *Knowing Women: Origins of Women's Education in Nineteenth Century Australia*, Cambridge University Press, Cambridge, 1996.

Thomas, Dylan, *Collected Poems 1934–1952*, J. M. Dent & Sons, London, 1959.

Tisdall, Constance, *Forerunners: The Saga of a Family of Teachers*, F. W. Cheshire, Melbourne, 1961.

Toennies, Ferdinand, *Community and Association (Gemeinschaft and Gesellschaft)*, translated and supplemented by Charles P. Loomis, Routledge and Kegan Paul, London, 1974.

Tong, Rosemary, *Feminist Thought: A Comprehensive Introduction*, Unwin Hyman, London, 1989.

Turner, I. S., *The Training of Teachers in Australia: A Comparative and Critical Survey*, Melbourne University Press, Carlton, 1943.

Turney, C. (ed.), *Pioneers of Australian Education. Vol. 3: Studies of the Development of Education in Australia 1900–50*, Sydney University Press, Sydney, 1983.

Vicinus, Martha, *Independent Women: Work and Community for Single Women*, University of Chicago Press, Chicago, 1985.

Wake, Roy & Denton, Pennie, *Bedales School: The First Hundred Years*, Haggerston Press, London, 1993.

Weatherhead, Leslie, D., *Jesus and Ourselves*, Epworth Press, London (1930), 1939.

—— *Psychology, Religion and Healing*, Hodder & Stoughton, London, 1951.

Webber, Horace, *Years May Pass On: Caulfield Grammar School 1881–1981*, Wilke, Clayton, 1981.

Weber, Max, *The Theory of Social and Economic Organization*, translated by A. M. Henderson and Talcott Parsons, Free Press, New York, c. 1947.

White-Rosh, Naomi, *School Matters: The Preshil Alternative in Education*, Mandarin, Port Melbourne, 1995.

Wollheim, R., *Freud*, in Frank Kermonde (ed.), Fontana Modern Masters, Collins, London, 1971.

Woodhouse, Fay, *Anti-Communism and Civil Liberties: The 1951 Communist Party Dissolution Referendum Debate at the University of Melbourne*, The History of the University Project, Working Paper, no. 3, University of Melbourne, 1989.

Woodworth, R. S., *Psychology. A Study of Mental Life*, Methuen, London (1922), 1940.

Yapp, R. H., *Botany: A Junior Book for Schools*, edited by Dorothy J. Ross, Cambridge University Press, Cambridge (1934), 1949.

Zainu'ddin, Ailsa, *They Dreamt of a School: A Centenary History of the Methodist Ladies College Kew 1882–1982*, Hyland House, Melbourne, 1982.

Articles, Journals

Australian Educational Quarterly, vols. 1–4, 1924–28.

Australian Educational Review, vols. 5–10, 1929–40.

Connell, W. F., 'The education of a professor of Education', in *Melbourne Studies in Education*, 1984, pp. 1–30.

Palmer, Imelda (ed.), *Melbourne Studies in Education*, Melbourne University Press, Carlton, 1984.

Ross, Dorothy J., 'Some impressions of the Elsinore Conference', in *Australian Educational Quarterly*, vol. 5, no. 2, October 1929, pp. 20–3.

—— 'Dr Montessori's Elsinore address', in *Australian Educational Quarterly*, vol. 6, no. 1, First Term, 1930, pp. 29–30.

—— 'The First Estate', in *Australian Educational Quarterly*, vol. 6, no. 2, October 1930, pp. 10–12.

—— 'Random but expurgated thoughts of an examiner', in *Australian Educational Quarterly*, vol. 7, no. 1, First Term, 1931, pp. 12–17.

—— 'NEF principles—a reminder', in *New Horizons in Education*, The Journal of the New Education Fellowship, no. 24, July–August, 1960.

Simons, Patricia, 'Women in frames: the gaze, the eye, the profile in Renaissance portraiture', in *History Workshop*, issue 25, Spring 1988, pp. 4–30.

Theobald, Marjorie, 'Women teachers' quest for salary justice in Victoria's registered schools, 1915–1946', in *Melbourne Studies in Education*, 1983, pp. 1–43.

New Horizons in Education, no. 20, Spring 1958 (State Library of Victoria).

New Horizons in Education, no. 24, July–August 1960 (State Library of Victoria).

New Education Fellowship Newsletters (State Library of Victoria).

Index

educational aims balanced, 125–6

educational democracy, 69, 92–5

educational psychology: of Adams, 58–9; of Freud, 56–9; of Neill, 60; of Steiner, 59–60; of Weatherhead, 60–1

Ellis, Henry Havelock, 143–4

Elmhirst, Leonard and Dorothy, 62

Empire Youth Sunday, 109

employment barred by marriage, 141

Ensor, Beatrice, 45

Epstein, June, 21–2, 108, 159

eros, 58

Europe, communication with, 33

Fabian Society of Victoria, 153

Falk, Barbara, 121

Falk family, 106

Farmer, Miss Constance, 151

Fascism predicted, 69

Fintona Girls School, 150

Fitzpatrick, Dorothy, 25–6

Forerunners (Miss Constance Tisdall), 147–50

Foster, Dr John, 116

Foundations of Secondary Education series (ACER), 134

Free Kindergarten Union, 34–5, 68

Freud, Sigmund, 161; *The Future of an Illusion*, 168; theories as applied to education, 56–9, 168

friendship, 58

Froebel, Friedrich, 22–8, 57

Gainford, Rubina, 20

Gamble, Miss, 108

Garnett, T. R., 129

Garton, Miss Addie, 16, 30

Geelong Grammar School, 67–8; Timbertop, 68

Geelong Kindergarten, 27

gendered forms of address, 141

generational change, 156

genetics, 131–2

Gesell, Arnold, 76

Gheeb, Paul, 45

Gilman Jones, Miss Kathleen Annie, 36–8; Anglican ceremonial rituals, 75; attitude to teacher training, 16; care for staff, 37; educational philosophy, 37–8; feminist stance, 37; head of MCEGGS, 4, 36; leadership skills, 73; membership of organizations, 36–7; NEF association, 37; professional guidance of D. J., 3, 38, 41, 71, 123; religious views, 39–40; teaching experience, 36

Gipson, Miss Dora, 151

Golden String: The Story of Dorothy Ross, A, (June Epstein), 21–2

Goodman, Jean Victoria (later Mrs Jean Cohen), 31

Gordon, Olive, 119

Gottschalk, Miss, 119

Grieve, F. E., 41

Haire, Norman, 57

Hall, Miss Kathleen, 106

Hall, Radclyffe (*The Well of Loneliness*), 57, 144, 148, 154

Head, Archbishop, 170

Headmistresses' Association of Victoria, 18, 37, 71

Headmistresses' Conference (England), 116

headmistresses of girls' schools; characteristics of, 146–7; close friendships with female colleagues, 152; dealing with school councils, 151; educational and personal responsibilities, 151; relationships with colleagues, 147

Herschfeld-Mack (art and music teacher at Geelong Grammar), 68

Herschfeld-Mack, Olive (née Russell), 108

structure, 90; Advisory Council, 78, 92; after wartime evacuation, 76; age of entry to secondary school, 78; alternative education programme, 39; Anglican nature of, 75; *An Australian School at Work* (D. J.'s monograph), 134–6; authority structure, 78, 86; boarders, 102–3; boarding-house staff, 102; *Brick* (student magazine), 100; building programme, 37; changes during 1950s, 123; Chapel, 75; choice of classmates, 99; Constitution, 75; curriculum streams, 99; democratic community, 26, 88, 89, 93, 139; devolution of power, 114; diagnosis of pupils' potential, 98–9; at Eastern Golf Club, Doncaster, 22, 88; enrolment numbers, 39; evacuation in WWII, 81–3, 85; examination results, 95; Executive Council, 92–5, 103; Field Day, 79–80; future after D. J.'s resignation, 114–15; house system, 38; Howard Plan, 37–9; letter of loyalty to Edith Mountain, 122; leavers going to university, 101; at Marysville, 85; New Education principles used, 19, 38; non-academic course, 79; nursery school, 78; Old Girls of the school, 97–8; Old Grammarians' Association, 72, 96–9, 116; Parents' Association, 39, 72, 97–8; political right-wing members of community, 125; population (staff and students), 90; post-Leaving Certificate, 101; practical stream, 99; prayer of School Council, 94, 148; prefects, 78; principal's position, 72–3; prizes not given during wartime, 108; pupils' card index, 98; religious education, 171; return to South Yarra after evacuation, 86–8, 104; salaries for teachers, 37; school captain's appointment, 78; School Council, 72, 97, 116; school counsellor, 90–1, 98; school magazine, 100; Silver Jubilee celebrations, 110; Social Studies curriculum, 100–1; sporting achievements and programme, 73, 79–81; staff, 20, 76, 90, 103–4, 108, 111, 124, 164; staff meetings, 89–90; student behaviour criticized, 110; student memories of evacuation period, 83; team games, 80–1; Wildfell, 83, 103

Melbourne Church of England Girls' Grammar School Jubilee History (*Nisi Dominus Frustra*, 1953), 110

Melbourne Grammar School, 68, 81–2, 87

Melbourne High School, 82

Menzies, Robert, 107

Mercer House, 115, 126–7, 174; *see also* Associated Teachers' Training Institute (ATTI)

Merz, Mrs Blanche, 23

Methodist Ladies' College (MLC), 66–7

Montessori, Dr Maria, 37, 43–4, 46, 63, 76

Morey, Dr Elwyn, 117

Morrison, George, 9, 143

Mountain, Miss Edith: at AMAV 1958 conference, 128; arrives at MCEGGS, 24, 121; barriers to communication, 125; 'crisis' and staff resignations (1958), 22–3, 24–6, 91, 121–5; D. J. meets, 116–17, 119; dogs, 121, 155–6

Murray, Miss Betty, 125

Murray, Rev. Charles, 171

National Council of Women of Victoria, 37

Neild, J. C., 68
Neill, A. S., 60, 61, 66
New Education Fellowship (NEF), 3, 18, 41, 42–5, 49, 63, 69, 115, 117
Nisi Dominus Frustra (Jubilee History, 1953), 110

Old Ruytonians' Association, 150

Parkhurst, Helen, 45
political conservatism, 107
political leadership, Weber's analysis of, 113–14
post-war migration, 107
post-war social and political changes, 107
Pownall, Miss Elizabeth, 22–3, 108
prayer of School Council, 94, 148
Preshil school, 49, 66, 128
Princess Ida Club, 8, 11
Principles of Gestalt Psychology (Kurt Koffka), 161
Priory, The, St Kilda, 10
'progressive education', 25
Psychology, A Study of Mental Life (R. S. Woodworth), 160
psychology and philosophy, 160–1, 175

Radford, Dr W. C., 134
reciprocal relationships, 139
Reddie, Dr (English educationalist), 62
relationships: in context of Christian doctrine, 154; significance in education, 57–9; and social mores, 59; staff, 120, 153; women, 167
Remington, Miss Catherine, 45–6, 49, 123
returned servicemen, education of, 33–4
Richardson, Mr (IARTV), 48
Rivers, Wilga, 20, 25

Riviere, Joan, 161
Rosbercon school, 147–9
Ross, Alfred George (D. J.'s father), 9, 10, 12, 167, 171
Ross, Charlotte ('Lottie', née Walden, D. J.'s mother), 9, 84–5, 171
Ross, Dorothy Jean
childhood and family: birth certificate, 9; childhood, 8–10, 27, 57, 140, 166; education (primary and secondary), 10, 27; family background, 8–10, 166–7; name, 1; parents' religious orientation, 171
described by: *Age* 1981 article, 26; Prof. G. S. Browne, 19; Margaret Connell, 18; Prof. William Connell, 17–18, 44, 88–9; Dr Gwyneth Dow, 19–20, 25; June Epstein, 21, 159; Mrs Gwenda Lloyd, 104–5; Dr Ethel McLennan, 16; Mrs Blanche Merz, 23; Elizabeth Pownall, 22–3; Dr W. C. Radford, 134; Wilga Rivers, 25; Arthur Sandell, 18
early adult years: academic results, 11; botany studies, 16, 30, 36, 47; at Crosby Hall, 41–2; Dip. Ed. studies, 13–16, 28; first teaching position, 14; prizes, 11; registration as primary teacher, 29–30; Science degree, 32, 34, 36; teaching practice, 14–15; at the University of Melbourne, 11
MCEGGS period of life: accessibility, 2, 90, 139–40; accusation of 'left' tendencies, 109; administrative skill, 39, 99; ambitions and abilities, 175–6; Anglican Low Church stance, 75–6; applicant for principal position at MCEGGS, 72–3; appointment of Edith Mountain, 123; ATTI involvement, 3–4, 41, 45, 50; atti-